A Guidance Approach
to Discipline

A Guidance Approach To Discipline

Daniel Gartrell, Ed.D.

D **Delmar Publishers Inc.**™

Ⓘ Ⓣ Ⓟ™

NOTICE TO THE READER

Cover photo design courtesy of Monte Draper
Cover design by Spiral Design Studio

Delmar Staff
  Executive Editor: Lucille Sutton
  Associate Editor: Erin J. O'Connor
  Project Editors: Carol Micheli
          Andrea Edwards Myers
  Production Coordinator: Sandra Woods
  Art and Design Coordinator: Karen Kunz Kemp

For information, address Delmar Publishers Inc.
3 Columbia Circle, Box 15-015
Albany, New York 12212

Copyright © 1994
by Delmar Publishers Inc.
The trademark ITP is used under license.

Printed in the United States of America
Published simultaneously in Canada
by Nelson Canada,
a division of The Thomson Corporation

1 2 3 4 5 6 7 8 9 10 XXX 00 99 98 97 96 95 94

Library of Congress Cataloging-in-Publication Data
Gartrell, Daniel.
    A guidance approach to discipline / Daniel Gartrell. — 1st ed.
      p. cm
    Includes index.
    ISBN 0-8273-5520-3
    1. School discipline—United States. 2. Child psychology—United
States. 3. Problem solving in children. 4. Interpersonal relations
in children—United States. I. Title.
LB3012.2.G37 1994
371.5'0973—dc20   93-25150
                                                    CIP

In memory of Two Education Professors:

Ben Thompson of Antioch College,
Yellow Springs, Ohio

and

Maurice Lucas of the
University of North Dakota,
Grand Forks

Contents

Preface

Content of the Text

The text presents an approach to discipline that is positive, preventive, and problem-solving in nature. Many of the ideas in the text apply to learners of all ages, infant to adult. The focus, however, is on the early childhood age group, children aged three to eight years. This is the period during which most children complete the transition from the private, informal life of the family to the institutionalized world of the school. For reasons of development and experience, this age group encounters, and poses, particular challenges that require study and understanding by the teacher.

As an introduction to the text, the reader will appreciate an overview of its contents. The work includes ten chapters, grouped under three units:

Foundations of a Guidance Approach
Reducing the Need for Mistaken Behavior
Solving Problems in the Classroom.

The first unit, Foundations of a Guidance Approach, has four chapters. Chapter one traces the guidance tradition in educational thought and quotes education reformers of the past to indicate the historic strength of the guidance approach. Chapter two develops a new construct that extends the guidance tradition, three levels of mistaken behavior. Chapter three discusses principles that define "the bottom line" for guidance discipline. Chapter four examines considerations important for readers who wish to implement the guidance approach in their classrooms.

Unit two, Reducing the Need for Mistaken Behavior, has three chapters. Chapter five discusses management of the classroom, particularly through the use of learning centers and routines, and the recruitment of parent volunteers. Chapter six explores management of the daily program, including the daily schedule, the balance of reliability and novelty in the program, the place of large groups, managing transitions, and working with volunteers. Chapter seven presents clear communication strategies with children designed to reduce the need for mistaken behavior. Techniques for communication with parents are also discussed.

Unit three, Solving Problems in the Classroom, has three chapters. Chapter eight provides conflict resolution strategies for the mistaken behaviors that teachers commonly encounter in early childhood classrooms. Five strategies are examined. The chapter includes a section on enlisting the assistance of parents. Chapter nine addresses steps teachers take when they encounter serious (strong needs) mistaken behavior. A comprehensive approach is developed that involves collaboration with the family, staff, and other professionals. Chapter ten defines liberation teaching as a bridging concept between guidance discipline and anti-bias curriculum. The chapter discusses the use of liberation teaching with parents.

Because the text discusses guidance at both the preschool and grade school levels, a word of practical orientation is warranted. In the work the term "early childhood" describes the full 3–8 age group. "Preschool" refers to the age range and programming at the pre-kindergarten level. "Pre-primary" addresses children and programming before first grade. "Primary" refers to children and the grade levels one through three. "School age" and "grade school" pertain to children and programming in kindergarten through third grade. Finally, because the whole child enters the classroom, the term "child" (and not "student") is used to define the learner.

Features of the Text

The text presents a guidance approach to discipline. The guidance approach does not punish children for having problems, but teaches children to solve them. The approach addresses mistaken behaviors, but at the same time protects self-esteem. The text builds upon a long-standing guidance tradition in educational thought. It brings together the thinking of education reformers of the last 150 years, the self-psychologists of the 1960s and 1970s, and developmental theorists and early childhood practitioners of the past three decades.

The book marks a new generation of works in the area of guidance. It was written after the monumental document of the National Association for the Education of Young Children (NAEYC) on **developmentally appropriate practice** (Bredekamp, 1987); the landmark text, *Anti-Bias Curriculum* (Derman-Sparks, 1989); and the occurrence of debate about "assertive" discipline systems prevalent in the 1980s. The reader might watch for several features influenced by these events, and other current trends:

a. The NAEYC work, *Developmentally Appropriate Practice in Early Childhood Programs Serving Children From Birth through Age 8*, is redefining educational practice at the preschool and elementary levels in terms responsive to child development. With redefinition of appropriate educational practice has come new understanding about the role of discipline. The NAEYC work documents persuasively that children learn best when they are active participants in the education process. A process of education that is interactive means that the purpose of discipline has changed. The teacher no longer uses discipline to control, but to manage, to teach, to coach, and to guide.

A feature of the text is that it inter-relates positive discipline practice with developmentally appropriate education. Chapters one, three, four, five, six, and ten utilize ideas about developmentally appropriate practice in the discussion of guidance discipline.

b. In distinct ways the events contributing to the writing of the text have done more for me than define the nature of guidance discipline. They have reinforced my conviction that close teacher-parent relations are needed in the successful education of the child. Family life no longer conditions children to a "seen and not heard" role that transfers to the classroom. As Dr. Bredekamp's eloquent foreword suggests, the plethora of conditions that affect modern families mean that the teacher cannot practice as though the only life that matters is the life of the child at school.

The child is an extension of the family unit, and the teacher must include the family to reach and teach the child. Moreover, acceptance of the family means acceptance of the cultural background of each child in the class. Chapters three, four, and ten address the need for guidance practices to be culturally sensitive. The term, "liberation teaching," introduced in chapter three and explored in chapter ten, links together the concepts of guidance discipline and anti-bias curriculum. As well, each chapter of the text includes a section on building productive teacher-parent relations.

c. In the guidance perspective the nature of the child is dynamic, developing, and tending toward good. Appropriate curriculum and methods encourage active learning, problem-solving, and social responsiveness—and so reduce the need for problem behavior. Building from the work of the self-psychologists—and in contrast to the proponents of obedience discipline systems—I suggest a new construct for understanding children when problems occur: three levels of mistaken behavior.

The skills of expressing strong emotions acceptably and getting along with others are complex and take into adulthood to learn. In the process of learning, children—like all of us—make mistakes. The mistakes occur at any of three different levels: experimentation, socially influenced, or strong needs. While the responses of teachers vary depending on the level, the goal of intervention remains constant: to help children learn positive behavioral alternatives from their mistakes.

Though perhaps not in theory, for many teachers the term "misbehavior" connotes punishment. Because in the guidance perspective punishment is dysfunctional to children's learning, the term "misbehavior" has not been used. Instead, the construct of mistaken behavior is developed in chapter two and is used throughout the text. The concept of "mistaken behavior" may be the most controversial aspect of the text. I suggest that whether readers grow comfortable with the concept or simply use the term "misbehavior" more consciously, the guidance approach will stand on its merit.

d. Like the NAEYC document on developmentally appropriate practice, the text crosses the "institutional barrier" between preschool and elementary school. To illustrate just one difference that the bridging effort encounters, many writers at the preschool level reject the very term "discipline." They do so for the same reason that I have chosen not to use "misbehavior." In everyday practice, the distinction between discipline and punishment is often blurred. "Guidance" implies an approach to children's behavior that provides direction yet is essentially non-punitive. It is the term of choice in the preschool literature.

Writers at the elementary level who address similar concerns have come to use terms like "positive discipline" or "cooperative discipline" to distinguish discipline models that do not rely on punishment. I have chosen to retain the term discipline in the text because it is still commonly used at the elementary school level. I wish to assure prekindergarten educators, however, that when I use the terms "a guidance approach to discipline" or more concisely, "guidance discipline," I am thinking about guidance as distinct from punishment.

In creating a "bridging text" some reviewers have commented that the discussion leans too heavily to preschool, others that it develops too fully primary grade material. The period of childhood from three to eight years roughly defines the age span when most children have entered Piaget's preoperational stage of development and when most children have exited from it. Piaget argues that children in the preoperational stage show common characteristics in learning and behavior that adults do well to understand. I accept Piaget's views in this matter and believe the developmental commonalities of young children outweigh the traditions of differing institutional practice. Developmentally appropriate education is the right of learners throughout the education process, and not just in preschool and kindergarten.

e. In keeping with the spirit of "inclusion," or teaching children with disabilities in the mainstream classroom, I have not created separate sections for addressing the needs and behaviors of young children with disabilities. Such children either may show mistaken behavior because of unmet needs and still developing social skills; or, they may be the victims of mistaken behavior as a result of vulnerabilities due to their circumstances. Chapter three develops the concept of unconditional positive regard, which certainly pertains to young children having disabilities. Chapter ten discusses liberation teaching, which is teaching that assists children to accept and learn from their own and others' human qualities. In the guidance classroom all children are welcome as accepted members of the group.

f. Finally, many references to other authors are used throughout the text. I've done so to illustrate the broad base of agreement about guidance ideas in the literature of progressive educators over time. Even the "new" ideas given expression in the work build from a strong and vibrant tradition—a commitment to the potential and worth of the developing child. Going back to Froebel and Montessori, early childhood educators have always been in the forefront of progressive educational thought. Through this textbook, my hope is that you and I will continue this tradition.

Foreword

"How do I get the children to behave?" "How do I control the classroom?" "What can I do with Scott . . . he's ruining the experience for the other children?"

These are always the first questions, often the second and third questions. Whenever someone decides to work with young children, the *primary* area of interest is discipline. Every teacher educator knows the sound of panic in a student teacher's voice when the issue of discipline arises. Every child care center director knows that classroom management is the greatest challenge for the inexperienced staff member. Every principal has grappled with a teacher who desperately wants the principal "to handle the problem child" so that the teacher can get on with the curriculum. Without overstating the case, discipline is usually the primary concern of parents as well.

At a recent NAEYC national conference, a presenter came into headquarters and irately demanded to know why her session was scheduled for a room that holds 500 when she had anticipated a small interactive group. "What's your topic?" she was asked. "Time-out," she replied. "That's why!" came the chorus of replies.

We all know the teachers who could be so good if only they didn't yell so much (with the resulting tension among the children in their classes). We have encountered the child who seems to spend more time on the time-out chair than in productive activity. Many of us have seen the classrooms where children respond like robots because any false move seems to result in their name going on the blackboard. The children in these classrooms are victims of what Gartrell calls, "mistaken behavior." In these cases, however, it is the teachers rather than children who are making mistakes. Too many teachers do not understand that discipline is not something that needs to be taken care of so that they can get on with the curriculum. They miss the point that children do not learn social problem solving skills when they are sitting on a time-out chair; as Lilian Katz says, what they learn is how to cultivate revenge. In developmentally appropriate early childhood programs, guiding young children to develop self-control and effective social skills *is a primary goal* of the curriculum.

The need for early childhood programs to promote the development of positive self-esteem and social competence through a guidance approach has never been greater than it is today. More and more children are growing up in stressful environments. Almost one fourth of young children lives in poverty. A high percentage of children live with only one parent and a growing number live with no parent, in foster care or other arrangements. Even families that may be relatively affluent suffer the stresses caused by divorce, substance abuse, and domestic violence. The communities, and the homes, in which many children live are not safe havens in which to develop a sense of security and trust. Some children do not have homes at all. In communities throughout this country, children are killing children. Is it any wonder that children enter child care, preschool, or school with some emotional problems?

Into this enormous area of need, Dan Gartrell wades with patience and clear-sighted thoughtful advice. The problems do not seem overwhelming when they are stated precisely, simply categorized, and clear strategies for solution are offered. The tone of his book is so calming, just like the tension-easing tone of a caring, knowledgeable teacher. A guidance approach to discipline is not rocket science, but it is soundly based in child development research and theory. Sometimes, the solutions may seem like common sense; but unfortunately, the sense to treat children with respect as rational human beings is all too uncommon in our society and in our schools.

A long time ago, a mentor of mine, Carol Seefeldt, taught me several rules about guiding young children. She carefully explained, "When you are having difficulty with a child, first change the environment, then change yourself, and if those two strategies fail, then and only then, should you attempt to change the child's behavior." Gartrell takes this simple piece of advice and elaborates on it with clear suggestions for strategies to try in each case. Changing the environment is often all that is needed. Frequently, the environment and the classroom expectations do not respect children's developmental needs. Too often, children are judged as bad when they are just acting like normal, healthy children—active, talkative, impulsive, for example. Too often, the adults are the problem, expecting too much or expecting the wrong thing. Sometimes, the child does have a real emotional problem. But punishing the symptom will not cure the ill. These children need clear limits, loving support, and specific coaching as they develop more constructive ways of coping. Gartrell offers adults, both parents and teachers, the help they need to find such constructive answers.

My mentor taught me another simple strategy for guiding young children that I have never forgotten. Every early childhood classroom needs three rules (and only three rules, I might add): Don't do anything to hurt yourself. Don't do anything to hurt other people. Don't do anything to hurt our classroom environment. Gartrell would undoubtedly phrase these rules in the positive, but the point is made. Kindergarten classrooms with fifty rules to memorize and elaborate punishment systems for violators should be relics of a distant, Dickensian past.

Guiding young children is hard work, as every parent knows. One of the greatest strengths of Gartrell's approach is the close collaboration he promotes between teachers and parents. Every chapter in this book involves parents just as every chapter in a child's life must involve the family. The principles of appropriate guidance are not unique to educational settings. As teachers become better guides of children, their effective strategies are emulated by parents and children experience greater continuity and support from home to program.

Guiding young children may be hard work, but it is perhaps the most important work that parents and teachers do. It will do no good if we accomplish 100 percent literacy and lead the world in math and science, and accomplish hundreds of other academic goals, if we can't all get along. The emotional health of our nation hangs in precarious balance. This book won't solve all the problems, but knowledge is a powerful tool. This book brings that power to adults who will, in turn, guide the children.

Sue Bredekamp
Director of Professional Development
National Association for the Education of Young Children

Acknowledgments

There are many persons who have made this book possible. First acknowledgments go to my mother, Beth Goff, for raising me this way, and to my wife, Julie Jochum, for her love and unending assistance. Thanks are due to the many teachers with whom I have worked over the years who have practiced guidance. I wish I could recognize them all, but a few who have contributed to the anecdotes and case studies are Pat Sanford, Sue Bailey, Vicki Wangberg, Judi Faymoville, Lynn Hart, Gayle Gish, Denise Ellis, Betty Schoenborn, Diane Lerberg, Ina Rambo, Nellie Cameron, John Ostby, Dee Bretti, and the entire staff of three programs: Bi-County Head Start, Bemidji Early Childhood Family Education, and the Paul Bunyan School Early Intervention Program.

I wish to thank the undergraduate and graduate students in my classes and workshops at Bemidji State University over the years. Their ideas, reactions, and responses have provided a valued sounding board for the concepts and suggestions in this text. As well, recognition is due to the Child Development Associate (CDA) candidates and student teachers whom I have supervised in classrooms across northern Minnesota for so long. This contact with children and staff alike has kept my ideas fresh and relevant to teaching in the field.

A special acknowledgment is due to Mrs. Haim Ginott who gave permission for five quotes of her husband to be used. More than others, the writings of Haim Ginott were a source of inspiration for the text—his ideas pertain to "little" and "big" learners alike. Thanks also are due to Dr. Steven Harlow for permission to duplicate his important discussion of "relational patterns" from the monograph, "Special Education: The Meeting of Differences"; the material forms a basis of the discussion in chapter two. Appreciation is expressed to Dr. Sue Bredekamp for contributing her eloquent foreword. Thanks go to Mrs. Ray Morin for permission to use her late husband's classic cartoon, "Joanie's Parents."

For assistance in Minnesota with reading and revision, I wish to thank Diane Lerberg, who offered major encouragement early on, and Julie Jochum and Catherine McCartney, both of Bemidji State University, who provided helpful feedback and suggestions for every chapter. Thanks also go to John Halcrow for his support and his humor.

My appreciation is extended to the reviewers enlisted through Delmar for their constructive criticism and helpful suggestions. They include:

Mary Ann Baggett
   Kilgore College
Jeffrey I. Gelfer
   University of Nevada-Las Vegas
Scott Hewit
   State University of New York-Plattsburgh

Margaret King
  Ohio University
Sharon McCluskey
  Portland Community College
Rosanne Pirtle
  Marian College
Marilyn Shelton
  California State University-Fresno
Joann M. Wood
  San Antonio College

For technical assistance with the photography, many thanks go to Monte Draper, more than a newspaper photographer. Bob Smith of Image Photography in Bemidji helped with late night developing to meet a deadline. Lin Wahlberg, Michael Crowley, and Richard Faulkner contributed artful photos to supplement those that I took for the text. I am grateful to the administrators, teachers, and parents who let me visit their classrooms and photograph the many goings-on: the Blackduck, Kids Konnection, and Bi-Cap Centers of Bi-County Head Start, Bemidji, Minnesota; The Onigum Center of Leech Lake Head Start, Cass Lake, Minnesota; the classrooms of Pat Sanford and the Early Intervention Program at Paul Bunyan School, Bemidji, Minnesota; the Shirley G. Moore Laboratory Nursery School at the University of Minnesota, Minneapolis; and the classrooms of Ina Rambo and Diane Lerberg at Audobon School, Minneapolis, Minnesota.

Clerical assistance was provided by Cherry Brouwer of the Child Development Training Program at Bemidji State University; thank you for momentous computer inputting. Gratitude is also expressed to Joan Abbott, for clutch final reading.

The entire editorial staff at Delmar, headed by Erin O'Connor, have been supportive, professional and efficient. They made the task easier. Special thanks go to Erin for bringing new life to the project.

About the Author

Dan Gartrell began as an elementary school teacher in an inner-city school in Ohio during the 1960s. He moved to Minnesota in 1968 to teach in the Head Start program of the Red Lake Band of Ojibwe at Red Lake, Minnesota. In the early seventies he attended Bemidji State University to obtain his Masters Degree. At the university he became field instructor for the Child Development Training Program (CDTP) and delivered coursework on-site to non-degreed Head Start staff.

Dan went on to complete a doctoral program at the University of North Dakota. His dissertation was on the topic "Self-Concept Development and the Teacher-Child Relationship." He returned to Bemidji State University as a field advisor for the Child Development Training Program, which was one of 13 pilot projects nationally field testing the Child Development Associate program. Dan was made director of CDTP in 1975. He is currently director of CDTP and professor of early childhood and elementary education at Bemidji State University.

Dan has given over 100 workshops and presentations locally, regionally, and nationally on the topics of guidance discipline and liberation teaching. He has written articles for *Young Children* and other publications on these topics, creative art, and outcomes-based education. He has long been active in the Minnesota Association for the Education of Young Children having served two terms as secretary. In 1988 he drafted a position document, for the Association, "Developmentally Appropriate Guidance of Young Children." With the Association's permission the document is included as Appendix C. of the text.

Dan is a member of a blended family that includes his wife, Dr. Julie Jochum, five children in their teens and twenties—Jesse, Kateri, Adam, Sara, Angie—and granddaughter, Julia. Dan comments that the family has added much to his understanding about guidance. Of his granddaughter he says, "I've got pictures! They're in the book."

(Courtesy Monte Draper, *Bemidji Pioneer.*)

Unit One

Foundations of a Guidance Approach

Unit One Chapter Summary

Chapter 1: *The Guidance Tradition*

Chapter one provides historical overview of the guidance tradition. Direct quotes by "giants in the field" are included to provide their own thoughts about child development, education, and the role of guidance. The tradition of teacher-parent partnerships in early childhood education is explored.

Chapter 2: *Mistaken Behavior*

Chapter two presents a concept in line with the work of the self psychologists for understanding young children's behavior: that behavior traditionally considered as "misbehavior" is more constructively viewed as **mistaken.** Three levels of mistaken behavior are analyzed. Considerations for acquainting parents with the construct are provided.

Chapter 3: *Guidance Discipline: The Bottom Line*

Chapter three develops four principles of a guidance approach: that it builds from positive teacher-child relations; reduces the need for mistaken behavior; takes a solution-orientation; and involves teamwork with other adults—particularly parents—on behalf of the child.

Chapter 4: *Creating the Climate for a Guidance Approach*

Chapter four examines considerations important for implementing the guidance approach: (*a*) The teacher is a professional; (*b*) a learning dynamic is intrinsic to the child; (*c*) developmentally appropriate practice defines the nature of teacher-child relations; (*d*) the teacher practices liberation teaching; (*e*) the teacher creates a climate for partnership with parents.

1

The Guidance Tradition

GUIDING QUESTIONS

As you read chapter one, you will discover answers to the following questions:

- **Who were the pioneers of the guidance tradition?**
- **Who were mid-century influences on the guidance tradition?**
- **What was the significance of discipline trends in the 1980s?**
- **What is the state of the guidance tradition today?**
- **What is the role of parents in the guidance tradition?**

A guidance approach to discipline has roots in the history of Western education and is tied to the thoughts of progressive educators over the last two centuries. The basis of guidance, the empowering of productive human activity, lies in the view that human nature, in the embodiment of the young child, has potential for good. In this view the role of the adult is not to "discipline the child away from evil" but to assist the child to develop the personal strength and understanding necessary to make ethical decisions. This learning process takes into adulthood to accomplish. Given the fragile nature of childhood, learning these difficult skills requires caring adults.

In the guidance tradition, the outcomes of classroom discipline are clear: to instill in children the abilities to get along with others, express strong feelings in acceptable ways, and solve problems using words. At bottom, these are the goals for citizens of a democratic society (Gartrell, 1992). For this reason, a guidance approach transcends the role and functions of traditional classroom discipline (Gartrell, 1987; Greenberg, 1988, 1992).

Unit one provides the foundations of a guidance approach. This first chapter documents that over the years progressive educators consistently have called for an integrative discipline model, one that links the positive potential of the

Figure 1–1 Guidance discipline is based on the view that human nature has the potential for good.

child, the interactive nature of appropriate curriculum, and the role of the caring teacher as democratic leader. The tradition that has lead to guidance as the necessary approach to relations in the classroom is traced in the chapter.

PIONEERS OF THE GUIDANCE TRADITION

A principle in the guidance tradition is that discipline cannot be separated from the curriculum used, and that both are tied to views of human nature (Gartrell, 1992). This three-way relationship is no recent occurrence and can be seen in the seventeenth century in the writings of the educators of the time—the

Figure 1–2 Believing that children tended toward evil, school masters of previous times found it necessary to "beat the devil" out of children—corporal punishment that would be considered child abuse today. (Courtesy Berger, *The Developing Person through Childhood and Adolescence*, New York: Worth Publishers, Inc.)

clergy. Osborn's informative chronology, *Early Childhood Education in Historical Perspective*, frames a fundamental disagreement about the nature of childhood that still affects education and discipline practice today (1980). Osborn documents that within the clergy two contrasting reasons were given for the importance of education. The 1621 treatise, *A Godly Form of Household Government*, states:

> The young child which lieth in the cradle is both wayward and full of affection; and though his* body be small, yet he hath a wrongdoing heart and is inclined to evil. . .If this spark be suffered to increase, it will rage over and burn down the whole house. For we are changed and become good, not by birth, but by education (p.24)."

An opposing point of view portrayed the child as a **tabula rosa** (blank slate). This point of view can be seen in Earle's *Microcosmography* (1628):

> The child is a small letter, yet the best copy of Adam. . .His soul is yet a white paper unscribbled with observations. . .and he knows no evil (p.24).

Among western cultures, the prevalence of the first view meant that strict discipline based on obedience and corporal punishment has been widely practiced into the twentieth century (Berger, 1991; deMause, 1974). Corporal punishment as an issue is still unresolved in the nation's schools. There has been progress toward humane educational practice, however, and some teachers

---

* For purposes of accuracy, masculine pronouns are retained in quotes by others. Otherwise, the author has sought to reduce and balance gender-specific pronoun

of the attitude expressed by Earle always have used tenets of the guidance approach.

During the nineteenth century such European educators as Herbart, Pestalozzi, and Froebel fundamentally reformed educational practice, in no small part as a result of their views about human nature. Herbart and Pestalozzi recognized that children learned best through real experiences rather than through the rote recitation of facts. Pestalozzi put into practice schools for the "less well-to-do" and so modelled the beginning of universal education. He also co-wrote *Manual for Mothers*, which provided guidance for mothers of very young children and inspired Friedrich Froebel's interest in early childhood education (Lilley, 1967). Herbart wrote effectively about the importance of motivating students to take an interest in learning, a fundamental **preventive** guidance strategy (Osborn, 1980).

Froebel's Kindergarten

Froebel was the originator of the kindergarten, at the time intended to serve children three to six. The purpose of the kindergarten was to provide an extension of the family life that Froebel thought all children should have. Education for Froebel was guidance so that the "innate impulses of the child" could be harmoniously developed through creative activity. In line with his early views about the role of development in education, Froebel believed that the nature of the child was essentially good and that "faults" were the product of particular experiences. In *Friedrich Froebel: A Selection From His Writings* (1967), Lilley quotes the educator:

> There are many faults. . .which arise simply through carelessness. When children act on an impulse which in itself may be harmless or even praiseworthy, they can become so entirely absorbed that they have no thought for the consequences, and indeed from their own limited experience can have no knowledge of them. . . .

> Moreover, it is certainly true that as a rule the child is first made bad by some other person, often by the educator himself. This can happen when everything which the child does out of ignorance or thoughtlessness or even from a keen sense of right and wrong is attributed to an intention to do evil. Unhappily there are among teachers those who always see children as mischievous, spiteful. . .whereas others see at most an overexuberant sense of life or a situation which has got out of hand (Lilley, p. 135).

In these views about children and their behavior, Froebel showed clear understanding of the need for a guidance approach to discipline.

Maria Montessori

As a transition figure between a pedagogy dominated by the philosophy of nineteenth century and the psychology of the twentieth, Maria Montessori was the first woman psychiatrist in modern Italy as well as a guiding force in early childhood education. Similar to Froebel, Montessori maintained that a fundamental principle in "scientific pedagogy" was that "the child is in a continual state of growth and metamorphosis, whereas the adult has reached the norm of the species." (Standing, 1962).

Montessori—as well as her American contemporary, John Dewey— abhorred traditional didactic practices, with children planted behind desks and expected to recite lessons of little meaning in their lives. Both criticized approaches to discipline based on this pervasive schooling practice. In her comprehensive, *The Montessori Method* (written in 1912 and translated in 1964), the educator asserted:

> We know only too well the sorry spectacle of the teacher who, in the ordinary schoolroom, must pour certain cut and dried facts into the heads of the scholars. In order to succeed in this barren task, she finds it necessary to discipline her pupils into immobility and to force their attention. Prizes and punishments are ever-ready and efficient aids to the master who must force into a given attitude of mind and body those who are condemned to be his listeners (1964, p. 21).

Montessori went on to devote an entire chapter of her text to an alternate discipline methodology that was more respectful of the child's development. For Montessori the purpose of education and discipline is the same: to encourage the development of responsible decision-making (1964).

John Dewey

John Dewey is considered the architect of progressive education in the United States. Over a sixty year period, Dewey raised the nation's consciousness about the kind of education needed in an industrial society. Like Montessori, Dewey viewed discipline as differing in method depending on the curriculum followed. In the 1900 monograph, *School and Society*, Dewey commented:

> If you have the end in view of forty of fifty children learning certain set lessons, to be recited to the teacher, your discipline must be devoted to securing that result. But if the end in view is the development of a spirit of social co-operation and community life, discipline must grow out of and be relative to such an aim. . . There is a certain disorder in any busy workshop; there is not silence; persons are not engaged in maintaining certain fixed physical postures; their arms are not folded; they are not holding their books thus and so. They are doing a variety of things, and there is the confusion, the bustle that results from activity. Out of the occupation, out of doing things that are to produce results, and out of doing these in a social and co-operative way, there is born a discipline of its own kind and type. Our whole conception of discipline changes when we get this point of view (pp. 16-17).

With Dewey's writings, the guidance approach to discipline became established in American educational thought.

Figure 1–3 When the classroom becomes a "busy workshop", our conception of discipline changes.

MID-CENTURY INFLUENCES: THE DEVELOPMENTAL AND SELF PSYCHOLOGISTS

Jean Piaget

Decidedly clinical in his orientation, Jean Piaget was the pre-eminent developmental psychologist of the 20th century. Writing in French, the Swiss psychologist shared with Montessori the precept that the developing child learns most effectively by interacting with the environment. Further, Piaget shared with Dewey a basic regard for the social context of learning—that peer interaction is essential for healthy development. Piaget agreed with both that education must be a cooperative endeavor and that discipline must respect and respond to this fact. In his landmark work, *The Moral Judgement of the Child* (1932), Piaget stated:

> The essence of democracy resides in its attitude towards law as a product of the collective will, and not as some thing emanating from a transcendent will or from the authority established by divine right. It is therefore the essence of democracy to replace the unilateral respect of authority by the mutual respect of autonomous wills. So that the problem is to know what will best prepare the child for the task of citizenship. Is it the habit of external discipline gained under the influence of unilateral respect and of adult constraint, or is it the habit of internal discipline, of mutual respect and of "self government"?. . . If one thinks of the systematic resistance offered by pupils to the authoritarian method, and the admirable ingenuity employed by children the world over to evade disciplinary constraint, one cannot help regarding as defective a system which allows so much effort to be wasted instead of using it in cooperation (pp. 366-367).

Among the developmental psychologists and educators in the United States who have built upon Piaget's foundation are Constance Kamii, David Elkind, David Weikart, and Rosalind Charles. Each is mentioned in subsequent chapters. By redefining education in a **constructivist** perspective that the child constructs knowledge by acting upon the environment, the developmental psychologists have changed the way teaching, learning, the curriculum, and discipline all are defined.

The Self Psychologists

During the 1960s the writing of such psychologists as Erickson (1963), Rogers (1961), Maslow (1962), and Combs (1962) focused on the developing self as the primary dynamic in human behavior. These theorists suggested that to the extent children felt safe in their circumstances and valued as members of the group, they would see themselves positively and not need to act out against the world. Numerous studies of self-image (the collection of feelings about who one is) and self-concept (the conscious picture of who one is) were conducted. Collected in works by Purkey (1970) and Havacheck (1970), the trend in these studies was that children who felt better about themselves got along better

with others and did better in school. Moreover, the studies found a high corre-
lation between schooling practices and heightened or lowered self-esteem.
Purkey stated:

> The indications seem to be that success or failure in school significantly influence
> the ways in which students view themselves. Students who experience repeated
> success in school are likely to develop positive feelings about their abilities, while
> those who encounter failure tend to develop negative views of themselves (p. 26).

Purkey discussed schooling practices that reinforced failure and frustration:

> Traditionally, the child is expected to adjust to the school rather than the school
> adjusting to the child. To insure this process, the school is prepared to dispense
> rewards and punishments, successes and failures on a massive scale. The child is
> expected to learn to live in a new environment and to compete for the rewards of
> obedience and scholarship. . .Unfortunately a large number of schools employ a
> punitive approach to education. Punishment, failure, and depreciation are charac-
> teristic. In fact, Deutsch (1963) argues that it is often in the school that highly
> charged negative attitudes toward learning evolve. The principle that negative
> self-concepts should be prevented is ignored by many schools (p. 40).

The **self psychologists** provided insights that assisted educators with
learners of all ages. Their ideas were valued especially in schools practicing
"open education" and programs serving preschool children. Such writers as
Dreikurs (1968, 1982) and Ginott (1972) adapted principles from self-
psychology into general models of discipline, still studied and utilized today.

Figure 1–4 Repeated success experiences help children build positive feelings
about their abilities.

Theodore Dreikurs

Theodore Dreikurs made a substantial contribution to educators' understanding of the "goals" of misbehavior. Building on his background in Adlerian theory, Dreikurs emphasized that all behavior is goal-directed and that the preeminent goal of behavior is social acceptance.

> Behavior is purposive or goal-directed. . .Humans are social beings with the overriding goal of belonging or finding a place in society. . .The child's behavior indicates the ways and means by which he tries to be significant. If these ways and means are antisocial and disturbing, then the child did not develop the right idea about how to find his place. The antisocial ways or "mistaken goals". . .reflect an error in the child's judgment and in his comprehension of life and the necessities of social living. To understand a child, we must understand the child's purpose of behavior, a purpose of which the child may be unaware. (1982, p. 9)

In such books as *Psychology in the Classroom* (1968), Dreikurs developed a theory, using four levels, for why children misbehave. A clear synopsis of the "four mistaken goals of misbehavior" is provided in *Building Classroom Discipline* (1989) by C.M. Charles:

> Dreikurs identified four mistaken goals: **attention getting, power seeking, revenge seeking, and displaying inadequacy.** These goals identify the purposes of student misbehavior. They are usually sought in sequential order. If attention getting fails to gain recognition, the student will progress to power-seeking behavior. If that is not rewarded they move on to getting revenge and then to inadequacy. (p. 75)

As important as Dreikurs' theories are, they have not been correlated with recent understandings about the development of the young child. Neither have they received scrutiny for consistency with ideas about personality development contributed by the self psychologists. Stated in Dreikurs' writings, the "overriding goal" of student behavior is acceptance by important others. This view differs from theory based on developmental research and the writing of psychologists like Maslow and Combs. In the view of developmental and self psychologists, social acceptance *is* a significant factor in children's behavior, but it is regarded more as a foundation for healthy personal development than an end in itself. Between three and eight years, children make tremendous strides in thinking processes, the communication of ideas and feelings, perceptual-motor skills, self-concept development, cultural identity, and social responsiveness. They are engaged in a process of **total development**. Yet with the natural insecurities of childhood and limited ability to understand the needs of others, children make mistakes. Social acceptance of each child even while addressing mistaken behavior, sustains **healthy personal development**, the primary goal in human behavior (Maslow, 1962; Rogers, 1961).

In his insistence that unacceptable behavior has purposes that adults can understand, Dreikurs nonetheless has made a vital contribution to the guidance tradition in educational thought (Charles, 1989). Dreikurs' writings argue persuasively that unacceptable behavior is a result of mistakes that children make in the "purposeful" goal of getting along with others (1968, 1982). By placing misbehavior in the context of social acceptance, Dreikurs raised the discussion of discipline from judgments about children's morality to strategies for helping children learn acceptable behavioral alternatives.

Halm Ginott

If Dreikurs has contributed to the theory of the guidance tradition, Ginott has contributed to its language. The opening lines from the chapter, "Congruent Communication" in his classic book, *Teacher and Child* (1972), illustrate the eloquent phrasing that typify Ginott's "psychology of acceptance":

> Where do we start if we are to improve life in the classroom? By examining how we respond to children. How a teacher communicates is of decisive importance. It affects a child's life for good or for bad. Usually we are not overly concerned about whether one's response conveys acceptance or rejection. Yet to a child this difference is fateful, if not fatal.
>
> Teachers who want to improve relations with children need to unlearn their habitual language of rejection and acquire a new language of acceptance. To reach a child's mind a teacher must capture his heart. Only if a child feels right can he think right (p. 69).

Virtually all early childhood education texts written in the last twenty years have emphasized a need for discipline methods that respect the feelings and dignity of the individual child. Although Ginott's writings do not address the early childhood age group per se, they speak to adult-child relations at all levels and are in agreement with the tone and philosophy of the guidance approach. Ginott's words will be cited frequently in chapters to come. His writings nurture the caring spirit that infuses the guidance tradition.

THE EIGHTIES: GUIDANCE OR PUNISHMENT?

For all of the contributions of writers in the guidance tradition, many of the criticisms made by Froebel, Montessori, Dewey, Piaget, Ginott and others still apply today. With the "back to the basics" emphasis and the "educational reform" of the late seventies and eighties, curriculum and teaching methods became more prescribed. Though the emphasis clashed directly with increased understanding about how young children learn (Bredekamp, 1987), the prescriptive academic influence has meant increasing numbers of young children at school spending long hours in their seats, following directions passively, and completing endless work sheets.

In some kindergarten and many primary classrooms the prescribed academic program was not new—classrooms had always been run this way. But on a

Figure 1–5 To reach a child's mind a teacher must capture his/her heart. (Courtesy Lin Wahlberg, Early Childhood Family Education Program, Bemidji, Minnesota.)

broad scale, kindergarten programs were expected to become academic, and preschool programs felt pressures to "get children ready for kindergarten." The emphasis on academic programming with younger children lent themselves to tightly controlled classrooms (Elkind, 1987). Except for the occasional teacher who made human relations a priority, the interactive nature of the guidance approach did not fit the regimen of the prescribed, academic classroom.

Assertive Discipline

Looking for methods to increase student compliance, administrators and teachers embraced new, "more effective" discipline systems. Predominant among these programs was Canter's Assertive Discipline, "a take-charge approach for today's educator" (1976). Developed in a clinical setting for emotionally disturbed students, assertive discipline gained rapid acceptance in school systems across the country (Canter, 1989). Though its effects on long term development are still unknown, it was used with kindergarten children and high school students—and even in some prekindergarten programs.

As followed in the 1980s, common practices under assertive discipline included:

- making rules and establishing consequences with children;
- obtaining consent agreements from parents for use of the system;
- recording names, often publically, of children who break rules;
- issuing "disciplinary referral slips" to repeat offenders—which commonly include trips to the principal, phone calls home, and "in-school suspensions";
- holding periodic popcorn parties or class outings for children who have complied with the system—and excluding those who have not.

By the end of the 1980s, debate about the effects of assertive discipline had become heated and ongoing (Brewer, 1992; Canter, 1988, 1989; Curwin & Mendler, 1988; Curwin & Mendler, 1989; Gartrell, 1987a; Hitz, 1988; Render, Padilla & Krank, 1989).

Canter (1989) points out that assertive discipline clearly establishes the authority of the teacher and the role of the student. The model teaches students to choose between the rewards of compliance and the consequences of disobedience. It provides a consistent system of rewards and punishments for teachers within a classroom and across a school or district. It involves parents. In the eyes of Canter and his adherents, it "works."

Critics, including Brewer (1992), Curwin & Mendler (1989), Gartrell (1987a), and Hitz (1988), argue that assertive discipline has negative implications for children and for teachers.

Effects on Children. Because the model does not allow for individual circumstances—rules and their consequences are cast in stone—children who make innocent mistakes suffer. The tendency toward public identification of "culprits" causes humiliation and begins negative self-fulfilling prophecies. Students frequently identified and punished grow immune to the system and become stigmatized as "out-groups" in the classroom and school (Render, Padilla, & Krank, 1989).

Though the system includes positive recognition for compliance, even the public rewards set up "winners" and "losers" within the class. Classrooms in which teachers have become entrenched in the negative aspects of the system are unpleasant, anxious places to be. The emphasis on obedience in the assertive discipline classroom inadequately prepares children to function in a democracy (Curwin & Mendler, 1989; Render, Padilla & Krank, 1989). Directing their comments to early childhood, Gartrell (1987a) and Hitz (1988) assert that the Canter model is inappropriate for use with children during their most impressionable years.

Effects on Teachers. A second criticism is that the system seriously reduces the teacher's ability to use professional judgment (Gartrell, 1987a). Because of the "obedience or consequences" emphasis, the teacher cannot react to the uniqueness of individual situations or individual children's needs. Neither can the teacher accommodate developmental, social/cultural, or learning style differences that manifest themselves in behaviors outside of acceptable limits (Hitz, 1988). As well, because it is essentially authoritarian, the model cannot adapt itself to democratic, interactive teaching styles—necessary for developmentally appropriate practice; the system pressures the teacher to be an authoritarian. Where schools or districts have mandated the system, teachers are expected to use it even if they are uncomfortable with it; the danger is that they may become technicians rather than professionals (Curwin & Mendler, 1989; Gartrell, 1987a; Render, Padilla, & Krank, 1989). In some situations, parents who object to use of the system may find themselves at odds with teachers and administrators charged with soliciting parental compliance. Often, parents who object are the very ones who might otherwise become productively involved (unpublished correspondence of parents with the author).

In their text, *Discipline With Dignity*, Curwin and Mendler say this about the "obedience models of discipline" of the 1980s:

> It is ironic that the current mood of education is in some ways behind the past. The 1980s might someday be remembered as the decade when admiration was reserved for principals, cast as folk heroes, walking around schools with baseball bats, and for teachers and whole schools that systematically embarrassed students by writing their names on the chalkboard. But we do have hope that the pendulum will once again swing to the rational position of treating children as people with needs and feelings that are not that different from adults. Once we begin to understand how obedience is contrary to the goals of our culture and education, the momentum will begin to shift. Our view is that the highest virtue of education is to teach students to be self-responsible and fully functional. In all but extreme cases, obedience contradicts these goals (p. 24).

The very term "discipline with dignity" supports and reinforces the guidance approach.

THE TRANSITION FROM DISCIPLINE TO GUIDANCE

At the same time that obedience discipline systems were taking hold in many school systems, a different trend was occurring. Inspired by the nursery school movement earlier in the century and the work of the developmental psychologists, writers at the preschool level were declaring their independence from the conventional role and functions of classroom discipline. Textbooks in the nursery school tradition, such as Read (1950, ninth edition—1993), phrased the setting of the preschool as a "human relations laboratory" in which the teacher models positive guidance skills. In the writings of Stone (1978), Shickedanz & Shickedanz (1981), Cherry (1983), Marion (1986, third edition—1991), Clewett (1988), and Greenberg (1988), careful distinction was drawn between positive and negative discipline practices. Teachers using negative discipline relied on

Figure 1-6 The guidance approach addresses children's behaviors, but in ways that support self-esteem.

punishment to enforce compliance or impose retribution (Clewett, 1988). Teachers using positive discipline in contrast, worked to prevent problems and, when they occurred, intervened in ways respectful of the child's self-esteem (Gartrell, 1987b; Greenberg, 1988; Wickert, 1989).

Significantly, after the debate about the place of obedience discipline systems began, textbooks not specific to early childhood education have renewed the need for positive discipline practices. Albert's *Cooperative Discipline* (1989) features the subtitle: "How to Manage Your Classroom and Promote Self Esteem." Based on the theories of Dreikurs, the book stresses diagnostic and communication skills to build cooperative relations not just between teacher and student, "but also between teacher and parent, teacher and teacher, and teacher and administrator" (1989, p. 3). Two other discipline texts, *Discipline with Dignity* (Curwin & Mendler, 1988) and *A Guide to Positive Discipline* (Keating, Pickering, Slack, & White, 1990), are guidebooks that present specific classroom management approaches. Each offers a coordinated system that can be used school-wide but still allows the teacher room for professional judgment while respecting the integrity of the learner.

In the early childhood literature, discomfort with the term "discipline" itself has emerged. Despite the claim that discipline is "value neutral" and an "umbrella term" (Marion, 1991), "discipline" still carries the baggage of negative connotations. The term to "discipline a child" suggests punishment, a practice unacceptable in the guidance approach. Gartrell (1987b) points out that in problem situations, teachers tend to blur the distinction between punishment and discipline, and not to think about "guidance" at all. He comments that unless handled so that a logical consequence is logical from the child's point of view, the child tends to perceive the act of discipline as punishment. For this reason, the teacher needs to emphasize guidance, which involves carefully teaching children about consequences and behavioral alternatives (1987).

In *Guiding Young Children* (1990), Reynolds provides a problem-solving approach that begins with setting up the environment and includes specific communication and problem-solving strategies and techniques. Reynolds argues that the problem-solving approach precludes the necessity of the term "discipline." She does not use the term in her text "in order to avoid confusion and misinterpretation" (1990, p. 3). In fact, the term "discipline" generally is fading from the early childhood literature, supplanted by "guidance." For some teachers, however, unless the connection between the two terms is made, there may be a tendency to think of "guidance" in one set of circumstances and "discipline," perhaps lapsing into punishment, in another. For this reason, the present text highlights "a guidance approach to discipline," shortened to either the "guidance approach" or "guidance discipline." It is the hope of many that in the future the term "guidance" alone will suffice.

The Contribution of Developmentally Appropriate Practice

In 1987, the National Association for the Education of Young Children (NAEYC) published *Developmentally Appropriate Practice in Early Childhood Programs Serving Children From Birth Through Age 8* (Bredekamp). This NAEYC policy statement has synthesized prevailing trends in research and theory pertaining to the education of young children. Significant is the fact that chapters in the work are supported by 550 separate references to authorities in the child development and early childhood fields. The position statement advocates educational practices that allow for an interactive approach to learning and teacher-child relations. Developmentally appropriate practices discussed reflect the guidance-oriented approach to discipline advocated by Froebel, Montessori, Dewey, Piaget, and the self psychologists. Clearly espousing the guidance tradition, the NAEYC document cites "positive guidance techniques" that encourage the teacher to: establish routines and expectations understandable to children; use methods such as modelling and encouraging expected behavior; redirect behavior toward more acceptable activity; and set clear limits. "Teachers' expectations match and respect children's developing capabilities" (p. 55). In addition:

> Children are provided many opportunities to develop social skills such as cooperating, helping, negotiating, and talking with the person involved to solve interpersonal problems. Teachers facilitate the development of these positive social skills at all times (p. 55).

According to the NAEYC document, **inappropriate** discipline practices are these:

> Teachers dominate the environment by talking to the whole group most of the time and telling children what to do. . . Teachers spend a great deal of time enforcing rules, punishing unacceptable behavior, demeaning children who misbehave, making children sit and be quiet, or refereeing disagreements (1987, p. 55).

> Teachers lecture about the importance of appropriate social behavior and use punishment or deprivations (such as no recess) when children who become restless and bored with seatwork whisper, talk, or wander around or when children dawdle and do not finish their work in the allotted time. . . Teachers place themselves in an adversarial role with children, emphasizing their power to reward acceptable behavior and punish unacceptable behavior. Their primary goal is maintaining control of the classroom. . .Whether or not the teacher intends, her attitude often feels demeaning to the child (p. 73).

This important document, pertaining to children three to eight, concretely contrasts guidance with developmentally inappropriate discipline practices based on obedience.

In summary, guidance discipline goes beyond the traditional goal of classroom discipline: to induce student compliance toward the authority of the teacher and the expectations of the educational program (Gartrell, 1992). A

Figure 1–7 Teachers facilitate the development of positive social skills at all times.

guidance approach teaches the skills children need in order to get along with others, express strong feelings in acceptable ways, and solve problems with words—in short to function as citizens of a democracy (Gartrell, 1987; Greenberg, 1988). Guidance discipline facilitates an interactive learning environment in which the adult functions as democratic leader and the child constructs meaning through developmentally appropriate activities (Greenberg, 1992). A guidance approach assists children to take pride in their developing personal and cultural identities and to view differing human qualities as sources of affirmation and learning. The approach links together teacher, parent and child as an interactive team.

PARENTS AND THE GUIDANCE TRADITION

A full history of parents and the guidance tradition would document events that have perpetuated both cooperative and adversarial trends in parent-teacher relations. Noted here are a few major events that have supported each trend. Significantly, parent-teacher partnerships have a tradition in early childhood education going back to the last century. Positive teacher-parent relations contribute at a fundamental level to the success of the guidance approach.

Parents and Froebel's Kindergartens

Froebel's first kindergartens called for cooperation between teachers and parents. As Lilley indicates, Froebel recognized the importance of the family in the education of the child:

> The child fully develops his driving need for creative activity only if the family, which is the vehicle of his existence, makes it possible for him to do so (1967, p. 94).

Home visits were a part of the first kindergarten programs, and Froebel included parents in his vision of early childhood education:

> The plan [for the kindergarten] is primarily to provide games and means of occupation such as meet the needs of parent and child, educator and pupil, and possess interest and meaning for adults as they share children's play or observe children sympathetically and intelligently (1967, p. 98).

In his writing Froebel called upon the mothers of Germany to take leadership in organizing kindergartens nationwide (Lilley, 1967). The original kindergartens, in Germany and then other countries, relied on parent involvement and began a practice that has continued in early childhood education ever since. The first kindergartens in America were run by immigrant parents who wanted the kindergarten experience for their own children. As the beginning point for K–12 education, kindergartens traditionally have enjoyed high levels of parent interest, allowing the opportunity for productive teacher-parent relations to this day.

Parents and Montessori's Children's Houses

Montessori, no less than Froebel, encouraged parent involvement in the Children's Houses of Italy. Perhaps due to her standing as doctor, psychiatrist, and educator, Montessori saw the directress (teacher) as a consummate professional, providing a model for children and parents alike. Montessori's "Children's Houses" were located in tenement buildings and were attended by the children of the residents. Directresses lived in the tenements in which they worked. In her definitive work, *The Montessori Method*, Montessori described the "modelling" role of the directress:

> The directress is always at the disposition of the mothers, and her life, as cultured and educated person, is a constant example to the inhabitants of the house, for she is obliged to live in the tenement and to be therefore a co-habitant with the families of all her little pupils. This is a fact of immense importance (pp. 61-62).

Despite a professional-client emphasis in the relationship, an element of partnership was also present. The parent and directress met each week to discuss the child's progress at school and home. Moreover, Montessori reported that the parents felt a sense of "collective ownership" toward the Children's Houses which she discussed this way:

> The parents know that the "Children's House" is their property, and is maintained by a portion of the rent they pay. The mothers may go at any hour of the day to watch, to admire, or to meditate upon the life there (pp. 63-64).

Parents and the Nursery School Movement

Between 1890 and the 1930s, the child study movement, along with the growing influence of Freudian psychology, sparked new interest in humane child-rearing practices and child-oriented education. The nursery school movement in Britain and the U.S. was an expression of these values. Cooperative nursery schools, administered by parents, began in Chicago in 1916 and continue on a nationwide basis today (Osborn, 1980). The nursery school model, with parent governing boards and close parent-teacher relations, has proven popular in other types of early childhood programs and private "alternative" schools as well.

Parents and Head Start

By the 1960s new knowledge about the importance of the early years in development began to infuse government policy. In 1965 Project Head Start began and parent involvement became an integral part of its operations. Head Start encourages cooperative parent involvement at several levels. In the home-based option, home visitors work with individual parents and children on a regular basis. In the center-based option, besides regular conferences with teachers and periodic home visits, parents are encouraged to volunteer in the classroom. Under both options, parents are given active policy roles on a local, agencywide and regional basis. Many trained Head Start staff began as parents with children in the program. As the families served by Head Start are predominantly low-income, the contribution of Head Start to parent involvement in American education is significant.

Parents and the Public Schools

Notably, two public school programs that have fostered close parent-teacher relations are early childhood programs. In many states, early childhood special education teachers may establish contact with parents before the infant has left the hospital. Teachers in early childhood special education work with the family in some cases for years before the child begins kindergarten. Parent-teacher collaboration is a hallmark of successful early childhood special education.

Run through school systems and other agencies, a new generation of parent-child programs include weekly parenting classes held in conjunction with preschool activities. Early Childhood Family Education, a state-wide system in Minnesota, provides a model for these programs, which involve parents directly (Kristensen and Billman, 1987). At the least, Head Start and the two school-based early childhood programs are increasing parents' confidence at communicating with professional educators and are contributing to the concept of the parent-teacher team.

Figure 1–8 Parent-teacher partnerships are accepted practice in Head Start, early childhood family education, and other types of preschool programs.

The Institution of the School. There has been a tradition in public K–12 education for school personnel to assume an authority-client relationship with parents. Between the end of the Civil War and 1920, the population of the United States more than doubled with many new citizens being non-English speaking immigrants. Universal education got its start during this time. In order to "Americanize the aliens," kindergarten teachers especially were requested to make home visits and start mothers' groups (Weber, 1919). The practice of the Bureau of Education in the Department of the Interior (with the encouragement of business leaders) was to reach children in the school and mothers in the home so that immigrant and other non-mainstream families could be made "good citizens" (Locke, 1919). Though diminished since the 1960s, this "melting pot" idea is still a part of American education. With the advent of compulsory attendance laws over time, American schools have assumed a powerful role in communities, as the institutions charged with socializing children to American society.

One result of the schools' growing institutional power is that opportunity for real parent input has become limited, especially for parents "out of the mainstream" (Greenberg, 1989). Though the parents of children with disabilities have led the way, the determination and confidence necessary to advocate for one's child at school remains for many a daunting task. In most school districts, it is up to the individual teacher to build cooperative parent-teacher relations, largely on his or her own time. Indeed, individual teachers can make a difference, and teachers and parents together can change school policy. From the perspective of a guidance approach to discipline, the situation will improve as schools give more recognition and resources to parent-teacher conferences, home visits, and innovative programs that help parents to feel they are valued partners in the education of their children.

The Role of Parents in Developmentally Appropriate Practice

The NAEYC position document is significant because it ties together research about child development and appropriate teaching practice. As shown, the discipline methods are those in the guidance tradition. A dimension of the guidance approach is close, cooperative relations between teachers and parents. As discussed, Froebel and Montessori each recognized parents as the primary educators of their children. They involved parents in their programs to ensure that differences in values and lifestyle did not negate the purposes of their programs. Following through to today, NAEYC's "Developmentally Appropriate Practices" identifies characteristics of parent-teacher relations that continue the guidance tradition:

> Teachers work in parent-teacher partnerships, communicating regularly to build mutual understanding and greater consistency for children (p. 57).

> Teachers have time for periodic conferences with each child's parents. Parents' visits to school are welcomed at all times and home visits by teachers are

encouraged. Teachers listen to parents, seek to understand their goals for their children and are respectful of cultural and family differences. Members of each child's family are encouraged to help in the classroom. . .to help with tasks related to but not occurring within the classroom. . .and to assist with decision making where appropriate (p. 75).

For the guidance approach to be effective, the teacher involves the parent as a team member on behalf of the child. The parent-teacher partnership is part of developmentally appropriate practice, and of the guidance tradition.

SUMMARY

Who were the pioneers of the guidance tradition?

A guidance approach to discipline has roots in the history of Western education and is tied to the thoughts of progressive educators over the last two centuries. A difference in viewpoints among Christian clergy as far back as the seventeenth century framed contrasting beliefs about the child, and hence the role of education and discipline. One view was that the child is inherently sinful and in need of strict instruction. Another view was that the child is essentially innocent and in need of careful guidance. With modern permutations, these contrasting views affect education and discipline practices today.

During the nineteenth century, Froebel considered the child to be "unfolding" toward goodness but vulnerable to the negative influences of others. He believed that the purpose of education was to guide the child along the path of wholesome development. Maria Montessori held that a mistaken practice of traditional education was to force obedience to the authority of the teacher. In her view discipline is an extension of education itself—the purpose of which is to provide for the development of responsible decision-making on the part of the child.

Like Montessori, Dewey believed that schooling practices of the day were outmoded and dependent on negative discipline. For Dewey, the classroom should be "a busy workshop," with teachers not enforcing silence, but instilling cooperation.

Who were mid-century influences in the guidance tradition?

The guidance tradition has been reinforced by many of the foremost psychologists of the last thirty years, notably from two fields of study. As the foremost developmental theorist of the 20th century, Piaget wrote that children construct the ability for intelligent, moral thought through social interactions. He argued that only when authority is shared by all members of the group can moral thought develop. Building on Piaget's work, the developmental psychologists established the importance of the child's construction of knowledge in the interactive classroom. The personality or self psychologists demonstrated the importance of supporting self-esteem in the classroom life of the child.

Two self psychologists who have contributed to the thinking of the guidance tradition are Dreikurs and Ginott. Dreikurs introduced the idea that children misbehave not because they are immoral, but because they adopt mistaken goals of behavior. Dreikurs has done much to shift our thinking about how to address children who misbehave. Rather than punish, teachers need to use strategies that redirect children's mistaken goals. Ginott has contributed much to the language of the guidance tradition. Ginott's position that teachers must show acceptance of the child even while they address unacceptable behavior is at the heart of the guidance approach.

What was the significance of discipline trends in the 1980s?

During the 1980s many school systems placed heavy emphasis on educational accountability, using such catchword phrases as "back to the basics" and "educational excellence." A consequence was an emphasis on academics even at the early primary, kindergarten, and preschool levels. In order to enforce compliance with these practices, schools began using new, "obedience" discipline systems, even with young children. While proponents argued that such systems as "assertive discipline" permitted "the teacher to teach and the student to learn," critics charged that there were often undesirable side effects. The atmosphere of many classrooms became more negative; children were being ill-prepared to function in a democracy; teachers were being reduced from professionals to technicians. Vigorous debate about the use of punitive discipline in the nation's schools has occurred.

What is the state of the guidance tradition today?

Due in part to the efforts of preschool educators, by the end of the decade arguments for guidance-oriented discipline again began to be heard. A landmark NAEYC publication edited by Bredekamp (1987) focused national attention on the need for education to be "developmentally appropriate"— responsive to the stage and needs of each child. Guidance rather than punishment empowered the active learning advocated by the NAEYC work. Some authors maintained that because of the punitive connotations attributed to "discipline," the term should be discontinued, or at least used with qualifiers. There is now general agreement that interactive, developmentally appropriate teaching techniques and a guidance approach to discipline go together. Each practice supports the other.

What is the role of parents in the guidance tradition?

Parent-teacher partnerships have been an important part of the guidance tradition. Froebel saw the kindergarten as an extension of family life and encouraged home visits and the involvement of parents. Montessori wrote of the need for collaborative relations between the directress and the parent, with parents welcome to visit the Children's Houses at any time.

Building on the tradition of British and American nursery schools, Head Start and other modern prekindergarten programs have demonstrated the value of close parent-teacher relations. The "professionalization" of the public schools during the century has given rise to paternalistic attitudes toward parent-teacher relations at this level (Greenberg, 1989). New awareness of the importance of parent-teacher partnerships is serving to change the mind set of many K–12 educators. The view that the child, teacher, and parent are on the same team, working together, is integral to the guidance approach.

FOLLOW-UP ACTIVITIES

Follow-up activities allow the student to interrelate material from the text with "real life" situations. The observations imply access to practicum experiences, the "interviews" access to teachers. When communicating about the activities, students need to respect the privacy of all participants in the observation or interview as an important professional courtesy.

1. **Who were the pioneers of the guidance tradition?**
   a. Each of the pioneers advocated teaching practices that empower children to be active, involved learners. Observe a classroom in which such teaching is in practice. What kind of guidance/discipline practices do you see in use?
   b. Interview an early childhood teacher or college professor who has studied the work of Froebel, Montessori, Dewey, or Piaget. What does the interviewee believe to be significant in how the pioneer educator thought about discipline issues.
2. **Who were mid-century influences in the guidance tradition?**
   a. An emphasis of the self psychologists is support of the child's self-esteem. Observe an instance in the classroom when an adult supported a child's self-esteem. What did the teacher say and do?
   b. Interview a teacher who values the ideas of either Dreikurs or Ginott. What is important to the teacher in the psychologist's writings?
3. **What was the significance of discipline trends in the 1980s?**
   a. One issue raised in the debate of the obedience discipline systems of the 1980s is the role of punishment. Interview a teacher about what s/he considers to be the difference between discipline and punishment? When, if ever, does the teacher believe punishment is justified?
   b. Observe an instance in a classroom where a teacher intervened to stop a conflict or disruptive situation. Respecting privacy, how did the adult teach/or fail to teach more appropriate social skills through the intervention?

4. What is the state of the guidance tradition today?

   a. Developmentally appropriate practice responds to the state of development and the needs of each child. Observe an instance of developmentally appropriate practice in a classroom. What are typical behaviors of the children? How does the teacher handle any problems that may arise?

   b. Interview two teachers at the preschool or primary grade level who are familiar with the term "developmentally appropriate practice." How are the teachers' comments similar? How are the comments different?

5. What is the role of parents in the guidance tradition?

   a. Observe an instance of productive parent-teacher relations at work. What seem to be the benefits of the productive relationship for the child in the classroom?

   b. Interview a teacher who has taught for five or more years. Talk with the teacher about how his or her views have changed/or stayed the same regarding parent-teacher relations.

SUGGESTED RESOURCES

Clewett, A.S. (1988). "Guidance and Discipline: Teaching Young Children Appropriate Behavior." *Young Children, 43*(4), pp. 26-36.

Dewey, J. (1900, reprinted 1969). *The School and Society.* Chicago: The University of Chicago Press.

Elkind, D. (1987). *Miseducation: Preschoolers at Risk.* New York: Alfred A. Knopf.

Gartrell, D.J. (1987b). "Punishment or Guidance?" *Young Children, 42*(3), pp. 55-61.

Kristensen, N. and Billman, J. (April, 1987). "Supporting Parents and Young Children," *Childhood Education.* Association for Childhood Education International.

Osborn, D.K. (1980). *Early Childhood Education in Historical Perspective.* Athens, GA: Education Associates.

Reynolds, E. (1990). *Guiding Young Children.* Mountain View, CA: Mayfield Publishing Company.

Stone, J.G. (1978). *A Guide to Discipline.* (rev. ed.) Washington, DC: National Association for the Education of Young Children.

REFERENCES

Albert, L. (1989). *A Teacher's Guide to Cooperative Discipline.* Circle Pines, MN: American Guidance Service.

Berger, S.K. (1991). *The Developing Person Through Childhood and Adolescence.* New York: Worth Publishers, Inc.

Bredekamp, S., (ed.),(1987). *Developmentally Appropriate Practice in Early Childhood Programs Serving Children From Birth Through Age 8* (expanded edition). Washington, DC: National Association for the Association of Young Children.

Brewer, J.A. (1992). *Introduction to Early Childhood Education: Primary Through the Primary Grades.* Needham Heights, MA: Allyn and Bacon.

Canter, L. and Canter, M. (1976). *Assertive Discipline.* Seal Beach, CA: Canter and Associates, Inc.

Canter, L. (1988). "Assertive Discipline and the Search for the Perfect Classroom." *Young Children*, *43*(2). p. 24.

Canter, L. (1989). "Let the Educator Beware: A Response to Curwin and Mendler." Reprinted article in: Noll, J.W., *Taking Sides: Clashing Views on Controversial Educational Issues.* Guilford, CT: The Dushkin Publishing Group, Inc.

Charles, C.M. (1989). *Building Classroom Discipline.* White Plains: Longman Inc.

Cherry, C. (1983). *Please Don't Sit on the Kids.* Belmont, CA: Pitman Learning.

Clewett, A.S. (1988). "Guidance and Discipline: Teaching Young Children Appropriate Behavior." *Young Children, 43*(4), pp. 26-36.

Combs, A.W. (ed.) (1962). *Perceiving, Behaving, Becoming: A New Focus for Education*. Washington, DC: Association for Supervision and Curriculum Development.

Curwin, R.L. and Mendler, A.N. (1988). *Discipline With Dignity*. Alexandria, VA: Association for Supervision and Curriculum Development.

Curwin, R.L. and Mendler, A.N. (1989). "Packaged Discipline Programs: Let the Buyer Beware." Reprinted article in: Noll, J.W., *Taking Sides: Clashing Views on Controversial Educational Issues*. Guilford, CT: The Dushkin Publishing Group, Inc.

deMause, L., ed. (1974). *The History of Childhood*. New York: Peter Bedrick Books.

Dewey, J. (1900, reprinted 1969). *The School and Society*. Chicago: The University of Chicago Press.

Dewey, J. (1944, reprinted 1966). *Democracy and Education*. New York: The Free Press.

Dreikurs, R. (1968). *Psychology in the Classroom* (2nd Ed.). New York.: Harper and Row, Publishers.

Dreikurs, R., Grunwald, B.B. and Pepper, F.C. (1982). *Maintaining Sanity in the Classroom*. New York: Harper and Row, Publishers.

Elkind, D. (1987). *Miseducation: Preschoolers at Risk*. New York: Alfred A. Knopf.

Erikson, E.H. (1963). *Childhood and Society*. New York: W.W. Norton and Company, Inc.

Gartrell, D.J. (1987a). "Assertive Discipline: Unhealthy for Children and Other Living Things." *Young Children, 42*(2), pp. 10-11.

Gartrell, D.J. (1987b). "Punishment or Guidance?" *Young Children, 42*(3), pp. 55-61.

Gartrell, D.J. (1992). "Discipline," Williams, L.R., Fromberg, D.P. (Eds.). *Encyclopedia of Early Childhood Education*. New York: Garland Publishing, Inc.

Ginott, H. (1972). *Teacher and Child*. New York: Avon Books.

Greenberg, P. (1988). "Avoiding 'Me Against You' Discipline," *Young Children, 43*(1), pp. 24-25.

Greenberg, P. (1989). "Parents as Partners in Young Children's Development and Education: A New American Fad? Why Does It Matter?" *Young Children, 44*(4), pp. 61-75.

Greenberg, P. (1992). "Ideas That Work With Young Children. How to Institute Some Simple Democratic Practices Pertaining to Respect, Rights, Responsibilities in Any Classroom," *Young Children, 47*(5) pp. 10-21.

Havachek, D.E. (1971). *Encounters With the Self*. New York: Holt, Rinehart and Winston, Inc.

Hitz, R. (1988). "Assertive Discipline: A Response to Lee Canter." *Young Children, 43*(2), p. 24.

Keating, B., Pickering, M., Slack, B. and White, J. (1990). *A Guide to Positive Discipline*. Boston: Allyn and Bacon.

Kristensen, N. and Billman, J. (April, 1987). "Supporting Parents and Young Children," *Childhood Education*. Association for Childhood Education International.

Lilley, I.M. (ed.). (1967). *Friedrich Froebel: A Selection From His Writings*. London: Cambridge University Press.

Locke, B. (July, 1919). "Manufacturers Indorse [sic] the Kindergarten," *Kindergarten Circular No. 4*. Washington, DC: Department of the Interior, Bureau of Education.

Marion, M. (1991). *Guidance of Young Children*. Columbus, OH: Merrill Publishing Company.

Maslow, A.H. (1962). *Toward a Psychology of Being*. Princeton, NJ: D. Van Nostrand Company, Inc.

Montessori, M. (1964). *The Montessori Method*. New York: Schocken Books.

Osborn, D.K. (1980). *Early Childhood Education in Historical Perspective*. Athens, GA: Education Associates.

Piaget, J. (1932, translated 1960). *The Moral Judgment of the Child*. Glencoe, IL: The Free Press.

Purkey, W.W. (1970). *Self Concept and School Achievement*. Englewood Cliffs, N.J.: Prentice-Hall, Inc.

Read, K.H., Gardner, P., and Mahler, B.C. (1993). *The Early Childhood Program: Human Relationships and Learning*. Fort Worth, TX: Harcourt Brace Jovanovich College Publishers (Ninth Edition).

Render, G.F., Padilla, JE.N.M. and Krank, H.M. (1989). "Assertive Discipline: A Critical Review and Analysis," *Teachers College Record, 90*(4). New York: Teachers College, Columbia University.

Reynolds, E. (1990). *Guiding Young Children*. Mountain View, CA: Mayfield Publishing Company.

Rogers, C.R. (1961). *On Becoming a Person*. Boston: Houghton Mifflin, Co.

Schickedanz, J.A. and Shickedanz, D.I., *Toward Understanding Children*. Boston: Little, Brown.

Standing, E.M. (1962). *Maria Montessori: Her Life and Work*. New York: The New American Library, Inc.

Stone, J.G. (1978). *A Guide to Discipline*. Washington, DC: National Association for the Education of Young Children.

Weber, S.H. (December, 1919). "The Kindergarten as an Americanizer," *Kindergarten Circular No. 5*. Washington, DC: Department of the Interior, Bureau of Education.

Wichert, S. (1989). *Keeping the Peace: Practicing Cooperation and Conflict Resolution with Preschoolers*. Philadelphia: New Society Publishers.

2
Mistaken Behavior

GUIDING QUESTIONS

As you read chapter two, you will discover answers to the following questions:

- **What is the concept of mistaken behavior?**
- **What are relational patterns?**
- **What are the three levels of mistaken behavior?**
- **Can mistaken behavior be intentional?**
- **How does the teacher communicate with parents about mistaken behavior?**

A guidance approach to discipline takes a positive view of human nature. With the assistance of caring adults, children develop healthy self concepts and grow toward social responsiveness. What explains, then, the "misbehavior" that young children show? If children have tendencies toward good, what is the reason for behaviors that adults label variously as "naughty," "willful," "rowdy," "aggressive," "hostile," "disruptive," or "defiant"? The answer to this question lies at the heart of guidance teaching. For most adults, at a cognitive level, the response is not hard to understand. At an affective level, however, adults sometimes have difficulty accepting the response. **The answer is that young children make mistakes** (Gartrell, 1987, 1991).

When children begin programs outside of the home, they typically are two months to six years in age. In the guidance approach, understanding about development is all important. Even seven- to eight-year-olds have lived only about one-tenth of the average life span. With limited experience and development, young children are in the beginning stages of learning prosocial behavior. In truth, it takes into adulthood for the individual to master the complex skills of expressing strong emotions acceptably and getting along with others—some adults in fact never master these skills. In this most complex of

30

Figure 2–1 How to share materials, as these kindergarten children are discovering, takes time to learn.

learning activities, children (and occasionally adults) make mistakes. A guidance approach requires that the adult regard behavior traditionally thought of as "misbehavior" as **mistaken** (Gartrell, 1987).

The second chapter of the unit provides the psychological foundation for a guidance approach to discipline. Building from the work of the developmental and self psychologists, the chapter explains why "misbehavior" is more constructively addressed when viewed as **mistaken behavior**. The chapter presents a construct of **three levels of mistaken behavior**, helpful in analyzing and responding to problems in the classroom. Chapter two also introduces typical teacher responses to mistaken behavior, intervention techniques that are used in guidance discipline. The chapter concludes by discussing use of the concept of mistaken behavior with parents.

THE CONCEPT OF MISTAKEN BEHAVIOR

As children learn skills and concepts, they make mistakes. Under the right circumstances, errors in the cognitive domain are accepted as part of the learning experience. Correction, when given, is responsive to the child's development and experience. It is offered in the form of helpful expansion or direction, and certainly is not given as criticism of the child's character. For example, a three-year-old says, "I gots itchy feets." A sensitive teacher is likely to show acceptance of the child's expression, gently model the standard terms in her response, and offer to help: "You have itchy feet; are your socks making you itch? How about if we take a look?"

Perhaps because of the higher emotional costs, adults find it difficult to react similarly to children's mistakes in **behavior**. Missing the opportunity to teach a constructive behavioral lesson—one that affirms the child even as it guides to acceptable alternatives—adults often resort to criticism and punishment. The adult may see the intervention as "a lesson the child has to learn," but for the child the result is humiliation. That an alternate, more constructive response could be used may not occur to the adult, unless s/he becomes aware of the possibility.

Anecdote: Inez and Hector were quarreling over who would use a car on the block road they had built. The teacher went to the children and declared: "You children don't know how to share the car properly, so I will put it away." As the teacher walked off with the car, Inez sat down at a table and looked sad. Hector frowned at the teacher's back, made a fist, and stuck one finger in the air. It was his index finger, but the sentiment was still expressed.

The teacher in this case was punishing the children for mistaken behavior, **not** teaching them how to solve their problem. As suggested by their responses, the likely message for the children was that they are incapable of playing together, solving their own problems, and using school materials. Because young children are actively engaged in self-concept development, such actions that result in perceptions of unworthiness need to be avoided.

In contrast, an adult might have used a guidance approach in the situation. One guidance response is to hold the car and talk with the children in order to reach a resolution. A variation would be to stop the play and have the children themselves work out a solution (Wichert, 1989). The adult might have said, "Looks like you both want to use the car. This is a problem. How can you solve the problem?" Guidance means teaching children how to solve their problems rather than punishing children for having problems they cannot solve (Gartrell, 1987, 1991).

In candid moments teachers recognize that they sometimes hold children to standards that they themselves do not always meet. Take the matter of "losing one's temper," a not unknown emotional state to most adults.

Anecdote: For a special first grade cooking activity, the teacher planned to have two teacher aides and a parent come in, so the children could work in small groups. The principal reassigned the aides at the last minute, and the parent failed to make it. The teacher did the best she could with the whole class and later improvised when the music specialist went home with the flu. In an after-school meeting with the other first grade staff, the teacher's proposal for more journaling and fewer work sheets was rejected. On the way home for a quick supper before an evening of parent conferences, the teacher got a speeding ticket. When she got home expecting supper to be ready, she discovered that her husband and children had forgotten to fix it. The teacher did **not** say, "That's OK dear family; I'm sure you had a hard day too." (What would you say?)

The ability to balance one's own needs with the needs of others is a high level human ability. Perhaps the one skill that is more difficult is assisting children to learn it. Adults frequently operate from the misconception that children know how to behave and that mistaken behavior is the result of a willful decision to do "wrong." In truth, the decision to act out or defy is made because the child does not yet have the cognitive and emotional resources necessary for more appropriate responses. Children gain these resources over time through the modelling and teaching of caring adults.

RELATIONAL PATTERNS: A PARADIGM FOR SOCIAL DEVELOPMENT

Building from the work of the developmental and self psychologists, Steven D. Harlow developed a system for understanding "levels of social relationships"

Figure 2–2 The adult accepts children as worthwhile individuals who, like all of us, sometimes make mistakes.

(1975). Although he directed his monograph to special education, Harlow actually provided a perspective about social development that pertains to all learners. Harlow's paradigm is helpful in that it also provides a model for understanding mistaken behavior. With Harlow's permission, portions of his monograph are presented:

> As a way of viewing children's functioning in the classroom setting, it might be helpful to examine general relational patterns that individual children disclose. By relational patterns, I mean ways in which children relate to situations, persons and things in the school environment. The patterns I would like to examine are: surviving, adjusting, encountering, all of which differ in their openness to experience, maturity, and their capacity to operate freely.
>
> The most immature and the least open of the relational patterns is that of survival. A child operating at the survival level is concerned with merely getting through time and space without disturbing his established ways of satisfying needs. For whatever reason—perhaps he has learned that his environment is a dangerous and painful place, and cannot by his efforts be mastered—the child wishes to keep things constant and reduce the amount of change in his world. Accordingly, his behavior is extremely stereotyped and rigid. When confronted by a new situation, he will ignore its special demands and treat it as if it were no different than previous situations.
>
> The second relational pattern is that of adjustment. At this level, the child is less preoccupied with predictability and is far more open to others than was true of the survivor. The adjustor's concern is that of learning what is expected of him by others and then producing corresponding behavior. His sensitivity to a reference group's norms and expectations is characteristic of David Riesman's other-directed individual. His reinforcements and rewards come from the response of others to his behavior. . .New ways of thinking and behaving are first sanctioned by an individual or reference group representing authority, before they are considered by the adjustor. . . .
>
> The relational pattern of greatest maturity (and it should be added that maturity has little to do with chronological age) is that of the encounterer. Many educators and psychologists (among them Jean Piaget, Eric Erikson, and John Holt) have described the individual functioning at this level. In contrast with the adjustor and survivor, the encounterer is less concerned with security and certainty and much more occupied with what Erikson referred to as the inner mechanism that permits the individual "to turn passive into active" and to maintain and regain in this world of contending forces an individual sense of centrality, of wholeness, and of initiative (Erikson, pp. 28-31).

Relational Patterns and the Teacher

In regard to the teacher's understanding of relational patterns, Harlow is clear that the teacher should not label children by the patterns they show. Instead, the teacher should consider how the situations children are in affect their social behavior. Harlow states:

The purpose of the paradigm is to help describe and understand a child's functioning in order to encourage him to a higher level of functioning. Rather than a label that indicates to school personnel a condition of some endurance, the typology describes functioning that is amenable to change. Further, the paradigm permits a child to be described in different terminology, as the situation indicates, for example, a child may be a "survivor" in confronting reading activities but an encounterer during free class time (p. 28).

Children at each relational level pose challenges and opportunities for teachers. The child at the survivor level is difficult for teachers to accept because of the non-social, at times anti-social, character of the child's behavior. Yet, it is the trust made possible by a positive adult-child relationship that empowers the child to progress to a higher relational pattern (Harlow, 1975).

Children at the adjustor level also can be challenging. Daily, teachers must respond to children who, fearing criticism, show anxiety over the completion of activities. Some children put off starting tasks, or don't start at all. Others ask the teacher or a friend to do it for them—or copy. Even when they have finished, many young children show taxing persistence in pursuing the blessings of authority. As the following anecdote shows, teachers of young children must work hard to encourage progress from the adjustor pattern of relations:

Anecdote: After much encouragement by her kindergarten teacher, Emily completes a creative "family day" card for her mother.

Emily: Did I do it good?

Teacher: You worked hard and your mother will love it.

Emily: But did I do it good?

Teacher: What's important is that you like it.

Emily: But is it good?

Teacher: Emily, I like whatever you make, just because you are you.

Emily: (Smiles.) Now, I'm gonna do one for my sister.

Some teachers are notorious for preferring the obedience of children at the adjustor level to the independence of children who relate as encounterers. Yet, Harlow's paradigm indicates that children at the encountering level are learning most effectively about themselves and the world (1975). As psychologists ranging from Piaget (1960) and Kamii (1984) to Maslow (1962) and Combs (1962) have written, children need freedom to interact and problem-solve in order for healthy development to occur. The Harry Chapin song, "Flowers are Red" (1978), illustrates the effect an emphasis on conformity has on a young child. In the song a child wants to paint flowers every color of the rainbow. His kindergarten teacher admonishes that "Flowers are red, young man, and leaves are green." Later in a new school, the teacher asks the boy why his flowers are only red. The child responds with the words he was taught. The challenge to the teacher is to maintain harmony in the classroom at the same time that s/he encourages the creative behavior of children at the encountering level.

Figure 2–3 Children who learn in ways that are creative and interactive learn best. (Courtesy Michael Crowley, Family Service Center, Koochiching-Itasca Head Start, Grand Rapids, Minnesota.)

At any relational level, the cause of mistaken behavior in the young child is insufficient understanding about how to act maturely in the complex situations of life. With the internal need to go forward and to learn—but limited ability to balance one's own needs with those of others—mistaken behavior will occur. Using Harlow's relational patterns, **three levels of mistaken behavior** are easily derived. Knowledge of the three levels assists the teacher to understand and work with children when they make mistakes.

THREE LEVELS OF MISTAKEN BEHAVIOR

Mistaken behavior is a natural occurrence, the result of attempts by the inexperienced, developmentally young child to interact with a complicated, increasingly impersonal world. When mistaken behavior occurs, adults significantly affect what children learn from the experience. Guidance-oriented responses that encourage children to keep trying and to continue learning empower healthy self-concepts and full personal development. On the other hand, punitive responses coerce children to abandon the need to experience fully and to adopt defensive behaviors, usually in compliance with the teacher's expectations. Punishment can even create a well of unmet emotional needs and lead to survival level relational patterns: withdrawing from situations, reacting with overt or covert hostility, or showing anxiety.

Adults help children toward healthy development if they regard mistaken behavior as an opportunity to teach and to learn, and if they realize that we all, including adults, make mistakes. It is not the child alone but the interactions of the adult and child together that determine the path of the child's behavior in the educational setting.

Over many years of observing young children in classrooms, the author has noted patterns in mistaken behavior that parallel the levels of social relations discussed by Harlow. In fact, by extending Harlow's paradigm, a model for understanding and addressing mistaken behavior emerges, one that treats mistaken behavior as occurring at three different levels. Level one is **experimentation level** mistaken behavior. Level one mistaken behavior is the equivalent of Harlow's category of encountering. Experimentation level mistaken behavior occurs when the child reacts to one of two motives: curiosity—the child acts to see what will happen; or involvement—the child's actions in a situation do not get the results expected (an "experiment" in daily living does not work out). In a previous anecdote Hector and Inez argued about a car; this incident illustrates experimentation mistaken behavior, as a result of their total involvement in the situation.

Corresponding to "adjustor" social relations is level two mistaken behavior, which is **socially influenced**. Socially influenced mistaken behavior happens when children are reinforced in an action, sometimes unintentionally, by others important to them. Examples are a child's learning an expletive from someone at home, or being influenced by classmates to call another child a name.

Level three denotes the most serious kind of mistaken behavior: The social relations pattern of the **survivor** is close in concept to mistaken behavior at the **strong needs level**. Children show level three mistaken behavior as a reaction to difficulty and pain in their lives that is beyond their capacity to cope with and understand. Most often, strong needs mistaken behavior occurs because of untreated health conditions or painful life experiences. Serious mistaken behavior in the classroom happens because a child is reacting to strong unmet needs, acting out against a perceived hostile world.

Common Sources of Motivation

The relationship of Harlow's relational patterns and the levels of mistaken behavior is close. The motivational sources of each are the same. At the level of encountering *and* experimentation mistaken behavior, the motivation is curiosity or involvement. At the level of adjusting *and* socially influenced mistaken behavior, the motivation is the desire to please and identify with others. At the level of the surviving *and* strong needs mistaken behavior, the motive is unmet basic needs. When a child at any of the three relational patterns acts in a way that is disruptive to the group or harmful to self or others, the child is showing mistaken behavior at that level. In other words, mistaken behavior is the result of miscommunication at the child's particular level of relational pattern in the situation.

Table 2.1

Common Sources of Motivation
Relational Patterns and Levels of Mistaken Behavior

Motivational Source	Relational Pattern	Level of Mistaken Behavior
Desire to explore the environment and engage in relationships and activities	Encounterer	One: Experimentation
Desire to please and identify with significant others	Adjustor	Two: Socially influenced
Inability to cope with problems resulting from health conditions or life experiences.	Survivor	Three: Strong needs

---

In the chapters to follow, the levels of mistaken behavior serve as a reference for understanding children's behavior. The remainder of this chapter further examines each of the three levels of mistaken behavior.

Level One: Experimentation Mistaken Behavior

As children begin to master the social expectations of the classroom, the continuous process of making decisions results in mistaken behavior. In early childhood classrooms, it is natural for children to do things to see what will happen, or because they are totally involved in a situation. For reasons of curiosity and involvement, children who are responding at Harlow's encountering relational level will sometimes show experimentation mistaken behavior.

Anecdote: (Level one mistaken behavior as a result of involvement)

At lunch in a Head Start classroom, Rodney, a three-year-old, said to the teacher, "Gimme the bread."

With a serious look, the teacher responded, "What are the magic words, Rodney?"

Not hesitating for a moment, Rodney raised his arms, spread his fingers and chanted, "Abra-cadabra!"

Smiling about the response, the teacher passed the bread. She commented, "Those are great magic words, Rodney, but the magic words for the table are 'please' and 'thank you,' OK?" Rodney nodded, took the bread and said, "Thank you."

Sometimes there is an element of charm in mistaken behavior at this level, especially in young children. The novelty of children's responses in familiar situations is an elixir of great worth to many an early childhood teacher. The ability to understand that the child is trying to learn through experimental mistaken behavior is the hallmark of the guidance approach at this level. A sense of humor and the avoidance of over-reaction are useful guidance techniques.

Some mistaken behaviors, such as the use of unacceptable words, can be shown by the child at any of the three levels. The intensity and frequency of the mistaken behavior tend to identify the level for the teacher. "Swearing" provides a useful illustration of this crossover pattern; an example of using unacceptable words at the experimentation level follows:

Anecdote: (Level one mistaken behavior as a result of curiosity)

A teacher enjoyed having Karen in the kindergarten for her enthusiasm and spontaneity. One day during choice time Karen approached her and said with a grin, "Shit, teacher."

Figure 2–4 A sense of humor and the ability to avoid overreaction are useful guidance techniques.

> The teacher looked at Karen, hid a smile, and responded: "Some words bother people, Karen, and that is one of them. You are learning new words every day, though, and I like that. You just need to use other words in kindergarten."

No moral issue was made, and the child was not punished for attempting to learn about the limits of acceptability in the classroom. Instead the teacher reinforced the limits in a matter-of-fact way without putting down Karen's efforts at "vocabulary development." Had the teacher made this more of an issue, the word's power would have been reinforced, and Karen might have used it in a level two or level three situation. This possibility still existed but was reduced by the teacher's response. In line with the guidance approach, the teacher let Karen know that her status as a member of the group was not in question.

Level Two: Socially Influenced Mistaken Behavior

Level two mistaken behavior is **learned behavior**. At the second level, the child is reacting to the influence of others, repeating behavior that is modelled, taught or suggested. In accord with Harlow's adjustment relational pattern, at level two children are conforming to the authority of persons important in their lives. Typical sources of social influence—intentional or unintentional—that can result in level two mistaken behavior are:

- parents or other adult family members;
- siblings or other relatives who are peers;
- friends and neighbors;
- other children in the center or school;
- the teacher or care giver;
- another adult in the center or school.

Anecdote: (Family influence) Every so often Matt's dad got quite upset at home, especially when his handyman efforts went wrong. When dad got upset, he swore. In second grade, when Matt spilled too much glue on his paper one day, he declared loudly, "Damn it to Hell!"

The teacher heard the comment and saw what had happened. She quietly told Matt that she didn't blame him for getting upset. The teacher said the next time he was having trouble, he could use other words like "ding-dong it" and come to her for help.

Reality suggests that on occasion many adults use language not dissimilar to Matt's dad. Matt's frustration was real and the expletive was understandable, if not appropriate. The teacher understood the situation, knew that Matt had heard the expression outside of class, and took a guidance rather than a punishment approach.

If the teacher had put Matt's name on the board or withheld a privilege, she would have made a simple problem into something possibly lasting and serious. Of course, additional intervention is needed if Matt continued to use unacceptable language. As Ginott wrote in *Teacher and Child* (1972), firmness without harshness is essential in guidance discipline.

Adjusting to the Situation

The difference in teacher response to level one and level two mistaken behavior is often the degree of firmness. At the experimentation level, children are in the process of learning new behaviors. Teachers need to appreciate the tentative nature of this situation and not over-react. At the socially influenced level, it is important to recognize that learning has already occurred, and the course of the learning needs to be changed. Children, like all of us, are more able to change if they know they are accepted, their efforts are appreciated, and there are definite expectations about their behavior. While on the one hand the teacher avoids harshness, on the other s/he practices being both friendly and firm (Ginott, 1972).

Sometimes, teaching to alter socially influenced mistaken behavior consists of reminders about limits and requests for alternate responses—as happened with Matt. Other times, the teacher works at consciousness raising in order to help children become more sensitive to a child or situation. The following

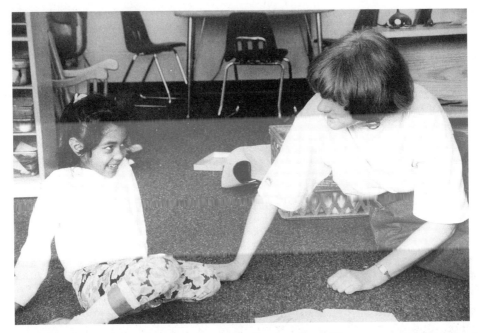

Figure 2–5 With friendliness and a smile, the teacher still can respond firmly to a mistaken behavior.

anecdote involves level two mistaken behavior that is peer-influenced, involving children in a prekindergarten special education classroom:

Anecdote: Charlie had just progressed from crutches to a new leg brace. Several children noticed that the brace squeaked. By the end of the day, they were laughing among themselves about "Squeaky leg, Charlie."

The next day the teacher talked with Charlie and at sharing time announced that he had something to show everyone. With a grin, Charlie pulled up his pant leg and announced, "Look, guys, I got a new leg brace. It squeaks some, but it works pretty good." With that he invited the children to come over and look at the brace close-up. He flexed his leg for them and made the brace squeak. The children were impressed; the name-calling stopped.

The following day the teacher was absent. When she returned, the substitute called and reported, "I must tell you what happened yesterday. Just as I walked in the door, three children came up to me and said that Charlie has a new leg brace. They said it squeaks, but he gets around on it "really good."

The teacher adjusts to the situation, being firm about limits when needed, teaching alternatives, and raising consciousness. Teaching more than "disciplining" is standard in the guidance approach.

Level Three: Strong Needs Mistaken Behavior

The author agrees with Stone (1973), Warren (1977), and Erickson & Pianta (1989) that serious mistaken behavior is due to trouble in children's lives that is beyond their ability to cope with and understand. At level one, a child might experiment with a "swear word" to see what the reaction will be. A child at level two will use an expletive learned from others to express a spontaneous feeling (that passes quickly unless a teacher over-reacts). At level three, reacting from strong needs, a child might let loose a string of expletives over a simple frustration, having completely lost control. The primary sign of the **strong needs level** is dysfunctional behavior with a definite emotional underlay that tends to be repeated—in short, extreme behaviors, repeated over time.

On occasion, any child (or adult) experiences a **level three day**. Irritability, frustration, inattentiveness, hostility, withdrawal or fatigue are common level three behaviors. Any of these can result from a short term upset to an individual's physical or emotional health. With young children, "level one" situations occasionally generate "level three" reactions—children feel deeply about things. The teacher needs to watch for how quickly the child recovers from the upset and whether such episodes are infrequent or common. When serious mistaken behavior is repeated often or continues for more than a day, the teacher should be alert to the possibility that basic needs of the child are not being met.

There are two sources of strong needs mistaken behavior, that operate independently or together. They are **physical discomfort**, due to a health-related problem, and **emotional discomfort**, due to neglect or abuse of a child's needs.

Health Factors and Level Three Behaviors

In their concern for the whole child, early childhood professionals sometimes detect chronic physical conditions such as vision or hearing disabilities, speech impairments, atypical developmental patterns, or perceptual-motor difficulties. Teachers of young children regularly observe acute conditions such as hearing infections, allergy flare-ups, and untreated illnesses. In the last few years, teachers also have become more cognizant of possible neglect and abuse related conditions: hunger, hygiene problems, lack of sleep, parental drug and alcohol involvement, unexplained injuries. All of these conditions, with physical etiologies and emotional ramifications, affect the behavior of children at school. A review procedure in which mistaken behaviors are evaluated for possible health-related causes is important in all programs serving young children.

Emotional Factors and Level Three Behaviors

All young children have "level three" days now and then. When these days occur frequently, or when the serious mistaken behavior persists, basic needs are not being met. In the eloquent little book, *What About Discipline?* (1973), Stone discussed the connection between mistaken behavior and trouble in the child's life:

> People who persist in thinking of childhood as a time of happy innocence are fooling themselves. Every child's life includes some stress and frustration and it comes out in the child's behavior. Young children are not good at covering up their feelings or at expressing them in words.

> Teachers often see children fall apart "for no apparent reason," except that there is a reason even if it is not apparent. Here are a few reasons why a child might misbehave. . .: The child has been teased, or humiliated, by older brothers and sisters and neighborhood children, or even by parents. It is no wonder if such a child turns on the children at school to tease them. Children have to absorb difficult changes in their lives—changes which are hard for them to understand, like the loss of a parent, or the experience of divorce. Children who are victims of severe physical punishment at home have been observed in their centers to use violence themselves, as if it were the only way they knew to respond to other people.

> While most of these troubles fall under the category of normal stress, there are children whose lives are marked by deep unhappiness. Some children have to endure violence against themselves or other family members or the disruptive effects of drug dependency or mental illness by a family member. Children feel helpless at such times, as they do in the face of divorce, illness, and death.

> When people are going through trouble in their personal lives, most show it in other parts of their lives. Adults may be unable to concentrate, for example. They may brood about their problems and not see or hear what is going on around them. They may try to deny their feelings but then get into arguments or fights because they are angry or worried. It is the same with children (pp. 8-11).

Stone complements Harlow's discussion of the "survival" relational pattern. Harlow's words help the teacher to understand dynamics behind serious mistaken behavior in the classroom:

> When problems arise, the survivor unsuccessfully attempts to meet them with generally inappropriate behavior. He may, for example, be prone to lash out destructively or withdraw completely when a problem presents itself. To the observer, it would appear that such behavior is self-defeating—and it is—but it serves the function of preventing the child from involving himself and opening himself to something in his environment that may prove overwhelming. Here, after all, is a child with little confidence in his ability to alter matters by direct action (p. 34).

Responding to Level Three Mistaken Behavior. When a child shows behavior that is disruptive or harmful, teachers need to enforce limits and

Figure 2–6 Stress and frustration are a part of life, even for young children.

protect the general need for safety. If mistaken behavior is serious, and especially if it continues over time, however, disciplinary responses in themselves will be inadequate to improve the situation. The "catch 22" with children behaving at level three is that although they need a helping relationship with a teacher the most, they are often the most difficult to work with and accept. A reminder from Warren applies here: while it is impossible to love every child, the teacher must work to build a helping relationship with each child based on acceptance and respect. Such a relationship is essential if the teacher is to guide the child toward more productive patterns of behavior (1977).

The beginnings of such a relationship include effort by the teacher to understand reasons for the mistaken behavior. Such efforts go beyond the common disclaimer, "He has a rough home life," to learning about the actual circumstances affecting the child.

Anecdote: After five weeks of school, a second grade teacher noted the following pattern in a child's behavior: During the middle of the week Wendy showed an interest in activities and cooperated easily with fellow students and the teacher. By Friday, however, Wendy was less able to concentrate, avoided contacts with other students, and was irritable in dealings with the teacher. It usually took until Tuesday of the following week before Wendy was fully back into the swing of things.

The teacher contacted the mother who disclosed that she and Wendy's father had separated. Until a divorce was finalized, Wendy was living with her mother during the week and with the father on weekends. Fortunately in this case, the mother expressed confidence that the father was caring for Wendy. The teacher hypothesized that the separation and the transition from one home to the next were affecting her. The teacher encouraged each parent to help Wendy understand the situation and to assist her during the transitions. For the teacher's part, she became less judgmental about Wendy's behavior and did her best to support Wendy during times of greatest need. Over a few weeks, Wendy began to adjust, and the mistaken behavior decreased

As illustrated in the anecdote, the teacher seeks to understand what is going on with the child. Full understanding may not occur, but new information almost always is attainable and can help in building relations. Efforts to increase understanding should include discussions with the parent and the child. Discarding the myth that the professional teacher works alone, s/he needs to communicate with other personnel, i.e. through "teaming arrangements," "staffings," and "cross-agency collaborations." Informal discussions with trusted colleagues about the situation are also important.

Strong needs mistaken behavior requires a multi-step problem-solving strategy that involves a clear, but flexible plan. The plan should include components for: (*a*) getting more information, (*b*) building a helping relationship with the child, (*c*) preventing problem situations, and (*d*) intervening in nonpunitive ways. When the plan is working, in Harlow's words:

> What occurs then, over time, is that the survivor's need for predetermined constancy is replaced by a new network of dependable relationships, which are based upon his successful actions on, or mastery of, at least a portion of the classroom environment. . .As the child begins to sense his powers of mastery, a new self-regard emerges. This self-regard enables the child to open himself to endeavors that before would have proven to be defeating (p. 34).

The discussion of level three mistaken behavior has been more lengthy than levels one and two for a particular reason. Children at level three pose the most difficulties for teachers. Their situations are the most complex and responses by the teacher need to be more comprehensive. (See Chapter 9). We shall suggest strategies for assisting children who are showing each level of mistaken behavior in the chapters to come.

MISTAKEN BEHAVIOR AND INTENTIONALITY

Because the concept is new, readers may be tempted to associate mistaken behavior with "accidents" and misbehavior with acts "done on purpose."

Figure 2–7 With trust in the environment, the child succeeds at tasks that before would have been self-defeating.

Mistaken behavior includes both accidents and intentional actions. A preschooler on a trike who runs over the toe of another child by accident has shown level one mistaken behavior. The accident was the result of loss of control or failure to look where one is going. The accident was unintentional but was level one because it was a mistake that arose from involvement.

A child may run over another's foot for a second reason related to level one: The trike rider hits the other's foot "accidentally on-purpose" to see what will happen. The lack of development of young children means that they have difficulty understanding how another child would feel under such circumstances. The act was intentional, but was done without full awareness of the consequences and so is level one mistaken behavior. The importance of the term "mistaken behavior" is that it reminds the adult that the trike rider needs guidance about human feelings and the consequences of actions, not punishment for making a mistake.

Of course, hitting another child's foot might also be a level two or three mistaken behavior. At level two, one child follows another on a trike. The second rider sees the first swing close to a bystander and follows suit, but strikes the bystander's foot. At level three, a trike rider comes to school with feelings of hostility and acts out against an innocent child. In either case, the teacher gives attention first to the "victim" (who deserves it), then speaks with the trike rider. The teacher decides a reasonable consequence with the trike rider but also gives some thought to the rider's motives. If the situation indicates strong needs mistaken behavior, the teacher might follow-up as suggested for level three. The follow-up is important because serious mistaken behavior is shown when children are victims of life circumstances that they cannot control. The acting out may have been intentional but the motive was not understood by the child. The mistaken behavior was an unintentional request for assistance, not punishment.

Adults sometimes comment that they can accept mistaken behavior in children, who have not attained the capacity to make mature social judgments. They continue that with adults the concept of mistaken behavior does not apply. As long as an individual disagrees with the idea that mistaken behavior can be intentional, this viewpoint is understandable. Another view is that a crime is a mistake, though of a grievous nature. The definition of a mistake in this case is "an error in moral judgment," and intentionality may well be involved.

Again, the value of the term "mistaken behavior" is that it has different implications than the conventional term, "misbehavior." Misbehavior tends to connote a judgment of character that leads to punishment. Mistaken behavior precludes character assessment and asks that the other be accepted as a person of worth (by virtue of being alive). The person may need to face consequences, but at the base of those consequences is guidance, so that the possibility of change is maximized.

A premise in the guidance approach is that even "willful acts" that are done "on purpose" still constitute **mistaken behavior**. A child who deliberately bites or intentionally disobeys **has made a mistake**. The adult able to approach children as worthwhile individuals who make mistakes is in a philosophically strong position to assist with healthy personal development. The adult who judges children negatively as a result of their mistaken behavior is not.

Visual Summary: Three Levels of Mistaken Behavior

Mistaken behaviors have distinct motivational sources. Behaviors that appear similar can be a result of differing motivations, and so be at different levels. The teacher must observe carefully to infer the motivation and the level of mistaken behavior in order to respond effectively. Figure 2.2 illustrates how sample mistaken behaviors can be at different levels.

In the guidance approach, the teacher responds to children not just on the basis of the discrete behavior shown, but on a judgment about the meaning of the behavior for the child. This is a high level skill that takes practice and sensitivity toward children. The chapters to follow assist the adult to interpret and respond to mistaken behavior in ways that enforce limits yet respect children's needs.

Table 2.2

Classifying Sample Mistaken Behaviors by Level

Incident of Mistaken Behavior	Motivational Source	Level of Mistaken Behavior
Child uses expletive	Wants to see teacher's reaction	One
	Wants to emulate important others	Two
	Expresses deeply felt hostility	Three
Child pushes another off trike	Wants trike; has not learned to ask in words	One
	Follows aggrandizement practices modelled by other children	Two
	Feels need to act out against world by asserting power	Three
Child refuses to join in group activity	Does not understand teacher's expectations	One
	Has "gotten into the habit" of not joining in	Two
	Is not feeling well or feels anxiety about participating	Three

COMMUNICATING WITH PARENTS ABOUT MISTAKEN BEHAVIOR

Parents' views about their children and the subject of discipline vary a great deal: "My kid is basically a good kid who just needs some 'T.L.C.' " "My child is willful and will try to get away with things unless the teacher is strict." In discussing children's behavior with parents, the teacher first seeks to understand how the parent views the child. This step will help in deciding how to communicate in terms the parent can accept. Second, the teacher needs to realize that however they see their children, parents want the best for them.

Parents who have positive views about their children generally accept the concept of mistaken behavior and its three levels. Out of an adult sense of fair play, however, parents neither want their child "to get away with things"

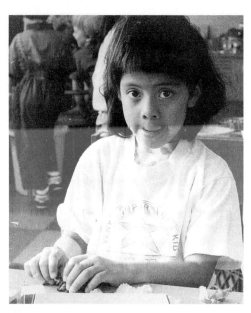

Figure 2–8 Parents who feel positively about their children generally accept the concept of mistaken behavior.

nor other children to treat their child unfairly. In explaining behavior in terms of "making a mistake," the teacher needs to emphasize that the child is in a developmental process of learning more acceptable alternatives and that the teacher is providing guidance to help the child do so. With relatively mild level one and level two mistakes, the teacher might say that s/he doubts the behavior will occur again but will continue to watch the situation.

Especially with more serious behaviors, the teacher must be clear to the parent that children, like all of us, make mistakes. At the same time it is important that the child learn from the mistake, and the role of the teacher is to help. That a hurting or disruptive behavior is "a mistake" does not justify it. Guidance discipline is not necessarily permissive. In the terms of Haim Ginott, "Helpful correction is direction":

> Frank, age five, pinched his friend, Sam. . .The teacher who witnessed the event said to Frank, "I saw it. People are not for pinching." Frank said, "I am sorry." The teacher replied, "To be sorry is to make an inner decision to behave differently." "O.K.," replied Frank. He went over to Sam to resume his play (p. 129).

Although Frank may not have understood the teacher's exact words, he probably got the message. The teacher was firm, but not harsh. She educated Frank about his actions and so modelled a guidance approach.

The goal in communicating with the parent is to convey a stance of acceptance of the child and of firm guidance in relation to the child's behavior. The levels of mistaken behavior provide a helpful vocabulary for the teacher in working toward this goal. If a child is having problems, the teacher also needs to communicate about the progress and achievements the child has accomplished. Parents, like all of us, accept suggestions for improvement more easily when progress is recognized.

At times, parents will seem more critical of the child than the teacher. Parents can express skepticism about their children's behaviors and still be nurturing parents. Occasionally, however, a teacher encounters a parent who has overly negative views about the child or unrealistic reactions to the child's mistaken behavior. One important comment needs to be made here. If a teacher believes that difficulties in parent-child communication are posing level three problems for a child, then the teacher needs to take a comprehensive problem-solving approach that includes collaboration with others. The teacher works with the family as well as with other professionals in order to solve difficult problems. Succeeding chapters will discuss parent-teacher communication under these circumstances.

Figure 2–9 (Reprinted with special permission of King Features Syndicate.)

SUMMARY

What is the concept of mistaken behavior?

With limited experience and development, young children are in the beginning stages of gaining social competence. The difficulty in helping children learn high level social skills leads some adults to the misconception that children know how to behave; they show "misbehavior" as the result of a willful decision to do "wrong." In truth, the decision to act out or defy is made because the child does not yet have the cognitive and emotional resources necessary for more mature responses. Children make mistakes. When adults think of behavior traditionally considered "misbehavior" as **mistaken behavior**, they are in a better position to accept the child as a worthwhile individual and teach the child more appropriate ways to act.

What are the relational patterns?

Building from the work of the developmental and self psychologists, Steven D. Harlow has developed a system for understanding "levels of social relationships," which he calls, **relational patterns**. The three relational patterns he has identified are **surviving, adjusting,** and **encountering**. A child operating at the survival level is concerned with merely getting through time safely. Due perhaps to a perception that the environment is a dangerous place, the child resorts to extreme behaviors, and may act out as a means of protection from perceived harm.

The second relational pattern is that of adjustment. A child at the adjustor level has as a primary motive the desire to please others, especially those in authority. The child looks for the approval of the adult authority or reference group before changing thought and behavior patterns.

The third relational pattern, which Harlow calls the pattern of greatest maturity, is that of the encounterer. A child at the encountering level is less concerned with security and certainty and more occupied with exploring new ideas, materials, and experiences.

Children at each level of social relationship pose particular challenges for the teacher. The teacher attempts to build relations and a sense of trust with the survivor, in order to make learning safe. With the child at the adjustor level, the teacher works to lower anxiety levels and nudge toward independence. The teacher must temper a personal need for control and develop a spirit of partnership with a child at the encountering level. In general, the teacher needs to avoid labeling children by relational pattern, but assist children across the range of classroom experiences to progress in the differing patterns they show.

What are the three levels of mistaken behavior?

The levels of mistaken behavior correspond to the three relational patterns. Level one is experimentation mistaken behavior, which corresponds to the relational pattern of encountering. Children show level one mistaken behavior through curiosity or involvement. When children do things in order to see what will happen, they are showing curiosity-related mistaken behavior. When children are involved in ongoing activities and encounter a conflict, they are showing involvement-related mistaken behavior. With level one mistaken behavior, the teacher avoids over-reaction but may educate to more appropriate alternatives of behavior.

Level two is socially influenced or "learned" mistaken behavior. Children show level two mistaken behavior when they are influenced toward an inappropriate act by significant others, either peers or adults. The influence can be either intentional or unintentional. The child who uses an expletive in the classroom just the way a family member might at home is showing socially influenced mistaken behavior. A child who marks a desk or calls a name because classmates also are is showing level two mistaken behavior. With level two, the teacher acts in a firm but friendly manner to reinforce a limit, raise consciousness levels, and teach alternative behaviors.

Level three is strong needs mistaken behavior. All serious mistaken behavior is caused by strong unmet needs that the child cannot cope with and understand. The source of the unmet needs might be health conditions that are untreated or emotional suffering from experiences either at home or school. To deal with strong needs mistaken behavior, the teacher takes a multistep approach that includes: (a) getting more information, (b) building a helping relationship with the child, (c) preventing problem situations from arising, and (d) intervening in nonpunitive ways. Almost always, the teacher collaborates with others—including the child, the parent, and other professionals—to set and implement a guidance plan.

Can mistaken behavior be intentional?

Readers may be tempted to associate mistaken behavior with "accidents" and misbehavior with intentionality. Mistaken behavior includes both. Because young children do not yet possess the social awareness of the adult, they do not have the personal resources to act "properly" in all situations— especially when emotions are running high. Young children cannot easily understand behavioral alternatives, personal motivations, or the resulting consequences. It is not that young children are bad, just that they have not yet learned how to act. In both psychological and social terms, children are vulnerable to making mistakes. For these reasons, teachers are better served by using the term mistaken behavior, whether intention is inferred or not. By thinking in terms of mistaken behavior, the adult is more able to accept the child as a worthwhile, developing person and to guide—in firm but friendly ways—toward more appropriate behaviors.

How does the teacher communicate with parents about mistaken behavior?

Parents' views about their children and the subject of discipline differ. In communicating with parents the teacher first seeks to understand how the parent views the child. Parents who see their children positively generally accept the concept of mistaken behavior and its three levels. Whether or not

the teacher uses the term, however, s/he needs to convey that children, like all of us, make mistakes. When discussing the problems a child is having in the classroom, the teacher needs to convey that the child is trying to get along and already has some strengths. The teacher and parent just need to work together to help the child learn from mistakes that might be made. If a teacher believes that level three mistaken behavior is involved, s/he collaborates with other professionals as well as the family to develop and implement a constructive plan.

FOLLOW-UP ACTIVITIES

Follow-up activities allow the student to interrelate material from the text with "real life" situations. The "observations" imply access to practicum experiences, the "interviews" to teachers and parents. When communicating about the activities, students need to respect the privacy of all participants in the observation or interview, as an important professional courtesy.

1. **What is the concept of mistaken behavior?**
   a. Observe a problem situation in a prekindergarten–primary grade classroom. Analyze the situation using the concept of mistaken

behavior. In what ways does the concept apply or not apply to the situation observed?

b. The concept of mistaken behavior is a new one for many teachers. Talk with a teacher about the concept. What parts of it are they comfortable with; what parts are they not sure about? What more would they like to know about the concept?

2. **What are relational patterns?**

a. Observe one child who is at two different relational patterns in two differing classroom situations. Which two relational patterns seemed to be operating? Reflect why the situations may have elicited different responses from the child.

b. Observe children at each of the three relational patterns. In what ways does Harlow's writing apply to the children? In what ways does Harlow's writing not seem to apply?

3. **What are the three levels of mistaken behavior?**

a. Observe an example of level one, experimentation mistaken behavior. What did you observe that makes you think the mistaken behavior is at this level? In what ways does recognizing this level of mistaken behavior help you to understand the child?

b. Observe an example of level two, socially influenced mistaken behavior. What did you observe that makes you think the mistaken behavior is at this level? In what ways does recognizing this level of mistaken behavior help you to understand the child?

c. Observe an example of level three, strong needs mistaken behavior. What did you observe that makes you think the mistaken behavior is at this level? In what ways does recognizing this level of mistaken behavior help you to understand the child?

4. **Can mistaken behavior be intentional?**

a. Observe an act of harm or disruption by a child that you believe to be intentional. Try to explain the behavior using the concept of mistaken behavior. In what ways does the concept apply? In what ways does it not apply?

b. Interview a teacher about the approach s/he takes when intervening in a problem situation. In what ways is the approach different if the teacher believes a child caused the problem by accident or on purpose? In what ways is the approach the same?

5. **How does the teacher communicate with parents about mistaken behavior?**

a. Talk with a teacher about the approach s/he uses when talking with a parent about a problem the child is having in the classroom. What is important for the teacher to convey to the parent? How does the teacher's approach relate to the concept of mistaken behavior?

b. Talk with a parent about the approach s/he would like a teacher to use if the parent's child were having a problem in the classroom. How do the parent's comments relate to the concept of mistaken behavior?

SUGGESTED RESOURCES

Erickson, M.F. and Pianta, R.C. (July 1989). "New Lunchbox, Old Feelings: What Kids Bring To School." *Early Education and Development, 1*(1). pp. 35-49.

Gartrell, D.J. (1991, revised edition). *Developmentally Appropriate Guidance of Children Birth to Eight*. St. Paul, MN; Minnesota Association for the Education of Young Children. (In Appendix).

Ginott, H.G. (1972). *Teacher and Child*. New York: Avon Books.

Harlow, S.D. (1975). *Special Education: The Meeting of Differences*. Grand Forks, ND: University of North Dakota.

Warren, R. (1977). Caring: *Supporting Children's Growth*. Washington, DC: National Association for the Education of Young Children.

Wichert, S. (1989). *Keeping the Peace: Practicing Cooperation and Conflict Resolution with Preschoolers*. Philadelphia: New Society Publishers.

REFERENCES

Combs, A.W. (1962). "A Perceptual View of the Adequate Personality," in Combs, A.W. (ed.). *Perceiving, Behaving, Becoming: A New Focus for Education*. Washington, DC: Association for Supervision and Curriculum Development.

Erickson, M.F. and Pianta, R.C. (1989, July). "New Lunchbox, Old Feelings: What Kids Bring To School." *Early Education and Development, 1*(1). pp. 35-49.

Gartrell, D.J. "Punishment or Guidance?" *Young Children*, March, 1987. Washington, DC: National Association for the Education of Young Children.

Gartrell, D.J. (1991, revised edition). *Developmentally Appropriate Guidance of Children Birth to Eight*. St. Paul, MN: Minnesota Association for the Education of Young Children.

Ginott, H.G. (1972). *Teacher and Child*. New York: Avon Books.

Harlow, S.D. (1975). *Special Education: The Meeting of Differences*. Grand Forks, ND: University of North Dakota.

Kamii, C. (February 1984). "Autonomy: The Aim of Education Envisioned by Piaget." *Phi Delta Kappan*. pp. 410-415.

Maslow, A.H. (1962). "Some Basic Propositions of a Growth and Self-Actualization Psychology," in Combs, A.W. (ed.) (1962). *Perceiving, Behaving, Becoming: A New Focus for Education*. Washington, DC: Association for Supervision and Curriculum Development.

Piaget, J. (1932, translated 1960). *The Moral Judgement of the Child*. Glencoe, IL: The Free Press.

Purkey, W.W. (1970). *Self Concept and School Achievement*. Englewood Cliffs, NJ: Prentice Hall, Inc.

Stone, J.G. (1973). *What About Discipline?* Cambridge, MA: Education
      Development Center.
Warren, R. (1977). *Caring: Supporting Children's Growth.* Washington, DC:
      National Association for the Education of Young Children.
Wichert, S. (1989). *Keeping the Peace: Practicing Cooperation and Conflict
      Resolution with Preschoolers.* Philadelphia: New Society Publishers.

3

Guidance Discipline: The Bottom Line

GUIDING QUESTIONS

As you read chapter three, you will discover answers to the following questions:

- **How are positive teacher-child relations the basis of the guidance approach?**
- **How does guidance discipline reduce the need for mistaken behavior?**
- **What does it mean that guidance discipline is "solution-oriented"?**
- **Why is teamwork with staff and other professionals part of guidance discipline?**
- **How are parent-teacher partnerships important in the guidance approach?**

As discussed in chapter one, guidance discipline has a strong tradition in progressive educational thought. Infused by the work of the developmental and self psychologists, the approach builds upon the ideas of Ginott, Dreikurs and others who articulated discipline models based on mutual respect. Whatever title we give it, guidance discipline has a look and a feel that make it unmistakable. The present chapter continues the theme of unit one by introducing five principles of the guidance approach. If these principles are present in a classroom, then the reader may be assured that the guidance approach is being practiced. The principles are that guidance discipline:

1. depends on positive teacher-child relations;
2. reduces the need for mistaken behavior;
3. takes a solution-orientation;
4. means teamwork with staff and other professionals;
5. involves parent-teacher partnerships.

These principles define a guidance approach to discipline and identify the types of teaching practices consistent with it.

1. A GUIDANCE APPROACH DEPENDS ON POSITIVE TEACHER-CHILD RELATIONS

In *Caring* (1972), Warren perceptively comments that teachers cannot feel love for each child and need not feel guilty when they realize this. Warren states, however, that the teacher does have an obligation to build positive relationships with all children and to help them feel a sense of belonging with the group. Building relations with persons we don't feel comfortable around is hard for all human beings. The task may be especially difficult when children show level three mistaken behaviors, which can be extreme and violent. Still, as Weber-Schwartz points out, seeking to understand a child is an important step in increasing our level of acceptance (1987). Productive human relations is an essential life goal in a democratic society and an important professional goal for the teacher (Read, Gardner, & Mahler, 1993).

During an address at the 1989 conference of the Minnesota Association for the Education of Young Children, Marian Marion commented that the teacher needs to be "unrelentingly positive" in acceptance of children and belief in their ability to learn and grow. This is the essence of a guidance approach. Only through maintaining productive relations can we learn—and help children learn—positive lessons from mistaken behavior.

The early childhood teacher builds positive relations with children based on the role that s/he fills. The role is different from that of the parent whose relationship with the child is highly personal and subjective (Katz, 1980). The unique task of the early childhood teacher is to facilitate the transition of the child from the intense, private relationship with the parent to the more public and collectively driven relationship with the teacher (Katz, 1980; Erickson & Pianta, 1989).

The author resists terms like "removed" and "impersonal" in describing teacher-child relations. Adjustment to school is easier for children who feel positively about themselves in the school situation (Erickson & Pianta, 1989). The essential ingredient for this disposition is personal affirmation by the teacher, **unconditional positive regard** for the person of the child.

Figure 3–1 Productive human relations is an essential goal for the teacher.

Unconditional Positive Regard

A common practice in conventional discipline has been the use of embarrassment, making an example of a child in order to control the group. Many adults can recall being embarrassed by teachers, even if those incidents occurred years and years before (Gartrell, 1987a). When teachers use embarrassment to control behavior, they may think they are reacting to a situation of the moment, but the injury to self-esteem may last a lifetime. The premise that discipline techniques should communicate respect for the child (Curwin & Mendler, 1988) is a critical element in the guidance discipline. Central to the approach is Rogers' term, **unconditional positive regard**.

Unconditional positive regard means full acceptance of the child as a developing human being and member of the group. The adult comfortable with the concept creates a spirit in the classroom where all children feel welcome and that they belong. In order to prevent the effects of embarrassment, the teacher seeks alternatives to "singling children out."

Anecdote: A teacher was attempting to begin a large group activity with a group of four-year-olds. She **did not say**: "Mark and Clarice, we are all waiting for you."

She **did say**: "We are almost ready to start. I like the way you are coming to the circle so quickly."

Such generalized comments, which recognize actual (or anticipated) collective efforts, are not as direct as personal references, but with practice they work. At the preschool level, strategic placement of adult or child **before** the start of the large group activity is an effective strategy. During the activity if more than a few show inattentiveness, a change is needed, often by a new activity that allows for increased child involvement (Osborn & Osborn, 1989). The old teaching notion, that the teacher stays with the lesson plan no matter what, has no place in early childhood practice. A positive classroom atmosphere is preserved by the teacher who is flexible and knows when to go on to something new.

With older children at school, Jones advocates the intentional use of body language (1987) to maintain group attention. First interventions are a glance and a glance with a hand gesture. Rather than chastising a child on the other side of the room, the teacher continues teaching while making one's way toward the child. Usually establishing proximity restores attention. If necessary, the teacher whispers a few words, perhaps requesting a private conference later. Through body language, the grade school child is apt to get the message without experiencing humiliation (Jones, 1987).

Beyond Praise. A challenging idea to many teachers is that praise as well as criticism can work against positive teacher-child relations (Hitz and Driscoll, 1988). When a teacher praises a child, the child becomes the institutionalized winner in the situation, and all others become the losers. Resentment and hurt are felt by many of those not recognized, and the child "positively" singled out is apt to feel *mixed* emotions—pleasure *and* embarrassment (Ginott, 1975; Hitz & Driscoll, 1988). The use of praise to set a "positive example," remains a common teaching practice. Teachers fail to see that such praise is meant only secondarily for the recipient; the real motive is control of the class.

An indication of professional development is when teachers step back and review how they use praise. Often, they can praise less—and teach more effectively—when they look beyond children's behavior to possible changes in the daily program.

Anecdote: A group of five-and six-year-olds attended a day care center on alternate days when they were not at school. The center policy was a nap each day, even though the children did not rest at kindergarten. The teachers had a difficult time keeping the children quiet during "nap." One incentive they used was to praise the "best rester" each day and have that child lead the line. On this day the teacher chose Carrie. From the others, a chorus of complaints were heard:

Jeremy: "I was sleepin' too."

Neil: "She always gets picked 'cause she sleeps!"

Carole: "I didn't say nothin' during rest, and I never get to be first."

Darrell: "Who wants to lead the line anyway?"

Carrie: "It's OK, Teacher, somebody else can do it."

Post-Script: After a staff meeting, the teachers decided to replace nap with "quiet time." The group stayed on their cots, but each day a story was read followed by a "super silent reading time." The children liked the new guidelines and either looked at books or slept. After rest, a random system for lining up—"everyone wearing blue"—was introduced. The teachers found that the program change was a big improvement.

Recognition of achievement and progress, like criticism, should be given carefully. Unconditional positive regard means that the teacher avoids holding a child up for comparison, **either by praise or criticism**.

The Use of Encouragement. The notion that "all praise is good" has been taken for granted in childhood education. Hitz and Driscoll argue persuasively that what young children need is not praise but **encouragement** (1988). As discussed, praise focuses on achievements, tends to single out individuals, and builds dependence on the teacher. In contrast, encouragement recognizes effort, usually does not single out, and affirms self-esteem (Hitz & Driscoll, 1988). Encouragement can be private or public.

Private encouragement is honestly meant for the child being recognized. Control of the group is not a motive. Individual recognition of effort and progress means a great deal to the child; s/he knows that a remark made in private is meant only for her/him. Contrast the likely meaning of these two remarks for Sheila, a first grader:

Praise in front of class: "Sheila is such a good listener today. She gets to help with snack."

   or

Private encouragement to child: "You were really listening today, Sheila; thank you for your cooperation."

Public encouragement takes two forms. The first is group-focused recognition that addresses efforts and progress of the whole class, and not individuals. As distinct from praise of the individual, group-focused recognition builds group spirit and positive relations. Notice the likely effects of these two sets of comments:

Figure 3–2 Encouragement recognizes effort, often is private, and affirms self-esteem.

Praise: "Everyone needs to be sitting like a pretzel, just like Chad and Leslie."
or
Public encouragement: "You are sitting like a plate of curled up pretzels and are almost ready for the story."

Praise: "Veda and Marlene were the best workers today. They get to choose their free time activity first."
or
Public encouragement: "Everyone has been working so hard today that I think we all deserve a little extra free time."

The second form of public encouragement does recognize individuals. On occasion there is good reason for bringing class attention to an individual child—for instance, a child who has struggled against a problem or disability with which the class is familiar. In electing to use public recognition, the teacher needs to decide whether the comments are meant for the child's benefit or for "crowd control." S/he needs to think about what the recognition will mean to the child **and** the other children. The long term goal should be to affirm the child's self-worth and to nurture feelings of empathy in the group. At the same time, the immediate objective must be to maintain positive relations with each member of the group and so with the group itself.

A contention of the guidance approach is that inappropriate practice, and the **conditional acceptance** and competition that drive it, give rise to feelings of failure and low self-esteem (Purkey, 1970; Gartrell, 1987a). Most early childhood teachers agree that the young child needs to feel accepted by the group in order to participate in activities successfully (Bredekamp, 1988; Clewett, 1988). When teachers practice "discipline with dignity," then children feel less need to act out in school and later life. Unconditional positive regard is sound preventive practice. In classrooms where it is found, children try hard to learn and get along, because they know that they may make mistakes, but they will not fail.

Ginott's Cardinal Principle

Unconditional positive regard is a venerable idea that was used in the nursery school movement of the 1920s considerably before Rogers coined the term (Read, Gardner, & Mahler, 1992). In 1972, Ginott gave new articulation to the idea with his "Cardinal Principle." Since relationships grow from teachers' communication skills, then effective teacher-child communication is at the heart of guidance discipline. Ginott phrased his principle this way:

> At their best, teachers address themselves to the child's situation. At their worst, they judge his character and personality. This, in essence, is the difference between effective and ineffective communication (1972, p. 70).

This is also the difference between guidance discipline and punishment.

Anecdote: Cheryl spilled her juice for the second time in a week. The teacher **did not** say, "Klutzy Cheryl, you did it again. When are you going to learn to not be messy?"

The teacher **did say**, "It's OK, Cheryl, we all spill, even teachers. The sponge is in the bucket. If you need help, let me know."

Labeling. The teacher above recognized that "labeling is disabling," and avoided what Ginott calls "teaching at its worst" (Ginott, 1972). Labeling children, either intentionally or unintentionally, has two broad negative effects. *First*, as the **self-fulfilling prophecy** suggests, children learn to see themselves in the way they are labelled. The label is incorporated into the child's self concept and may influence future behavior. Without fortunate counter experiences that tell the child, "I'm not like that," the child's views and feelings about self may be permanently affected.

Second, the label causes adults to focus unduly on the particular behavior they have come to expect. They fail to see other important behavior patterns and qualities in the child. By labeling, adults limit their ability to work productively with children. Every child is greater than the sample of behavior that stands out to the teacher. So much development has yet to occur that the teacher must avoid constricting that development by labeling (Erickson & Pianta, 1989). The ability to value the child as a still developing person allows for teaching responses that the author terms "liberating."

Anecdote: After a few weeks of Head Start, a three-year-old named Jimmy began to show a strange behavior when he arrived in the morning: He began to kick the teacher in the leg! Sue, the teacher, tried an assortment of techniques none of which worked, but steadfastly refused to brand Jimmy with character references. Finally, she tried a new approach. When Jimmy first walked in the door, the teacher approached him quickly, gave him a hug and told him how happy she was to see him. After a few days of this new welcome, Jimmy would arrive, give the teacher a wide berth and say, "Hi, Teacher."

Four years later, Sue received a Christmas card from Jimmy and his mother. Written on the card were these words: "Dear Teacher, I'm havin' a nice Christmas. I hope you are. I still remember you. Do you remember me?"

A key understanding about labeling is that it occurs even when the adult does not specifically "call names." A teacher scolds a child by saying that what s/he did was "not nice." As a result of developmental immaturity and limited experience, the child internalizes the message as "I'm not nice" (Erickson &

Figure 3–3 When teachers intervene, they must select their words with care.

Pianta, 1989). As Ginott suggests, the challenge is to convey to children that although the teacher is upset with what happened, s/he still accepts them as individuals of worth and welcome members of the group (Ginott, 1972). In other words, **teachers must select words carefully when they choose to intervene**. Assess for yourself which intervention is more supportive of the child's developing self:

"Kyle, you are being rowdy." "If you don't work more quietly, I will move you."	"The talking is too loud. You choose, Kyle; work quietly or find a different seat."
"Zach, don't you be lazy. You used the blocks. If you don't put them away, you won't go outside."	"Zach, all who used the blocks need to put them back. As soon as they're away, we can go out."
"Class, you are being antsy again. Story time is now over; go and take your seats."	"OK, everybody, we need a break. Let's stand up and stretch. When the music starts, let's all 'get the wiggles out.'"

Firmness Not Harshness. An erroneous criticism of a guidance approach is that it is permissive, sacrificing limits to maintain relations. In fact, positive relations with children depend on the reliability of limits, responsibly set and enforced (Hendrick, 1992a). Children have the right to programming and practices that are appropriate for their development and personal backgrounds. Teachers have the responsibility to use guidelines that enable productive child activity. Ginott's Cardinal Principle illustrates that how—and not whether—teachers enforce limits is the issue.

Individual teachers have their own levels of tolerance and behavioral expectations. Such limits are the teacher's to decide. A guidance approach argues that when the teacher intervenes, s/he does so with appropriate firmness for the situation, but without the punishing effects of being harsh. Nonpunitive intervention takes experience and understanding. The Cardinal Principle gives direction to intervention that is firm but friendly, maintains limits, but still supports the self-concept of the child.

2. GUIDANCE DISCIPLINE REDUCES THE NEED FOR MISTAKEN BEHAVIOR

Because of the intrinsic dynamic that is a part of their biology, young children normally come to school ready to learn and grow. When children have trouble in the school environment, two factors tend to be involved.

The Nature of Childhood

The first factor has to do with the nature of childhood itself. All young children bring insecurities—the fear of abandonment, the fear of failure—into the early childhood classroom. These anxieties, combined with only a beginning understanding of social expectations, mean that young children make mistakes (Greenberg, 1988). Many such mistakes are the product of every day life in the classroom—not wanting to share the playdough, quarreling over a pencil—these the teacher monitors, but may not prevent. Through learning to solve problems and resolve conflicts in a climate of positive regard, the child gains life-long personal and social skills (Wichert, 1989).

While the teacher does not work to prevent all problems, neither does s/he manufacture additional problems. The caring teacher may pose **challenges**, but only if s/he believes the child has a good chance to succeed in the face of the challenge. Her role is to assist children, overcome the anxieties they feel, and come to understand social expectations (Erickson & Pianta, 1989). Anxiety levels of the children and the potential for harm are two determinants in the teacher's decision about whether and when to intervene.

A knowledge of the levels of mistaken behavior helps with guidance decisions. For example at level one, experimentation, children are likely to argue over material. The teacher may avoid a needless problem by providing an expanded choice of materials. Or, s/he may help to resolve the dispute by encouraging the child to negotiate a compromise. If necessary, s/he redirects a child to another material.

At level two, social influence, a child may repeat a name used by others, such as the timeless, "poopy butt." In this situation the teacher privately reinforces a guideline about name calling and teaches "non-hurting" words to use. A "class meeting" may also be called, even at the preschool level, to discuss (in terms that do not "single out") the need to appreciate each other (Greenberg, 1992b).

A child who frequently becomes upset over small frustrations is showing level three, strong needs mistaken behavior. As discussed in the previous chapter, children who show serious mistaken behavior have strong needs which they are unable to cope with on their own. The difficulties may be physical—health conditions and disabilities—or emotional, the effect of negative experiences and unhealthy attachments.

The teacher uses the multistep approach necessary with level three: reinforces limits non-punitively, seeks more information about the child, builds a collaborative intervention strategy, and develops the relationship. The relationship helps the child develop trust in the school environment. The strategy assists the child to avoid problem situations and express strong feelings in acceptable ways.

The job of the early childhood teacher is to be familiar with the kinds of mistakes children are likely to make, just because they are children. By preventing some problems and assisting children to resolve others, the teacher removes obstacles to the child's intrinsic construction of meaning based on successful experience (Erickson & Pianta, 1989).

The Match of the Child and the Program

A second factor in mistaken behavior lies in children's reactions to practices that are not **developmentally appropriate**. In recent years a shift in emphasis toward academic kindergarten curricula has occurred, based on two stereotyped beliefs: (*a*) by virtue of attending preschools, children are now "more advanced"; and (*b*) because of expanding societal knowledge, children have to be instructed more intensely and earlier (Nebraska State Board of Education, reprinted, 1990). Many preschools have followed this line of reasoning, beginning academic "readiness" programs (Elkind, 1989).

These beliefs have resulted in practices that are inappropriate for young children, who are not developmentally ready for conceptually oriented seat work until well into the primary years. A typical complaint as a result of this emphasis is that many, often boys with summer birthdays, "are not ready for kindergarten." They show such behaviors as difficulty in attending, short attention spans, perceptual/motor difficulties, and low frustration levels (Charlesworth, 1989).

With the trend toward earlier academics, schools have urged families to start "young five-year-olds" a year later than usual, so they can receive "the gift of time." As well, special classes have become popular for the "immature kindergarten child," sometimes called "developmental" or "junior kindergartens." Charlesworth (1989) argues that these stopgap measures have not proven effective and support essentially erroneous pedagogical conclusions about the characteristics of young learners. Works by the Nebraska Board of Education (reprinted, 1990), Bredekamp (1987), and Elkind (1989) argue persuasively that programs need to be developmentally appropriate for all children, not just for those who can sit still through formal academic programming.

Growing understanding about the importance of development in education is having an effect on how teachers interpret discipline issues. Behaviors that teachers previously regarded as immature and disruptive are now seen as an indication that programming is not appropriate for the development and learning style of a child. This new awareness shifts the responsibility for "program-caused" mistaken behavior from the child to teachers and administrators.

A basic factor in reducing the need for mistaken behavior, then, is the relevance of the educational program to the child. To further healthy development, the teacher uses programming that has meaning for children and at which they can succeed. In this effort, developmental characteristics must be accommodated by appropriate curriculum and methods. Family backgrounds must be affirmed by culturally responsive teaching practices. As a professional, the teacher works with colleagues to improve the acceptance of these ideas in the center or school (Bredekamp, 1987).

Within the classroom, the teacher designs and implements programming in line with accepted guidelines for appropriate and responsive practice. She monitors, and on occasion more formally assesses, the match between the

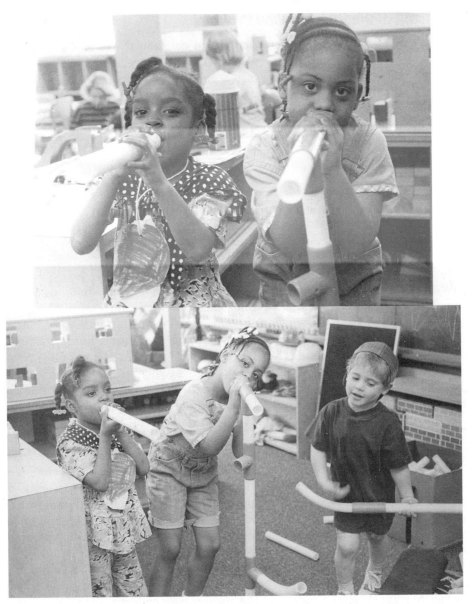

Figure 3–4 A factor in reducing mistaken behavior is the relevance of the educational program to the child.

needs and backgrounds of the children and the educational program. Deviations from expectations mean that revision may be necessary to improve the match (Osborn & Osborn, 1989; Evertson et. al., 1989). Modification of the program to improve learner-involvement is at the heart of reducing much mistaken behavior. The anecdotes that follow illustrate how two teachers "fine tuned" music activities to respond better to the developmental and cultural needs of their children.

Anecdote: [Improving the developmental match with rhythm instruments:]

A kindergarten teacher was working for the first time with rhythm instruments. He held up the various instruments—tambourine, triangle, rhythm sticks, bells, blocks—and asked who wanted to use each. Many hands shot up for the "exotic" instruments, not many for the rhythm sticks. He observed that some children were crestfallen when they didn't get the choices they wanted, and others pressured those near them "to trade."

After several minutes of stock market maneuvers, the teacher got the activity explained: He would start the cassette tape, call out the name of an instrument, and just that group would play. Unexpectedly, the children made "rhythms" at will, without much sense of either the beat or the instrument group called. The teacher saw that some adjustments were needed.

For the next two weeks during choice time, the music center materials included a set of each rhythm instrument. The children used the instruments each day while they listened to music on their headphones. After the two weeks of "exploration," the teacher resumed the large group rhythm activity, but with an expanded supply of instruments borrowed from another classroom. The rhythm band quickly developed its skills.

Anecdote: (Improving cultural responsiveness with rhythm sticks)

A teacher had been working with her preschoolers using rhythm sticks for a few weeks when two Native American (Ojibwe) children joined the program. The teacher told DJ and Cheyenne that they could participate with the group or sit and watch. The two boys watched, then noticed two extra sticks on a chair behind the teacher. They each picked up a stick, cupped one ear, and began drumming the sticks on the chair to the music. The teacher became upset, took the sticks, and told them to sit quietly for the rest of the activity.

Afterwards, a teacher aide who was also Ojibwe explained that the children were using the sticks as their older relatives did, to "beat the drum and sing like at a pow-wow." Embarrassed, the teacher asked the aide's help to organize a pow-wow for the preschool, which included two of the boys' relatives as singers. DJ and Cheyenne were proud to sit with the singers and dance with the rest of the class.

The teacher reduces the need for mistaken behavior by using practices that are developmentally appropriate and culturally responsive. These ideas are discussed further in chapters to come.

3. GUIDANCE DISCIPLINE TAKES A SOLUTION-ORIENTATION

Referring to child rearing practices of the past, Berger states:

> Except for a few dissenters. . .most people were much more interested in disciplining children to keep them from becoming sinners or degenerates than in nurturing them so that they would preserve their natural curiosity and enthusiasm (1989).

It is only in the twentieth century that empathy for the condition of childhood has become a broad-based social value (deMause, 1974; Osborn, 1980). That children show mistaken behavior out of developmental immaturity and unmet basic needs is a distressingly recent understanding.

A guidance view of discipline holds that children should not be punished for having problems, but assisted to develop the personal skills necessary to solve their problems (Gartrell, 1992). Rather than reinforce the labeling of children as good or bad, model students or rowdy, guidance discipline is about helping all children to get along, solve problems, and express strong feelings in acceptable ways (Greenberg, 1988).

Even young children are put into situations where they must make moral decisions (Osborn & Osborn, 1988). This ability cannot be built through punitive discipline. Only a guidance approach empowers children to build the self-control *and* self-acceptance necessary to say yes or no "because it is the right thing to do" (Gartrell, 1987b; Osborn & Osborn, 1989). Rather than moralistic in tone, guidance discipline is solution-oriented. Rather than authoritarian or permissive, guidance discipline is interactive. Guidance discipline requires positive leadership. It requires teachers to make firm decisions. The decisions need to model ethical considerations, however, and be based not on an infallible sense of authority but on an understanding of young children and their needs (Weber-Schwartz, 1987; Greenberg, 1992a).

Problem-Solving

In the guidance approach the adult teaches techniques for problem-solving as an ongoing part of the education program (Wichert, 1989). The vehicle for **conflict resolution** is **mediation**. Mediation skills are critical in a democracy, but the widespread notion that children are incapable of solving their problems is only now beginning to change.

At the grade school level, the Mediation in the Schools Program in Lancaster, Pennsylvania, illustrates one way that "life problem-solving" is becoming a part of K–12 education programs. In participating elementary schools, trained students wearing "Conflict Manager" jerseys assist other students to resolve playground disputes. Knowing that the conflict managers report each case back to the principal, students have incentive to make the mediation work. Drops in playground conflicts among schools using the program have proven significant (A.P. News Release, 1988). Mediation in the Schools practices have spread to other states, a positive trend.

Even preschool children can be empowered to mediate disputes (Greenberg, 1992b; Hendrick, 1992b; Wichert, 1989). In Wichert's schema, children operate at one of three skill levels to resolve classroom difficulties. At **high adult intervention** the teacher actively assists children to calm children, focus on the problem, and move toward resolution (Wichert, 1989). In **minimal adult intervention**, "children define the problem using their own language and the adult merely clarifies when needed" (Wichert, p. 56, 1989). At level three **children take charge**, removing themselves from the situation to discuss and solve the problem (Wichert, 1989)

The teacher works to help children understand that they have the ability to solve problems themselves. Wichert states:

> You should be just as aware of each child's skills level in negotiating as of other developmental areas like gross and fine motor skills. Do not underestimate the children's ability to engage in this kind of negotiation, but also be flexible in your

Figure 3–5 Frequently, the teacher waits to see if children can resolve a difficulty on their own.

expectations of a child who may be having a difficult day. . .Negotiation learning in children is a prime example of the importance of process over product. . . Sometimes there simply will be no solution that suits both parties one hundred percent. Life is like that, and your job is then to help children cope with their feeling about it (Wichert, p. 58, 1989).

A preschool in northern Minnesota set up **talk and listen chairs** for the resolution of conflicts. At the beginning of the year when two four-year-olds were having an argument, a teacher would accompany them to "the chairs." She would mediate while the children took turns talking, exchanging chairs, and listening until the difference was resolved. By spring, the use of the chairs was routine, and the children went to them on their own.

Views differ on the practice of having children leave the place of activity to resolve difficulties in a formal fashion. The prospect of using the chairs is often an incentive toward resolution in itself. In any case, "talk and listen" chairs provide a variation in conflict resolution strategies. The practice is documented at a first grade level by Chenfeld (1983).

The Teacher as Democratic Leader

If mediation is to be used successfully, then adults must be sure about their role in the classroom. In distinguishing the democratic classroom from the autocratic, Dreikurs characterized the teacher as a "leader" "winning cooperation" in the one and a "boss" "demanding cooperation" in the other. In the autocratic classroom, the teacher takes sole responsibility for transactions and takes the position, "I decide, you obey." In contrast, the teacher in the democratic classroom is more like a manager or coach who shares responsibility with the team (Dreikurs, 1972).

Student teachers sometimes find difficulty in assuming the leadership that is required in the teacher's role. Out of concern for children's feelings, they confuse leadership with dictatorship (Hendrick, 1992a). A teacher can be a friend to children, but the relationship must be that of an adult friend to a child. Even democracies need strong leaders.

In the democratic classroom, the teacher creates a climate of mutual respect. Children reciprocate this feeling when they are empowered to make choices on their own and decisions with others (Osborn & Osborn, 1989; Hendrick, 1992b). This is but one reason that play, or self-selected "work time," is important in the daily schedule. Play not only gives children the freedom to make mistakes and experience disagreements, but the opportunity to resolve these difficulties as well. The teacher knows s/he is using mediation well when children spontaneously use the communication skill on their own.

Crisis Intervention

Young children are just beginning to understand the complexities of social situations and they feel emotions strongly. Even under the best of circumstances they will not always resolve problems with words. On occasion they need to be rescued from their own behavior. The test of guidance discipline is when the adult must physically intervene to prevent harm. Although early intervention to head off a crisis is preferable, it is not always possible (Hendrick, 1992a). When communication has broken down and there is danger of physical or psychological harm, the teacher must act.

In guidance discipline physical intervention is limited to "passive restraint" and brief periods of supervised removal; these are methods of last resort (Gartrell, 1987). If a "time out chair" or other crisis resolution practices are used **often**, teachers need to review their approach because (*a*) the techniques are not working, and (*b*) the atmosphere may be becoming more punitive than is desired (Clewett, 1988). When the teacher does restrain or remove a child, after feelings have cooled s/he explains why the behavior compelled the intervention and how the child might respond differently next time. The teacher then assists the child to reenter the group. A point of distinction in a guidance approach is that after intervention the teacher works for **reconciliation** and helps the child to regain self-esteem (Gartrell, 1992). Further discussion of the solution-orientation to mistaken behavior can be found in chapters seven, eight and nine.

Learning While Teaching

In 1970, Kounin wrote about "withitness" to describe a teacher's ability to identify those key situations in the classroom that need to be addressed. Discussed since in texts by such authors as Charles (1985), Evertson et al. (1989), and Osborn & Osborn (1989), the term has become a staple in the literature of classroom management. From his classroom research, Kounin concluded that effective teachers—the ones with "eyes in the back of their heads"—have withitness; ineffective teachers do not (Kounin, 1970).

Withitness, like other teaching skills, takes time to master, and even experienced teachers can be fooled. When teachers recognize that becoming fully informed is the goal, but that they must often act on less than complete information, then withitness is put in its proper perspective. When teachers do miscalculate a situation, then perhaps a sensible practice is to recognize both their fallibility and their potential to learn, and go on from there (Hendrick, 1992a):

Anecdote: A "circus" was set up in a large room of a day care center. Different activities were occurring in various parts of the room, including a very popular cotton candy "concession." Brian, an after-school five, was standing in line when he was pushed from in front. He bumped against a three-year-old who fell down and was hurt. A teacher arrived on the scene, looked over the situation and told Brian to go to the end of the line for pushing. A few minutes later the teacher noticed that Brian was crying. A student teacher who had seen the incident explained what had happened. The teacher helped Brian get his place back in line, happily the next one to receive a wand of cotton candy.

It is difficult to know exactly what happened and how to intervene. These skills take continuing practice. An important guideline is that anytime a teacher can act more like a judge in a courtroom and less like a police officer on the street s/he is working to understand the situation. Quick judgments sometimes are necessary, but a more positive resolution may come about if the teacher delays action in order to gather information and collect thoughts (Hendrick, 1992a).

Anecdote: In a Minneapolis kindergarten, Jed, a child who rarely initiated conversations, was using a truck during a choice time. The teacher did not see exactly what happened, but heard Jed crying and saw Sharon pushing the truck to another part of the room. The teacher was tempted to confront Sharon, who was looking over her shoulder, but went first to Jed and quietly talked with him. When the teacher got up and walked to where Sharon was, the five-year-old did **not** argue that she had the truck first. Instead Sharon said, "I didn't mean to." This response allowed the teacher to assist Sharon to make amends.

A task of the professional teacher is to develop techniques for anticipating situations that may require intervention. Another important task is to be as familiar as possible with the child in the situation. A teacher cannot always learn what is bothering a child, but the attempt to learn is likely to yield positive results. First, the teacher gains new information that may increase understanding about the child. Second, the **effort** to gain new information tends to improve the teacher-child relationship. From a modification in relations, the child may come to see school in a different light.

Accepting Our Humaness

Teachers need to monitor their own feelings to retain consistency in their communications with children (Hendrick, 1992). They watch out for their own "level three" days.

Anecdote: After a night of little sleep, due to teething by an infant and a spouse out of town, a teacher (who also happened to have a sinus headache) modified plans about the intensity of activities. This became a day for more reliance on coworkers, soft-pedaling of expectations for the group, and increased use of videos and self-defining activities. The day proved long, but not as long as it might have. The spouse returned that evening, and the infant felt better.

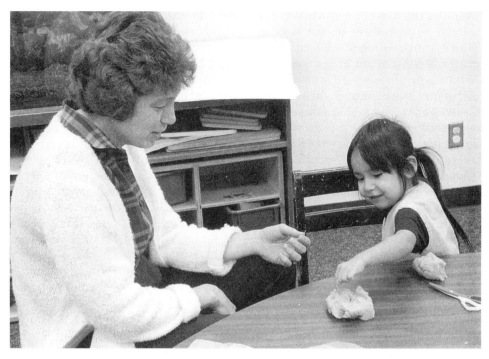

Figure 3–6 The teacher gains new information that assists in understanding behavior and building relations.

Often when teachers are affected by personal circumstances, they let the class know. In a caring classroom even three-year-olds will make an effort to "help teacher feel better." (Teachers report, however, that this practice loses its effectiveness if used on a daily basis.) Teachers who keep a list of strategies and activities to help them through physically or emotionally rough days have shown understanding about their importance in the lives of young children.

Finally, despite the best of intentions, because they are human, teachers too make mistakes. They may misinterpret situations, over-react to a child, be punitive toward a group, or unprofessional to an adult. Use of a guidance approach does not presume teaching perfection. A problem-solving orientation takes a long time to master. In guidance discipline, a teacher has a right to make mistakes, but what is important is that s/he learn from them. The professional teacher learns even while s/he teaches (Gartrell, 1992).

4. GUIDANCE DISCIPLINE MEANS TEAMWORK WITH OTHER ADULTS ON BEHALF OF THE CHILD

A myth that still afflicts education is that the teacher handles all situations alone. Perhaps the myth goes back to the one room schools of rural America past and the expectations upon the teachers who taught in them. Many adults wanted no part of the teacher's job which was seen as making unruly, undisciplined youth sit obediently and master the three Rs. Depending on their demeanor and perceived success, teachers were revered as saintly, like the first Montessori directresses in the tenements of Rome; respected for their iron discipline, like the school masters of British boarding schools; or made the butt of jokes, like the fabled Ichabod Crane. In any case, the adult community expected teachers to sink or swim on their own with minimal support from administrators, other teachers, or parents.

Until recently K-12 school systems have largely continued this practice. Through its power as the institution responsible for socializing youth, the public school has tended to put educators in a superior "professional" position, frequently casting parents as "friendly intruders" (Greenberg, 1988). The implication was that the teacher should not need the parent's input, deemed by its source to be of marginal value.

As well, in relation to first year teachers, administrators have been oriented more to performance reviews than mentoring relationships. To many administrators, their job was not so much to help a beginning teacher remediate deficiencies as to weed out those deemed unfit for the profession.

Happily, both of these trends are on the wane. Articles such as Katz's on the developmental stages of teachers (1977) have led the way in pointing out the need for new teachers to be eased into the profession by working with mentors. As well, a new consciousness about the importance of the home life in educational success is increasing the emphasis on true teacher-parent partnerships (Boyer, 1991). Reduced class sizes especially in the first few grades of school—called for by Boyer among others—is further indication that the myth of teacher as "supermarm" may be coming to an end.

The Teaching Team

There is **team-teaching** and then there is the **teaching team**. The two concepts are different. **Team-teaching** is the practice, mainly at the K–12 level, of having two licensed teachers working together with the same group of children. Thornton (1990) provides a useful account of the problems and promise when two teachers work together. For Thornton, mutual trust is a prime ingredient and this quality takes hard work, communication, and time.

When the relationship is established, the benefits are many. Cooperative planning, implementation, and evaluation of the program take pressure off each individual. Through teamwork, developmentally appropriate, active learning experiences are easier to initiate. The choice of two personalities with whom to relate can be empowering both for the children and their parents (Thornton, 1990). By virtue of their differing personalities, two teachers can respond more effectively to the wide array of learning and behavior styles represented in any group of young children. When team-teaching is working, each member has a built-in support system.

Not all teachers function effectively as in the teaching team situation, and care must be taken in setting up such assignments. When the relationship is a comfortable one, however, children and teachers both stand to benefit (Thornton, 1990).

The technical name for the **teaching team** is **differentiated staffing**, or the use of adults with differing credentials and experience-bases to serve the same group of children. The traditional teaching team format is the teacher and the teacher-aide. In actuality, classroom volunteers as well as staff can comprise the team. In modern educational settings, a teacher may work with volunteers, paraprofessionals, Chapter One teachers, special education teachers, and other specialists, all in the same class—a comprehensive staffing arrangement to be sure.

When an aide and teacher work together as a team, the teacher provides supervision for the learning environment, but the aide works with small groups, individual children, and on occasion with the full group. In other words the aide also teaches. Conversely, if the situation warrants, the teacher may wipe up a spill or help a child change clothes (Read, Gardner & Mahler, 1993).

In classrooms where there is a strict separation of professional and paraprofessional roles, it is generally thought that only the teacher does the teaching. Despite appearances, this view is incorrect. In reality, all adults in a

Figure 3–7 When the teaching team concept is used, children and the adults benefit.

classroom serve as models for young children, and so all are teachers. The adult who accepts this premise accepts the concept of the teaching team.

The advantages of the teaching team are similar to those of team-teaching, but the teaching team goes further in its model of democracy. When children see adults in differing social roles converse and work together, they learn that social and cultural differences need not be threatening. The teacher-parent relationship is the most direct example and offers the most benefit to the child. Nonetheless, when a teacher and aide work together amicably, the child's expanding social world becomes that much more reliable and friendly. The children are likely to follow the lead of the teacher and feel respect for all of the adults in the classroom.

When the efforts of the aide are appreciated, s/he feels affirmed. Negative feelings that result from being "stigmatized" (disqualified from full membership in the group) do not arise. Disagreements do not become conflicts, but get resolved. Like children, assistants who feel accepted participate fully (Read, Gardner & Mahler, 1993).

Of course, not all aides are prepared to function as "associate teachers" on the team. Using the criteria of state regulations, program policy, and personal readiness, the teacher, as team leader, determines how much responsibility other team members are to be given. Unpressured discussion about roles, along with ongoing communication about duties, are important to make teaming work.

Over the last twenty years, a variety of terms have been used to describe teaching team members. The terms usually reflect the education programs completed by the member and the roles ascribed by the program or district. The National Association for the Education of Young Children through its Institute for Professional Development, is trying both to standardize roles and qualifications and to advocate for better articulation (transferability) across training programs (Bredekamp, 1991).

Such terms as volunteer, teacher-aide, teacher-assistant, assistant teacher, associate teacher, Child Development Associate, teacher, lead teacher, and early childhood educator illustrate the complexity of the mix of roles. Whatever the titles of the staff who work together, where there is trust and communication, it is a teaching team. The positive atmosphere in such classrooms radiates to the children.

The Teaching Team in the Primary Grades. On the surface, the teaching team concept seems to have less relevance to K–3 classrooms. In most schools the system is set: one teacher, twenty to thirty-five children. When an aide is present, it is usually for a small part of the day. The aide likely has "para-professional" duties specified in the "master contract."

Primary grade teachers who wish to incorporate a team concept into their classrooms sometimes have limited options, but it is happening. The growing practice of **inclusion**, or broad-scale integration of children with disabilities in the "regular" classroom, is advancing the teaching team concept. Some teachers

Figure 3–8 The growing practice of inclusion is advancing the teaching team concept.

recruit parents, college students, or senior citizens to come into classrooms on a regular basis. These volunteers read to children, supervise learning situations, work with small groups, or otherwise lend their experience. In a growing number of schools, students from the upper grades assist in prekindergarten, kindergarten, and primary classrooms. Where such efforts are organized and supervised, programs run smoothly, and both older and younger children benefit.

Teacher as Team Leader. With the use of a teaching team, the teacher's role changes. S/he no longer undertakes all teaching transactions herself. Instead, s/he manages an active learning laboratory, teaching and modelling continuously, but also supervising others who are there to help. Informally, the new role approaches that of the "early childhood educator" written about by Almy in 1975. It is an uncomfortable role for many new teachers just entering the profession and for others, steeped in the traditional notion of what a teacher does.

We are still learning about the teacher's role in the differentiated staffing situation, and about the effects of the teaching team for the classroom and children's behavior. In some ways the role poses additional new tasks for teachers. In others it offers new freedoms and possibilities—in particular the ability to reach children who in the old system might have passed through unaided. Here is the connection with guidance discipline. With more adults in the classroom on a regular basis, the chances for positive relations with adults increases, and the need for mistaken behavior diminishes.

Working with Other Professionals. Besides team members in the classroom, the teacher communicates with other professionals: administrators and specialists in the program or school; specialists from other agencies. As Kagan and Rivera point out (1991), the "buzzword" for such communication is **collaboration**. The word is a useful one if it has the meaning the authors intend:

> We have defined collaborations as those efforts that unite and empower individuals and organizations to accomplish collectively what they could not accomplish independently (Kagan & Rivera, 1991, p. 52).

In early childhood settings, collaborations typically revolve around two agenda: (*a*) specifics of the program itself—resources, scheduling, content, methods; and (*b*) matters pertaining to the children in the class. When children show serious mistaken behavior, collaboration is often required. Information exchanges within the school or center, professionally done, assist the teacher to better understand the child and the situation. As Hendrick points out, however, discussions involving formal diagnosis or possible referral should not be effected between professionals by themselves. Professional ethics, and often statute and policy, warrant the involvement of parents.

When parents, the teacher, and other professionals meet for a possible referral or special services, the teacher assists the collaboration by remaining

"Oh, yes, Joanie's parents—I recognized you from her drawings!"

Figure 3-9 (Courtesy of Mrs. Ray Morin.)

sensitive to the discomfort that many parents feel in the presence of professionals. Such collaborations are strengthened when representatives of all concerned programs participate, such as day care staff with the kindergarten teacher, or Head Start personnel with early childhood special education teachers. The promise of collaboration is that the process allows for a comprehensive and unified plan that can assist a troubled child.

5. GUIDANCE DISCIPLINE MEANS PARTNERSHIPS WITH PARENTS

Anecdote: In a rural community in Minnesota, a principal informed a long time third grade teacher that she was assigned to a first grade class the next fall. The teacher requested that she be allowed to invite parents into the class to help with activities. The principal reluctantly agreed, but told the teacher the idea would never work.

By the end of mid-October, the teacher had seventy-five percent of the parents, including many working parents, coming into class on a regular basis. By December, the teacher reported that every parent had been into the classroom at least once. The principal responded warmly. She said she was sold on the idea the day a substitute had taught in the first grade and offered this reaction: Between the parents and the children, the classroom had run itself.

In an outspoken commentary in the NAEYC journal, *Young Children*, Polly Greenberg discusses roadblocks to effective parent-teacher relations, including the issues of gender bias, racism, and classism (1989). Greenberg develops the argument that as the century progressed, schools grew more "professional," and parents became less welcome in them—especially parents from cultural and income backgrounds different than school personnel. As well, the administrative structure of schools became male-dominated, making communication difficult for single parents, most of whom are women, and for the women teachers of young children (1989). Greenberg defines the resulting problem this way:

> If, when they were children, parents had a great many frustration and failure experiences in school, they may not like schools very much. This feeling can be contagious to their children. It can be true in any family. It seems to be particularly true of low-income minority families, though of course it's by no means always so. In this case, many children feel they have to choose to spurn the family and throw themselves into succeeding at school, or to spurn school success to win family approval. This is a tough spot to put a young child in! Children who have to buck school to avoid disapproval at home are often big-time discipline problems.

In further response to this issue, Greenberg concludes:

> Conversely, children whose parents expect them to cooperate and to do their best at school, and who are proud when they do, tend to have better self-discipline. They are striving to achieve family approval; to do this they must earn the teacher's approval. Encouraging a high degree of family enthusiasm for their children's public schools and child care centers is one of the best ways in which teachers can. . .build children's self-esteem and reduce discipline problems. . . (pp. 61–62).

For the reasons mentioned by Greenberg, partnerships with parents are integral to a guidance approach to discipline. Building such relations requires teachers to put aside biases and focus on what they and parents have in common, the well-being of the child (Galinsky, 1988; Gestwicki, 1992). Exceptional teachers always have gone out of their way to make parents feel welcome and esteemed. Authorities in the field make the point that the responsibility to reach even hard-to-reach parents lies with the teacher (Galinsky, 1988; Greenberg, 1989; Gestwicki, 1992).

Whatever the existing practices of a school or center toward collaboration with parents, the teacher does well to note two generally accepted ideas in early childhood about parents:

- There is no more important profession for which there is so little preparation as being a parent.
- Parents are the primary educators of their children; teachers only help.

Greenberg's call for prospective teachers to have more preparation in working with parents and for administrators to give more attention to parent-teacher relations is timely and important (1989). The child is an extension of the family unit. The teacher who knows and works with the family will be more successful in guiding the development of the child.

Awareness of the importance of parent involvement in their children's education is growing in the society. Despite busy schedules, many parents are willing to become involved. They need invitations, choices regarding their involvement, and support from the teacher. With increased parent participation, children learn they are supported at home and at school. The need for mistaken behavior then becomes less.

SUMMARY

How are positive teacher-child relations the basis of the guidance approach?

It is impossible to love all children, but as a professional, the teacher works to accept each child as a welcome member of the group. This "unconditional positive regard" does not mean the teacher is permissive, but that s/he separates the mistaken behaviors a child may show from the personality of the child—addressing the behaviors while affirming personal worth. The teacher avoids singling children out either for criticism or praise. S/he offers private, individual encouragement, or encouragement that is public, but group-focused. To maintain positive relations, the teacher practices the "cardinal principle," avoids labels, is firm but friendly, and practices liberation teaching. Children who feel accepted as individuals and members of the group have less need for mistaken behavior.

How does guidance discipline reduce the need for mistaken behavior?

The teacher recognizes that when children have trouble in the school environment, two factors tend to be involved. First is the nature of childhood itself. The teacher accepts the fact that young children come to school eager to learn, but in the process of learning they make mistakes. S/he assists children to learn from mistakes more effectively when s/he understands the three levels of mistaken behavior.

A second factor lies in children's reactions when teaching practices are not developmentally appropriate. The teacher improves the match by using developmentally appropriate and culturally responsive teaching practices. When their motivations, needs, and family backgrounds become the driving force for the educational program, children become not passive, bored, or frustrated, but active, involved, and successful.

What does it mean that guidance discipline is solution-oriented?

The teacher creates an environment in which problems can be resolved. S/he does so by teaching and modelling conflict-resolution skills. S/he does so as well by modelling democratic leadership skills; s/he is a friend to children but as an adult friend to a child. S/he intervenes non-punitively, using removal and passive restraint only as methods of last resort, when communication has broken down and there is a danger of harm. After direct intervention, s/he assists the child to reconcile with the group and salvage self esteem.

The teacher learns even while s/he teaches. S/he practices such skills as withitness, but recognizes that teachers usually do not know all that has happened in a situation. The teacher improves chances for problem resolution to the extent s/he can act more as judge than as a police officer. Not every situation will be successfully resolved, of course, and teachers will at times show human frailties. Being models to children, it is important for teachers, as professionals, to recognize their mistakes and to learn from them.

Why is teamwork with staff and other professionals part of guidance discipline?

Children benefit from positive relations with all adults who may be in the classroom. Effective communication among adults allows for comprehensive strategies for working with mistaken behavior. For these two reasons, the myth that the teacher handles all situations alone needs to end. In the guidance approach, the teacher moves toward a teaching team model in the classroom and involves fellow staff and volunteers of differing backgrounds to provide responsive programming. Children gain a sense of reliability in their expanding social worlds when they see adults of different backgrounds working together amicably. They gain in esteem and understanding from increased individual attention.

The teacher collaborates with other professionals: administrators and specialists in the center or school as well as specialists in other agencies. When such collaboration involves diagnosis of children's behavior or possible referral, the teacher involves parents as partners in the collaborative process. Through collaboration, adults can accomplish together what they might not be able to do alone.

How are parent-teacher partnerships important in the guidance approach?

The teacher recognizes that being a parent is a difficult job and that many parents, for personal and cultural reasons, feel discomfort in communicating with educators. It is the teacher's job to initiate relations even with hard-to-reach parents. Though busy, many parents respond positively to invitations to become involved in their children's education. The need for mistaken behavior diminishes when parents and teachers work together.

FOLLOW-UP ACTIVITIES

Follow-up activities allow the student to inter-relate material from the text with "real life" situations. The "observations" imply access to practicum experiences, the "interviews" access to teachers and parents. When communicating about the activities, students need to respect the privacy of all participants in the observation or interview, as an important professional courtesy.

1. **How are positive teacher-child relations the basis of the guidance approach?**
   a. Observe an instance in which a teacher affirmed positive regard for a child. What did the teacher say and do? What did the child say and do? How do you think the child's behavior might be influenced by such an exchange?
   b. Talk with a teacher about a sensitive topic: Explain that your textbook says that teachers do not always have natural positive feelings towards every child. Ask the teacher how s/he builds relationships with children who are "more difficult to like or understand."

2. **How does guidance discipline reduce the need for mistaken behavior?**
   a. Observe an instance when a teacher acted to "head off" or resolve a problem in a firm but friendly manner. Think about what level of mistaken behavior was at work. Reflect about how the teacher showed understanding of the child or children involved.
   b. Observe an activity that seemed a "good match" between the levels of development of the children and what the activity asked the children to do. Reflect about the amount of productive behavior and/or mistaken behavior that you observed in the activity.
   c. Ask a teacher to discuss a change s/he has made to the curriculum or schedule in order to improve the match between the needs of the children and the expectations of the program. How did the change make the day "go better" for the group or individual children, and for the teacher?

3. **What does it mean that guidance discipline is solution-oriented?**
   a. Observe an instance when a teacher assisted children to resolve a problem. Reflect about what the teacher said and did. How did the children react? What do you think they learned from the experience?
   b. Ask a teacher to recall an instance of when s/he assisted children to resolve a problem. Ask the teacher his or her feelings about the experience. What would the teacher do differently or the same if a similar situation were to arise again?

4. **Why is teamwork with staff and other professionals part of guidance discipline?**
   a. Observe a productive teaching team in operation. Note the kinds of communication that occur between the team members, verbal and non-verbal. What seems to characterize the communication you have observed?
   b. Interview a lead teacher and/or another member of a teaching team. Ask what is important to each in maintaining positive relations between the adults and a positive atmosphere in the classroom.

5. How are parent-teacher partnerships important in the guidance approach?
   a. Observe a classroom in which parents are participating as volunteers. What actions on the part of the teacher(s) seem to help the parents feel welcome. How are the parents participating?
   b. Interview a parent who is actively involved in a program. Ask how the parent's involvement has affected the parent and the child.

SUGGESTED RESOURCES

Charlesworth, R. (1989). " 'Behind' Before They Start? Deciding How to Deal With the Risk of Kindergarten 'Failure,' " *Young Children, 44*(3), pp. 5-13.
Erickson, M.F. and Pianta, R.C. (1989). "New Lunchbox, Old Feelings: What Kids Bring to School," *Early Education and Development, 1*(1), pp. 35-49.
Greenberg, P. (1989). "Parents as Partners in Young Children's Development and Education: A New American Fad? Why Does it Matter?" *Young Children, 44*(4), pp. 61-75.
Hitz, R. and Driscoll, A. (1988). "Praise or Encouragement?" *Young Children, 43* (5), pp. 6-13.
Katz, L.G. (1977). "Teachers' Developmental Stages," *Talks with Teachers, Reflections on Early Childhood Education*. Washington, DC: NAEYC.

Nebraska State Board of Education (Reprinted 1990), "What's Best for Five-Year-Olds? Position Statement on Kindergarten" in Jensen, M.A. and Chevalier, Z.W. (eds.). *Issues and Advocacy in Early Education*. Boston: Allyn and Bacon.

Thornton, J.R. (1990). "Team Teaching: A Relationship Based On Trust and Communication," *Young Children, 45*(5), pp. 40-42.

Weber-Schwartz, N. (1987). "Patience of Understanding," *Young Children, 42*(3), pp. 52-54.

REFERENCES

Almy, M. (1975). *The Early Childhood Educator at Work*. New York: McGraw Hill Book Company.

Berger, S.K. (1986). *The Developing Person Through Childhood and Adolescence*. New York: Worth Publishers, Inc.

Boyer, E.L. "Education: A New Look For the 90's." A Westminster Town Hall Forum Address (November 14, 1991). Minneapolis, MN: Westminster Presbyterian Church.

Bredekamp, S. (1987). *Developmentally Appropriate Practice in Programs Serving Children From Birth Through Age 8*. Washington, DC: NAEYC.

Bredekamp, S. (1991). "NAEYC to Launch New Professional Development Initiative," *Young Children, 46*(6), pp. 37-39.

Charles, C.M. (1989). *Building Classroom Discipline*. White Plains, NY: Longman Inc.

Charlesworth, R. (1989). " 'Behind' Before They Start? Deciding How to Deal With the Risk of Kindergarten 'Failure,' " *Young Children, 44*(3), pp. 5-13.

Chenfeld, M. (1983). *Creative Activities for Young Children*. New York: Harcourt Brace Jovanovich, Inc.

Clewett, A.S. (1988). "Guidance and Discipline: Teaching Young Children Appropriate Behavior," *Young Children, 43*(4), pp. 26-31.

Curwin, R.L. and Mendler, A.N. (1988). *Discipline With Dignity*. Alexandria, VA: Association for Supervision and Curriculum Development.

deMause, L., ed. (1974). *The History of Childhood*. New York: Peter Bedrick Books.

Dreikurs, R. (1972). *Discipline Without Tears*. New York: Hawthorn Press Books, Inc. Publishers.

Elkind, D. (1989). *Miseducation: Children At Risk*. New York: Alfred A. Knopf.

Erickson, M.F. and Pianta, R.C. (1989). "New Lunchbox, Old Feelings: What Kids Bring to School," *Early Education and Development, 1*(1), pp. 35-49.

Evertson, C.M., Emmer, E.T., Clements, B.S., Sanford, J.P. and Worsham, M.E. (1989). *Classroom Management for Elementary Teachers*. Englewood Cliffs, NJ: Prentice Hall, Inc.

Galinsky, E. (1988). "Parents and Teacher-Caregivers: Sources of Tension, Sources of Support," *Young Children, 43*(4), pp. 4-12.

Gartrell, D.J. (1987a). "Assertive Discipline: Unhealthy for Children and Other Living Things," *Young Children, 42*(2), pp. 10-11.

Gartrell, D.J. (1987b). "Punishment or Guidance?" *Young Children, 42*(3), pp. 55-61.

Gartrell, D.J. (1992). "Discipline," in Williams, L.R. and Fromberg, D.P. (eds.) *Encyclopedia of Early Childhood Education.* New York: Garland Publishing, Inc.

Gestwicki, C. (1992) *Home, School, and Community Relations.* Albany, NY: Delmar Publishers Inc.

Ginott, H.G. (1972). *Teacher and Child.* New York: Avon Books.

Greenberg, P. (1988). "Avoiding 'Me Against You' Discipline," *Young Children, 43*(1), pp. 24-31.

Greenberg, P. (1989). "Parents as Partners in Young Children's Development and Education: A New American Fad? Why Does it Matter?" *Young Children, 44*(4), pp. 61-75.

Greenberg, P. (1992a). "Why Not Academic Preschool? Part 2. Autocracy or Democracy in the Classroom," *Young Children, 47*(3), pp. 54-64.

Greenberg, P. (1992b). "How to Institute Some Simple Democratic Practices Pertaining to Respects, Rights, Responsibilities, and Roots in Your Classroom," *Young Children, 47*(5), pp. 10-21.

Hendrick, J. (1992a). *Whole Child.* Columbus, OH: Merrill/McMillan.

Hendrick, J. (1992b). "Where Does It All Begin?" Teaching the Principles of Democracy in the Early Years," *Young Children, 47*(3), pp. 51-53.

Hitz, R. and Driscoll, A. (1988). "Praise or Encouragement?" *Young Children, 47*(3), pp. 6-13.

Jones, F.H. (1987). *Positive Classroom Discipline.* New York: McGraw Hill Book Company.

Kagan, S.L. and Rivera, A.M. (1991). "Collaboration in Early Care and Education: What Can and Should We Expect?" *Young Children, 46*(1), pp. 51–56.

Katz, L.G. (1977). "Teachers' Developmental Stages," *Talks With Teachers, Reflections on Early Childhood Education.* Washington, DC: NAEYC.

Katz, L.G. (1980). "Mothering and Teaching—Some Significant Distinctions." Katz, L.G. (ed.) *Current Topics in Early Childhood Education.* Norwood, NJ: Ablex Publishing Corp.

Kounin, J. (1977). *Discipline and Group Management in Classrooms.* New York: Holt, Rinehart and Winston.

Nebraska State Board of Education (Reprinted 1990), "What's Best for Five-Year-Olds? Position Statement on Kindergarten" in Jensen, M.A. and Chevalier, Z.W. (eds.). *Issues and Advocacy in Early Education.* Boston: Allyn and Bacon.

Osborn, D.K. and Osborn, J.D. (1989). *Discipline and Classroom Management.* Athens, GA: Daye Press, Inc.

Read, K.H., Gardner, P. and Mahler, B.C. (1993). *The Early Childhood Programs: Human Relationships and Learning.* Fort Worth, TX: Harcourt Brace Jovanovich College Publishers.

Thornton, J.R. (1990). "Team Teaching: A Relationship Based on Trust and Communication," *Young Children, 45*(5), pp. 40-42.

Warren, R. (1972). *Caring*. Washington, DC: NAEYC.

Weber-Schwartz, N. (1987). "Patience of Understanding," *Young Children, 42*(3), pp. 52-54.

Wichert, S. (1989). *Keeping the Peace: Practicing Cooperation and Conflict Resolution With Preschoolers*. Santa Cruz, CA: New Society Publishers.

4

Creating the Climate for a Guidance Approach

GUIDING QUESTIONS

As you read chapter four, you will discover answers to the following questions:

- **What are the main differences between a teacher who is a technician and a teacher who is a professional?**
- **What do developmental psychologists say about the learning dynamic that is intrinsic to young learners?**
- **How does developmentally appropriate practice define the teacher-child relations necessary for guidance discipline?**
- **Why does liberation teaching empower the guidance approach?**
- **How does the teacher create a climate for partnership with parents?**

It may seem that in earlier times there were "magic answers" to problems in the classroom. Children were more obedient, and the teacher's rule was absolute. Yet, the nature of the "remedies" of yesteryear—the hickory stick, the dunce cap, a statement written 500 times—made school a place that many children feared.

In this day and age we recognize that there are no magic answers. Human motivations, relationships, and behaviors are complex, including when young children are concerned. All intervention methods have consequences that last beyond the act of intervention (Gartrell, 1987; Ginott, 1972). For this reason, teachers no longer can regard effective discipline as merely the decisive response at the precipitous moment. The whispered comment, the friendly

Figure 4–1 Human motivations, relationships and behaviors are complex, including when young children are concerned.

joke, the non-verbal cue all have their place in a guidance program. But effective guidance, guidance at its best, is **preventive**. Effective guidance is effective teaching, so that much mistaken behavior becomes unnecessary.

Unit one develops the foundations for guidance discipline. This final chapter in the unit presents five considerations important for a teacher using the guidance approach.

The five considerations conducive to guidance discipline are:

- **The teacher is a professional, not a technician.**
- **A learning dynamic is intrinsic to the human species and is at its height during early childhood.**
- **Developmentally appropriate practice defines the interactive teacher-child relations necessary for guidance discipline.**
- **The teacher practices liberation teaching.**
- **The teacher creates a climate for partnership with parents.**

The teacher who accepts these considerations and incorporates them into teaching practices moves comfortably into guidance as the mode of relations with children. The education program becomes one in which many common mistaken behaviors become unnecessary; children learn from the mistakes they do make; and the serious problems that some children face become more manageable.

A PROFESSIONAL, NOT A TECHNICIAN

In discussing discipline trends of the 1980s, chapter one took the position that obedience discipline is "reductionistic" both of the child and the teacher. When using obedience discipline, teachers are reduced to the status of "technicians," trained to follow a specific set of rules in predetermined, inflexible ways. The guidance approach asks that the teacher be a **professional**. How the teacher responds to situations in the classroom defines the difference between the teacher as technician and professional. **The professional teacher**:

1. *Uses diagnostic skills to assess the situation.* While the technician tends to determine only whether or not a rule has been violated, the professional recognizes that each situation is different and attempts to understand at a deeper level what actually is occurring.
2. *Makes judgments—actually hypotheses—about the situation and takes action based on the hypotheses.* While the technician responds in an inflexible manner—X behavior happened, therefore punishment Y is called for—the professional uses a problem-solving approach. S/he works to resolve the conflict and to teach the child alternative behavior patterns. (Another way of saying this is that the technician punishes a child for having a problem; the professional teaches the child to solve the problem.)
3. *Makes the effort to learn from the experience.* On a daily basis, the teacher makes quick assessments and takes quick actions. Even experienced teachers find that interventions do not always work out as intended. Professionalism means that even though the teacher does not always make the right decision, s/he endeavors to learn from the experience in order to improve the quality of relations with an individual child and the class.

Just as guidance supports the potential of the child to learn, so it does for the teacher. Although guidance discipline provides no magic answers for teacher-technicians, it offers ideas to think about, to try, and learn from—opportunities for teachers to feel better about who they are and how they are with children. Guidance offers the promise of professional growth, difficult for teachers locked into the technician role. Teachers who are professionals want nothing less for themselves in order to empower the learning and development of young children.

THE LEARNING DYNAMIC

Awareness of an unfolding human potential goes back at least to Socrates. Froebel, Montessori, and Dewey all wrote about the need to respect the dynamic of development within the child. Two midcentury psychologists, Jean Piaget and Erik Erikson, have added greatly to our understanding about development and its importance in teaching and learning.

Piaget and Developmental Stages

Jean Piaget's clinical studies with his own and other children brought developmental theory into the forefront of twentieth century psychology. Piaget discovered that in the process of growing and learning, each person passes through "a biologically determined sequence of stages" (Charlesworth, 1992, p. 329). Piaget identified four major stages of development:

- **Sensori-motor** (birth to two)
- **Preoperations** (two to seven)
- **Concrete operations** (seven to eleven)
- **Formal operations** (eleven through adulthood)

In Piaget's view, the way a child responds to a situation is linked to his or her stage of development. Although a child's mode of thinking is limited by the psychological characteristics of the developmental stage, the process of learning

Figure 4–2 The child constructs knowledge through interacting with the environment.

is always active. The child constructs knowledge (derives meaning) through interacting with the environment. As each new stage is reached, the old ways of thinking are not lost but are integrated into the new ways (Charlesworth, 1992).

Charlesworth's recent interpretation of Piaget is helpful in understanding about the development of thought. Cognitive development begins during the sensori-motor stage as the infant forms schemata (singular "schema"), or sensory impressions, of what s/he perceives. By the beginning of the preoperational stage, the toddler is linking similar schemata into "preconcepts" (Charlesworth, 1992).

Preconcepts represent the start of symbolic thought and often contain **overgeneralizations**, calling all four-legged animals "kiki" (for kitty), and **overspecializations**, expressing shock at seeing a teacher in an unexpected setting like a store (Charlesworth, 1992). Gradually, during the preoperational stage, the child forms new preconcepts and refines existing concepts in order to accommodate the outside world.

Until concrete operations at about age seven, the child's perception process is limited by a tendency to focus on the outstanding elements of what is perceived. The young child does not yet have the ability to perceive the complexities of situations. Within the limits of perceptual ability, however, the child notices and processes information with great efficiency. From the "Piagetian perspective," the role of the teacher is not to correct beginning concepts, but to act "as a guide and supply the necessary opportunities [for the child] to interact with objects and people" (Charlesworth, 1992, p. 316).

Anecdote: In a midwestern American Indian community, a Head Start class returned early from a trip to the beach on a very windy day. They were discussing why they had to leave early when the teacher asked, "What makes the wind blow anyway?"

A four-year-old named Virgil exclaimed, "Don't you know, teacher? The trees push the air."

Realizing that he could not explain to anyone what makes the wind blow, the teacher commented, "You are really thinking, Virgil; how do you know that?"

Amused at the teacher's obvious lack of knowledge, Virgil explained, "Cause the leaves is fans, of course."

(To this day the teacher—who happens to be the author—remains impressed with Virgil's preoperational stage thinking.)

As this anecdote illustrates, through experiences with peers, adults, and physical things, the learner perceives new, often conflicting, information. The child learns by mentally processing this information and constructing knowledge from it. The need to reach **equilibrium**, harmony between percep-

Figure 4–3 The motivation to do a puzzle lies in the need to create equilibrium through putting the pieces in place.

tions and understanding, out of **disequilibrium**, dissonance between what is perceived and understood, is intrinsic. Piaget believed that the disequilibrium felt by the child is a primary source of the intrinsic motivation to learn (Charlesworth, 1992).

Anecdote: Jinada and Lorenzo were playing house. Jinada commented, "I'm the momma so I'll get breakfast."

Lorenzo retorted, "Pappas get breakfast, so I will get breakfast." A heated exchange followed.

Having heard the argument, the teacher intervened: "Jinada, you have a momma in your house and she makes breakfast. Lorenzo, you have a pappa in your house and your pappa makes breakfast. Since you two are a momma and a poppa in the same house, maybe you can make breakfast together."

Jinada said, "Yeah, and I will make the toast and the cereal."

Lorenzo added, "I will put them dishes and spoons on the table." The two children proceeded to "make" and "eat" breakfast. Afterward, the teacher was amused to hear Jinada say, "But we got to go to work so we'll clean up later." Lorenzo said, "Yeah," and the two went off to work.

Developmental Egocentrism. In Piaget's concept of social and moral development, a key idea of Piaget is that young children show what the present author terms **developmental egocentrism**. Before the stage of concrete operations, brain development is occurring very rapidly. Still, preoperational stage children are just beginning to develop the concepts necessary to understand the viewpoints of others and the complexities of rules and standards (Kamii, 1984; Piaget, 1932). They see the world from their own perspectives and believe they are to blame when at times things don't go as they expect. Understanding these developmental characteristics, the task of the teacher is to adapt the curriculum to the social world of the child (Charlesworth, 1992).

Anecdote: Two student teachers organized a game of musical chairs with twelve preschoolers. To their amazement the first child "put out" began to cry, the second moped, and the third swept a book off a shelf. The two noticed that as the remaining children left the game, none looked happy. The last child out complained that the winner pushed and "It's not fair."

After discussion with their supervisor, the student teachers realized that the children were unable to comprehend the rules of the game. The children probably thought they were being punished by being put out and felt hurt, frustrated, and guilty.

Not to give up, the student teachers organized the game on another day, but with different rules. The children helped to tape their names to chairs. They were then asked to suggest the names of animals and came up with "chickens," "dolphins," and "elephants." When the music stopped, the children proceeded to their chairs, moving like the animal selected. The game went for 40 minutes, all of the children participated, and all—including the student teachers—had a good time.

Autonomy. In Piaget's perspective, the challenge for the adult is to assist children to build understanding about the perspectives of others, and the capacity for intelligent decision making. Piaget referred to the individual's ability to make intelligent, ethical decisions as **autonomy**. For educators who take a Piagetian perspective, **intellectual** and **moral autonomy** are the most important goals of education (Kamii, 1984). **Autonomy** means being governed by oneself—as opposed to **heteronomy**, or being governed by others. Writing of moral autonomy, Kamii—a leading authority on the concept states:

Autonomy enables children to make decisions for themselves. But autonomy is not synonymous with complete freedom. . .There can be no morality when one consider's only one's own point of view. If one takes other people's views into account, one is not free to tell lies, to break promises, to behave inconsiderately (p. 411, 1984).

Early childhood education provides the first institutional experience for children in relation to issues of autonomy. Yet, young children's limited social experience and developmental egocentrism make instruction for autonomy an exasperating part of preschool-primary instruction. Charlesworth phrases the teacher's dilemma concisely:

How often the adult says of the young child, "I know he knows better!" And the adult is right; the child does "know better," but is not yet able to reason and act consistently with his knowledge. It is not until the child is close to six that he begins to develop standards, to generalize, and to internalize sanctions so that he acts morally not just to avoid punishment but because he **should** act that way (Charlesworth, 1992, p. 497).

Clearly, given Piaget's discoveries about the course of development, autonomy takes throughout childhood—and into adulthood—to master. Teachers who recognize the young child's limited ability to conceptualize about moral decisions

Figure 4–4 The attainment of conscience, or inner control, happens through adult guidance.

understand the importance of an approach that teaches rather than punishes and allows the child to develop in healthy ways.

At all levels of education, Piaget regarded authoritarian adult roles as unhelpful in the process of empowering autonomy (Piaget, 1932). Interpreting right and wrong for children through the use of rewards and punishments reinforces **heteronomy** (Kamii, 1984, p. 410). More recently in agreement with Piaget, Kolberg and Lickona believe that the environment that empowers the development of autonomy is the "just community" (Kohlberg & Lickona, 1990). Charlesworth comments that:

> A just community is a developmentally designed school democracy that stimulates moral and social advancement. Some of the approaches used are:
>
> * encouraging student generated rule-making;
> * providing support structures (such as clear rules, a system for taking turns, etc.);
> * promoting group decision-making;
> * using spontaneous interpersonal conflicts as the basis of discussion;
> * fostering a moral community;
> * developing caring relations;
> * promoting cooperative learning (p. 498, 1992).

For developmental psychologists, knowledge is not fixed and finite, to be transferred by teachers to the minds of passive students. Learning in both the intellectual and moral spheres is a **constructive process**, that is the learner constructs meaning from interactions with peers, adults, and materials. From this perspective, social experience is fundamental to the education process. Through interactions with adults and peers, the individual constructs, alters, and integrates mental concepts—and in turn contributes to the thinking of others. Democracy within the classroom becomes the vehicle of society to further individual development and to replenish itself. A legacy of Piaget—like that of John Dewey—is the interrelation of the development of the child and the functioning of the society, with the common reference point being the interactive classroom and guidance discipline.

Erikson: Initiative and Industry

The psychologist, Erik Erikson, framed the nature of the intrinsic dynamic in his much quoted theory, "Eight Critical Ages" (1963). The third critical age, **Initiative versus Guilt**, identifies the drive in young children to explore, to try, and to discover. Healthy development during this period depends on responsiveness of the adult to these needs. The teacher structures the environment and provides guidance so that children can experience fully while learning nonpunitively about the limits of acceptable behavior. The saying, "The process is more important than the product," applies to this period, as children learn primarily from the doing and the gratification of *self-defined* results.

In *Miseducation: Preschoolers at Risk*, David Elkind (1987) discusses factors in schooling that affect young children's development. Elkind interprets the third critical age by referring to it as "initiative and belonging versus guilt and alienation." Elkind explains:

> Erik Erikson describes this period as one that determines whether the child's sense of **initiative** will be strengthened to an extent greater than the sense of **guilt**. And because the child is now interacting with peers, this period is also critical in the determination of whether the child's sense of "**belonging**" will be greater than the sense of **alienation**. (p. 115, 1987).

Elkind's inclusion of "belonging versus alienation" in the early childhood period is insightful. Studying the transition from preschool to kindergarten made by a sample of fifty-eight children, Ladd and Price (1987) found that preschoolers who had high levels of positive social relations were liked by their kindergarten peers. A contributing factor to peer acceptance, and fewer anxieties around the transition, was the presence of friends made previously in the preschool setting.

In a second study,

> Ladd (1989) found that the number of new friendships children formed in the first two months of the school year predicted higher levels of social and academic competence, fewer absences from school, fewer visits to the nurse, and less behavioral disruptiveness (Bukatko & Daihler, 1992, p. 669).

Figure 4–5 The development of both a sense of initiative and belonging during early childhood indicates the importance of this period.

The value of friendships and the ability to make friends, clearly are important skills, so important that they appear to be predictive of school success. Given these findings, the teacher who assists a prekindergarten-primary grade child with limited social skills to make friends contributes in a lasting way to the child's future.

During early childhood, children, hopefully, have been immersed in "initiative experiences" with the social and physical social world. This being the case, by the time they reach middle childhood at about age eight, they are ready for more sophisticated social interactions and learning expectations.

Erikson's fourth critical period, **Industry versus Inferiority**, occurs mainly during the primary grade years. A characteristic of children during this period is that they are greatly affected by the judgments of others. They are acutely aware of the possibility of failure, and sensitivity in teacher feedback is critical. Evaluative comparisons and reliance on competition result in classroom "losers"—in larger numbers than "winners." Conditional acceptance of children, dependent on their performance and obedience, is a significant contributor to feelings of inferiority in grade school children (Rosenholtz & Simpson, 1984).

Figure 4–6 As children approach middle childhood, they are greatly affected by the judgments of others.

A common view is that schools need to prepare children for "the competition of life" by "toughening them to it." In fact, public chastisement and evaluative comparisons are shown by Rosenholtz and Simpson (1984) to correlate with lower feelings of competence, i.e. inferiority. Teaching practices that tend to lower self-esteem include:

- Reliance on clearly defined ability groups—"the Bluebirds, the Robins, and the Turkey Vultures." (As Bukatko and Daehler [1992] point out, the practice persists.)
- Use of peer tutoring—as opposed to cooperative learning—having a clearly defined tutor (the "smart kid") and "tutee" (the "dummy").
- Teacher-domination of classroom transactions with children cast in passive and reactive roles.
- "Benign neglect" of children showing lower levels of academic achievement.
- Indifference toward children who are unpopular with peers or from "non-mainstream" backgrounds.
- Undue attention to incorrect responses in written and oral exercises.
- Stress on "power tests" and other comparative evaluation procedures.
- Punitive reactions to random mistaken behavior within the group.
- Repeated use of punishments with some children, such as time-outs, in-school detentions, or exclusion from special events.
- Distancing or other discriminatory reactions to the parents of some children.

In contrast, a corresponding list of teaching practices that promote industry in children includes:

- A variety of grouping arrangements—informal interest groups, cooperative learning groups, heterogeneous study groups, learning/social style "matched" groups, collaborative peer pairings.
- A variety of means for achieving success available for children.
- Promotion of autonomy through opportunities to make decisions and contribute to the group.
- Cross-age tutoring, using a diverse population of older students.
- Inclusion of other adults in classroom to maximize personal attention.
- Advocacy and support for unpopular and "nonmainstream" children.
- Specific, nonembarrassing teacher feedback.
- Low-key, supportive orientation to evaluation of children's work.
- Firm and friendly guidance orientation to mistaken behavior.
- Collaborative, problem-solving orientation to serious mistaken behavior.
- Involvement of parents of all children.

As children enter middle childhood, teaching at its best nudges children toward a sense of industry—confidence in their ability to achieve successfully.

Figure 4–7 Informal pairings of "neighbors" for projects is one example of multidimensional grouping.

Clearly, the principles of guidance discipline are congruent with teaching practices that promote industry as children proceed through the primary grades.

Adults who have seen the curiosity, openness, and perseverance of young children recognize that a learning dynamic is intrinsic to the human species. The presence of this intrinsic dynamic, the human potential to learn and respond, is regarded as a "given" by teachers who value guidance discipline. As the writings of both Jean Piaget and Erik Erikson indicate, teachers can severely limit or fundamentally empower that potential. Teachers taking the guidance approach recognize that teaching is about helping children to make the most of personal potential, regardless of labels the child might have received due to birth order, cultural heritage, family circumstance, or personal reputation.

DEVELOPMENTALLY APPROPRIATE PRACTICE AND TEACHER-CHILD RELATIONS

One still hears from some teachers that their children's ability to learn is limited by their "short attention spans." A knowing teacher replies that the activity determines the attention span—as a puzzle done several times in a

Figure 4–8 The presence of an intrinsic dynamic for learning is a given in the guidance approach.

row, extra time taken to write in a journal, or a "never ending" push on a swing will attest. If allowed the initiative of participation on their own terms, there may be no more effective learner than a concentrating young child. When the curriculum is developmentally appropriate, the child's attention span frequently is longer than the adult's.

The important NAEYC Publication defining **developmentally appropriate practice** (DAP) (Bredekamp, 1987) contributed this term to describe what many early childhood teachers have always done. Thanks to this document—and others such as Elkind's, debunking high pressure preschools (1987)—DAP has gained wide acceptance in the prekindergarten field. Moreover, despite a differing pedagogical tradition in the public schools, the "percolator up" phenomena is taking hold in an increasing number of kindergarten and primary grade classrooms.

From the guidance perspective, the increased use of DAP is vital. Although the human relations skills of exceptional teachers may permit them to use guidance techniques regardless of curricular expectations, most find it easier to use guidance when the curriculum is responsive to the developmental levels and cultural backgrounds of young children.

Common inappropriate practices—prolonged periods of sitting and listening, prescribed activities done to exacting standards, critical evaluation of children's work, teacher-communication that stigmatizes—invite mistaken behavior. As discussed in the previous chapter, **curriculum-driven** mistaken behavior is a primary cause of "the classroom as battle ground."

Within the classroom, a professional teacher works to maximize children's involvement in the learning process. Such "initiative-friendly" methods as daily child-chosen activities, creative art and journals (even before conventional script and spelling), manipulatives-based math, diverse small group experiences, and active, concise large group sessions allow children to find meaning and success in learning experiences (Brewer, 1992).

The following chart illustrates how DAP can reduce mistaken behaviors:

Table 4.1

Increasing Appropriate Practice to Reduce Mistaken Behavior

Moving from Inappropriate Practice	*To Appropriate Practice*	*Reduces Mistaken Behavior*
Prolonged sitting and listening	Active, concise large groups	Restlessness, bothering neighbors, confrontations with adults
Prescribed activities done to exacting standards	Child-choice, creative, "no one right answer" activities	Acting out of feelings of failure, frustration, inferiority
Critical evaluation of children's work	Supportive evaluation of children's work	Mix of reactions to lowering of self-esteem
Rejection of some children due to mistaken behavior	Acceptance of children as members of group	Acting out of feelings of rejection

DAP in the Primary Grades

In many elementary schools, support is growing for teachers to **supplement and modify** the traditional academic program. Such practices as integrated curriculum, outcomes-driven education, cooperative learning groups, site-based management, and authentic assessment techniques allow teachers to be fully professional and classroom practices to become developmentally appropriate (Bredekamp, 1991; Minnesota Education Association, 1989) In many schools, however, these changes have taken courage and ingenuity on the part of individual teachers.

Anecdote: (Kindergarten). Despite a kindergarten teacher's statements that they were not developmentally appropriate, a principal decided that the worksheet-based arithmetic system had to be used. Being tenured and known as an individual, the teacher decided she *would* use the worksheets but in her own way. On the last Friday of each month, the class had a worksheet party. The teacher made plenty of popcorn, and everyone did worksheets. Having used manipulatives to teach math concepts during the month, the teacher reported the children "whipped through the sheets, had fun doing them and took lots of papers home."

Anecdote: (First Grade). A first grade teacher felt compelled to use the basal series adopted by the school district, but found the reading program did not reinforce the children's excitement about learning to read. He supplemented the reading program with "super silent reading" times when he and the children read self-selected books. He introduced "just journaling and jotting" times, when he and the children recorded their own thoughts and feelings in journals. When the teacher discovered children reading and journaling during *other* parts of the day, he concluded he now had an **emergent literacy program** that met his expectations.

Like the teachers in the anecdotes, for years individual teachers have been "psychologizing" the curriculum, as Dewey termed it (1900). Many of these teachers have had to do so quietly, behind closed doors. Some—usually after receiving tenure—have "done their own thing" openly and endured the label from colleagues of being that "offbeat one at the end of the hall." As one teacher, known for being creative, commented, "I do as little of what I have to do and as much of what I want to do to stay out of serious trouble." Fortunately, times are beginning to change.

Working Together

Often, a committee can make a curriculum modification request seem more "studied" and "objective" than an individual teacher. For this reason, two or more teachers who attend a workshop or conference together may be successful in introducing developmentally appropriate practices into a school. When all of the teachers at a grade level, for instance, feel strongly about the need to modify practice, they may have success by working together.

Tact, patience, and incremental change—starting with the modifications that are most feasible—are the watchwords. As textbook sales persons and inspirational speakers have long known, educators tend to be receptive to changes that are linked to the latest trends. Movement toward DAP is sometimes easier when it is linked with other current buzzwords: "literacy development," "manipulatives-based math," "outcomes-driven education," "integrated curriculum," and/or "inclusionary education."

A noteworthy anecdote about riding the buzzword bandwagon is two first grade teachers who are alleged to have gotten play into their programs by calling it a "self-selected, self-directed autonomous learning period." In many locations, the term "developmentally appropriate practice" in itself is fueling elementary school reform.

Role of the Principal

The stereotype of the elementary principal is of the middle-aged patriarch, the male secondary teacher who got his administrator's license. A problem some primary grade teachers have experienced is that such principals neither know about nor seem to care about the needs of young children. As Greenberg has pointed out, sexism sometimes confounds the communication process (1989).

Contrary to this image, many administrators are open to improvements in programming at any time and for any grade level; they see becoming educated about early childhood education as a part of their jobs. They ask only for a clearly spelled out rationale and a projection of program implications (Goffman & Stegelin, 1992).

In the remaining years of the century, as a new generation of principals comes to the fore, an increase in administrators with backgrounds in early childhood education can be expected. Nonetheless, it makes sense to know the principal well as teachers work to introduce DAP into the school. In some situations, s/he will be the teacher's best ally (Goffin & Stegelin, 1992). In others, the teacher without tenure should work closely with, but stay in the shadow of, teachers who do.

To modify practice in a school or district, teachers need to plan carefully and organize well. Inviting educators from other areas who are using interesting ideas is a useful technique. The DAP book and *Changing Kindergartens* (Goffin & Stegelin, 1992), both published by NAEYC, provide useful information for moving ahead.

Anecdote: Two kindergarten teachers in an urban school became tired of worksheets and drills used to teach phonics and counting skills. They heard from a teacher at another school about alternate approaches using "whole language techniques" and a manipulatives-based math program. The two teachers began attending workshops, collecting sample materials, and talking with primary grade teachers. The teachers got the principal to agree that the new methods were more responsive to the developmental levels of kindergarten children. With the principal's support, the two teachers convinced the third kindergarten teacher to adopt a manipulatives-based math program to replace use of worksheets. They currently are negotiating to use a new approach to beginning reading/writing, more child-active and less dependent on a pre-primer phonics system. The first grade teachers are taking notice of what is going on in the kindergarten. The kindergarten teachers plan to involve them further.

School Anxiety

If a child wants to go to school when ill, something's right; if a child does not want to go when well, something's wrong. Young children who are unhappy at school cannot easily work through anxieties with words. In some children, **school anxiety** shows in direct mistaken behavior—inattentiveness, frequent frustration, irritability. In others, anxiety manifests itself in physical conditions situationally caused. Symptoms range from the twice-a-year "stomach ache" to actual ulcers, from occasional "headaches" to persistent allergies, from sporadic nervousness to high blood pressure and depressive reactions (Cherry, p. 1981).

School anxiety can result from specific situations, such as the morning bus ride or the afternoon power test. As well, the cause can be more pervasive factors—a general feeling of being:

- disliked by the teacher;
- alienated from other children;
- dislocated from the education program.

School anxiety is a major cause of level three mistaken behavior in children—strong unmet physical and/or emotional needs that the child acts out.

Educators sometimes miss school anxiety as a cause of serious mistaken behavior. With the plethora of problems besetting modern families, teachers

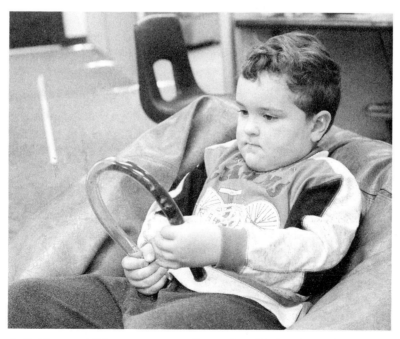

Figure 4–9 Young children cannot easily work anxieties through with words.

tend to look first to the home situation. In past years, serious mistaken behavior (and consequent punishment) were rationalized by the labeling of a "bad child." More recently, educators attribute "a bad home life" to children who act out—and seek to provide the controls not provided at home.

Much level three mistaken behavior is caused by situations outside of the school. But teaching practice that fails to accommodate the developmental levels and individual circumstances of young learners is a primary cause of mistaken behavior in many situations and a contributing factor in others. The use of DAP allows the teacher to interact with the child as an individual and empowers the child to succeed. DAP reduces the occurrence of problems in the classroom and sets the stage for the guidance approach.

LIBERATION TEACHING

Liberation teaching has its roots in the social psychology of Goffman (1963), the social commentary of such authors as Gottlieb (1973) and Boyer (1992), and the practices of countless caring teachers over the years. The term "liberation" is borrowed from such disparate sources as Catholic theology and the writings of Mazlich and Faber (1975). The self psychologists, notably Maslow (1962), have contributed to the construct.

Readers are probably familiar with Maslow's **hierarchy of needs**. A related concept, the dual needs for safety and growth (1962), sets in motion the practice of liberation teaching. Within every learner are two sets of needs, one for safety and one for growth. Of the two needs, the need for safety—security, belonging, identification, love relationships, respect—is the stronger. To the extent the child feels safety needs are unmet, s/he becomes preoccupied with meeting these needs and is likely to show mistaken behavior.

On the other hand, as safety needs are met, the child is empowered to address the need for growth and develop such qualities as openness, curiosity, creativity, problem-solving ability, responsiveness, and self-actualization (Maslow, 1962). **Liberation teaching is the ability to assist the child to meet safety needs and nudge the child toward growth**.

The work of other psychologists also apply to the liberation concept. In Piaget's terms liberation teaching is assisting the child to move toward autonomy (Piaget, 1932). In Erikson's modified construct, liberation teaching is empowering the child to grow from guilt, alienation, and inferiority to initiative, intimacy, and industry (Elkind, 1989). For Harlow, cited in chapter two, liberation teaching is helping the child to rise from the social relations of survival and adjustment to encountering.

An enduring vision of the teacher, sometimes attributed to Socrates, holds that s/he does not cram students' minds with facts but kindles enthusiasm in students with the knowledge of what they can become. Such descriptions of effective teachers clearly are not new. Why, then, use the term "liberation" when what is being described is plain old fashioned "good teaching"? The answer lies in the power of the teacher to affect the present and the future of the child.

Children come into early childhood classrooms vulnerable in many ways. Many come from non-traditional family situations or from minority cultural groups. Others have "established disabilities," such as hearing loss or speech delay; more recently diagnosed disabilities such as fetal alcohol syndrome; or less easily diagnosed conditions such as pervasive allergies. Children may be of unusual facial appearance, short or tall of stature, underweight or overweight. They are of different genders. Children may have unique learning styles, experience backgrounds, and developmental characteristics. They possess unique levels of need for attention, strong needs to act out or to be independent. Young children come into classrooms with a range of social attributes, physical characteristics, learning capabilities, and levels of self-esteem—any of which can impede or enhance their progress in the class.

The teacher responds to each child, given the mix of human qualities that comprise that child's developing personality. As the most significant adult outside of the child's family, the teacher has great influence. Responses that aggravate a child's need for safety and deny the possibility of growth are **stigmatizing**. In Goffman's terms, stigmatizing responses disqualify an individual from full participation in the group and so greatly diminish self-esteem (Goffman, 1963). Teacher-responses that affirm the child's sense of belonging, worth, and competence empower the child toward growth. Teachers who do so liberate children from the vulnerabilities they have, simply by being children. These adults practice liberation teaching. They are the consummate professionals because for them, the children come first.

A CLIMATE FOR PARTNERSHIP WITH PARENTS

A young child's anxiety in a new school experience may be lessened if there is not an abrupt division between home and school. Children thrive when they feel a continuity between parents and teachers that can be present only when adults have reached out in an effort to understand and respect each other. Just as a teacher's first task in relating to young children is to build a sense of trust and mutual respect, the same task is important in working with parents (Gestwicki, 1992, p. 103).

With the exception of the traditional "spring roundup," teachers create a climate conducive to partnership during the days immediately preceding and following the beginning of school. Several veteran kindergarten teachers from Minnesota have unique and effective approaches for building partnerships with parents. The "case study" that follows is a composite of the practices of these teachers, rolled into the approach of one teacher, whom we shall call "Judy."

Figure 4–10 The results of liberation teaching often speak for themselves.

Case Study: How Judy Builds Partnerships

Judy views both children and parents as her "customers." Her intent is to build "happy customers." Part of her approach is to reach the parents through the children. Another part is to reach the children through the parents. An axiom that she works with is "if the children are happy, the parents will be too." Judy knows that parents who themselves had unhappy school experiences will be more likely to accept a teacher if they know she cares about their kids. She puts this idea to work even before the first day.

About two weeks before school, Judy sends a letter to both the child and the parent(s). To the child she says how happy she is that the child is in her class and how many fun things they will do at school. The teacher encloses an animal sticker and tells each child to watch for that animal when they get to school. The animal emblem is prominently displayed by the classroom door, and Judy wears the emblem during the first week.

In the letter to the parents, she says the same things, but goes on to invite them to either of two orientation meetings (one late afternoon, the other at night) to be held during the second week of school. Before school begins, it is Judy's eventual intent to make home visits. So far, this plan "is still in the negotiation stage" with administration. Instead, Judy gets phone numbers for all parents who have recorded them on school enrollment forms. She calls each family a day or two before the start of school. She also calls on the evening of the first day, to make sure children returned home safely and to take care of any problems that may have occurred. To parents with no phone numbers listed, she sends notes and on a few occasions has made a home visit on her own time.

On the first day of school, Judy always has a parent volunteer from the year before to help with separation problems. Judy greets each child with a name tag as they arrive. There are two classes of children who attend on "A" days and "B" days. At the request of Judy and the other kindergarten teachers, the district allows half of each class to come in on separate days during the first week. This means that instead of 24 children on two first days, there are twelve children on each of four days. Parents are always welcome in Judy's class (and are put to use); they are especially welcome during the first week.

In the first days, Judy allows lots of exploration time, but also gets the children used to numerous routines right away. She comments, "A lot of problems never happen if the children know and are comfortable with the routines." Judy and the volunteer make sure all get on the correct buses at the end of the day. Before leaving the classroom, they have a "class meeting" to discuss how happy Judy will be to see them the next time they come to school. Judy hugs each child as they leave, a practice she continues all year. After they have completed kindergarten, she sends each a letter saying how much she enjoyed having them in her class and wishing them the very best when they begin first grade next fall.

Judy holds two orientation meetings, and families can attend either one. She gets high school students who had her as a teacher to care for children who

Figure 4–11 Parents are always welcome in Judy's class and contribute in many ways.

come with the parents to the orientation meetings. At the orientation, she
talks about her program, answers questions, and asks parents to fill out a brief
survey. The one-page survey includes items about their and their child's
interests, the child's family background, the kinds of activities the parents can
help with during the year, and other information "that would help me to understand and work with your child." Completing the survey is optional, but almost
all fill it out. The responses provide useful information to discuss at the first
conference later in the year.

The teacher attributes the high level of attendance at the orientation
meetings to the phone calls and letters at the beginning of school year. She
says the first week is exhausting, but the investment is worth it. "That phone
call the first night of school really wins them over. I remember how I felt the
first time my child left for kindergarten. I still get tears when I think about it."

Judy tries hard to communicate with each parent and has even held a
conference at a lounge, where a single parent worked afternoons and evenings.
Judy does have strong feelings about parents who she believes could be doing
more for their children. She attempts to be friendly with these parents, nonetheless. She knows that some parents are kids who never had a chance to grow
up themselves. She realizes that if she can get a parent involved, it may make a
difference in that child's life. She knows, because she's seen some parents get
involved and grow, and she's seen their children's attitudes and behaviors
change.

> It is not realistic to expect teachers to like all parents. However, it is essential
> and possible for teachers to respect all parents for their caring and efforts. In
> most cases, parents do care. This belief is the basis for all teacher interaction
> (Gestwicki, 1992, pp. 103-104).

Judy practices Gestwicki's recommendation.

SUMMARY

**What are the main differences between a teacher who is a technician
and a teacher who is a professional?**

Technicians view teaching as the effective implementation of pre-set curriculum and behavior management systems. They tend to react in rigid ways,
determined by prescribed materials and administrative expectations. Professionals use informed judgment, formulated through continuing education and
experience. They recognize that each child and each situation is unique. They
adjust teaching practice on the basis of experience to improve the social and
educational climate of the class. The need for mistaken behavior is reduced as
a result, and they feel better about themselves as teachers. Professionals learn
even as they teach.

What do developmental psychologists say about the learning dynamic that is intrinsic to young learners?

The writings of Piaget conclude that children construct knowledge by interacting with the environment and so are by nature active learners. In response to perceived disequilibrium, children adjust their thinking to better accommodate experience. Children think and respond as a function of their experience and the stage of development they are in. For teaching to be effective, it must be matched to the child's developmental level and active learning nature. Autonomy, or principled and intelligent decision-making, is, for Piaget, the goal of education.

Erikson theorized critical ages that all humans go through. In the age of initiative versus guilt, preschoolers need support for exploration and creative activity, through which they can define success for themselves. Elkind suggests that this age also includes the dilemma of belonging versus alienation, a crucial awareness for teachers working with children during their first years outside of the home.

During the primary years, the teacher's task is to ensure that the learner is building feelings of industry through successful learning transactions. Rigid standards, critical evaluation, and competitive teaching practices are likely to give rise to feelings of failure and inferiority, with consequent mistaken behaviors.

How does developmentally appropriate practice define the teacher-child relations necessary for guidance discipline?

Within the classroom, the teacher moves toward developmentally appropriate curriculum when she offers choices in learning activities; evaluates supportively; keeps large group activities active, enjoyable, and concise; and personalizes the curriculum. The use of developmentally appropriate practice is widely accepted in preschool education. Working with colleagues, teachers are making progress in increasing the use of developmentally appropriate practice at the kindergarten and primary grade levels. Practice which is responsive to the developmental level and individual circumstances of children reduces the occurrence of mistaken behavior.

Why is liberation teaching conducive to the guidance approach?

From Maslow's perspective, each individual has two sets of psychological needs: for safety and for growth. In children the safety needs are the stronger, for physical security, belonging, love, and esteem. The various physical, social, cultural, cognitive, and behavioral circumstances of children put them at-risk in relation to these needs. Insensitive or uncaring teacher reactions can cause children to be stigmatized. Mistaken behavior is the result. To the extent that the teacher assists children to meet the need for safety and to move toward growth, s/he is practicing liberation teaching.

How does the teacher create a climate for partnership with parents?

Before and during the first days of school, the teacher does much to create a climate for partnership with parents. Partnership is important because it

eases the transition of the child from home to school. If children are happy at school, relations with parents will be easier to build. Teachers cannot expect to like every parent, but by remaining friendly and accessible, parents may respond. Parent involvement in the education program can make a life-long difference to the child.

The chapter examined five considerations conducive to guidance. The teacher who accepts these five considerations and incorporates them into the education program moves into guidance as the predominant mode of relations with children. The program becomes one in which many common mistaken behaviors become unnecessary; children learn from the mistakes they do make; and the serious problems that some children face become more manageable.

FOLLOW-UP ACTIVITIES

Follow-up activities allow the student to interrelate ideas from the text with "real life" situations. The "observations" imply access to practicum experiences, the "interviews" access to parents and teachers. When communicating about the activities, students need to respect the privacy of all participants in the observation or interview, as an important professional consideration.

1. **What are the main differences between a teacher who is a technician and a teacher who is a professional?**
   a. Observe a teacher you regard as a professional as s/he responds to situations in the classroom. Note an incident or two that you believe s/he handled effectively. Talk with the teacher about his or her responses.
   b. Interview a teacher you believe to be a professional. Discuss decisions the teacher has made about the program that might be construed as difficult, innovative, or even controversial. Ask about the teacher's reasons for the decisions made.

2. **What do developmental psychologists say about the learning dynamic that is intrinsic to young learners?**
   a. Observe a young child for behaviors that reflect or contradict an idea of one of the developmental psychologists about the learning dynamic intrinsic to young children.
   b. Select a characteristic of young children as learners from this section of the chapter. Interview a teacher about how s/he accommodates this characteristic in her teaching.

3. **How does developmentally appropriate practice define the interactive teacher-child relations necessary for guidance discipline?**
   a. Observe the interactions between a teacher and child in an activity that you believe is developmentally appropriate. Decide why the activity is developmentally appropriate. Determine what you believe to be significant about how the teacher and child communicated.
   b. Interview a teacher who uses developmentally appropriate practice. Ask about adjustments to programming the teacher has made in the last week or two to accommodate the developmental characteristics of individual or the group of young children.

4. **Why is liberation teaching conducive to a guidance approach?**
   a. Observe an example of liberation teaching. Focusing on the responses of the teacher and the child in the situation, decide why you believe liberation teaching was at work.
   b. Ask a teacher to share about an experience when s/he was successful in helping a child who was at-risk for stigma. Inquire about how the child was helped and how the teacher felt about the experience.

5. **How does the teacher create a climate for partnership with parents?**
   a. Observe an activity that includes parents. Determine what you believe to be a feature of the event that would encourage continued parent involvement in the program.
   b. Interview a teacher about the steps s/he takes at the beginning of the year to involve parents in the program.
   c. Interview a parent about what is important for a teacher to do to create a climate for partnership with parents.

SUGGESTED RESOURCES

Bredekamp, S., (ed.) (1987). *Developmentally Appropriate Practice in Early Childhood Programs Serving Children From Birth Through Age 8.* (expanded edition). Washington, DC: National Association for the Association of Young Children.

Cherry, C. (1981). *Think of Something Quiet.* Belmont, CA: David S. Lake Publishers.

Dewey, J. (1902, reprinted, 1969). *The Child and the Curriculum.* Chicago: University of Chicago Press.

Dewey, J. (1900, reprinted, 1969). *The School and Society.* Chicago: The University of Chicago Press.

Elkind, D. (1987). *Miseducation: Preschoolers at Risk.* New York: Alfred A. Knopf.

Goffin, S.G. and Stegelin, D.A. (eds.). (1992). *Changing Kindergarten.* Washington, DC: National Association for the Education of Young Children.

Greenberg, P. (1989). "Parents as Partners in Young Children's Development and Education: A New American Fad? Why Does it Matter?" *Young Children, 44*(4), pp. 61-75.

Kamii, C. (1984). "Autonomy: The Aim of Education Envisioned by Piaget," *Phi Delta Kappan, 65*(6), pp. 410-415.

REFERENCES

Berger, S.K. (1986). *The Developing Person Through Childhood and Adolescence.* New York: Worth Publishers, Inc.

Boyer, E.L. (1991). *Ready to Learn: A Mandate for the Nation.* Princeton, NJ: The Carnegie Foundation for the Advancement of Teaching.

Bredekamp, S. (ed.) (1987). *Developmentally Appropriate Practice in Early Childhood Programs Serving Children From Birth Through Age 8.* (expanded edition). Washington, DC: National Association for the Association of Young Children.

Bredekamp, S. (1991). "The Outcomes Driven Developmental Model and Developmentally Appropriate Early Childhood Education: The Problem of the Match," *Quality Driven Education, 1*(5), pp. 44-52.

Brewer, J.A. (1992). *Introduction to Early Childhood Education: Pre-kindergarten Through the Primary Grades.* Needham Heights, MA: Allyn and Bacon.

Bukatko, D. and Daehler, M.W. (1992). *Child Development: A Topical Approach.* Boston: Houghton, Mifflin Company.

Cherry, C. (1981). *Think of Something Quiet.* Belmont, CA: David S. Lake Publishers.

Dewey, J. (1902, reprinted, 1969). *The Child and the Curriculum*. Chicago: University of Chicago Press.

Dewey, J. (1900, reprinted, 1969). *The School and Society*. Chicago: The University of Chicago Press.

Elkind, D. (1987). *Miseducation: Preschoolers at Risk*. New York: Alfred A. Knopf.

Erikson, E.H. (1963). *Childhood and Society*. New York: W.W. Norton and Company, Inc.

Faber, A. and Mazlish, E. (1974). *Liberated Parents Liberated Children*. New York: Avon Books.

Gartrell, D.J. (1987). "Assertive Discipline: Unhealthy to Children and Other Living Things," *Young Children, 42*(2), pp. 10-11.

Gestwicki, C. (1992). *Home, School, and Community Relations*. Albany, NY: Delmar Publishers Inc.

Ginott, H.G. (1972). *Teacher and Child*. New York: Avon Books.

Goffin, S.G. and Stegelin, D.A. (eds.) (1992). *Changing Kindergarten*. Washington, DC: National Association for the Education of Young Children.

Goffman, E. (1963). *Stigma*. Englewood Cliffs, NJ: Prentice Hall, Inc.

Gottlieb, D. (ed.) (1973). *Children's Liberation*. Englewood Cliffs, NJ: Prentice-Hall, Inc.

Greenberg, P. (1989). "Parents as Partners in Young Children's Development and Education: A New American Fad? Why Does it Matter?" *Young Children, 44*(4), pp. 61-75.

Kamii, C. (1984). "Autonomy: The Aim of Education Envisioned by Piaget," *Phi Delta Kappan, 65*(6), pp. 410-415.

Ladd, G.W. (1989, April). "Children's Friendships in the Classroom: Precursors of Early School Adaptation." Paper presented at the biennial meeting of the Society for Research in Child Development, Kansas City, MO.

Ladd, G.W. and Price, J.M. (1987). "Predicting Children's Social and School Adjustment Following the Transition from Preschool to Kindergarten." *Child Development, 58*, pp. 986-992.

Maslow, A.H. (1962). *Toward a Psychology of Being*. Princeton, NJ: D. Van Nostrand Company, Inc.

Minnesota Education Association (1989). "Teachers as Instructional Leaders: A Model for Teacher Empowerment," *Sharpening Our Competitive Edge: Educating a New Generation* (monograph series). St. Paul, MN: MEA.

Piaget, J. (1932, translated 1960). *The Moral Judgment of the Child*. Glencoe, IL: The Free Press.

Rosenholtz, S.J. and Simpson, C. (1984). "The Formation of Ability Conceptions: Developmental Trend or Social Construction?" *Review of Educational Research, 54*, pp. 31-63.

Unit Two

Reducing the Need
for Mistaken Behavior

Unit Two Chapter Summary

Chapter 5: *Managing the Classroom*

Chapter five discusses management of the classroom through the use of learning centers and classroom routines. The discussion includes: the role of learning centers in classroom organization; the use of learning centers at the pre-primary level; the use of learning centers at the primary level; a teacher's perspective on the place of routines in classroom management; and suggestions for encouraging parents to volunteer in the classroom.

Chapter 6: *Managing the Daily Program*

Chapter six explores management of the daily program in order to reduce the need for mistaken behavior. The first topics include the balance between reliability and novelty, daily schedules, and planning active and quiet times. The chapter then discusses the role of large groups in the developmentally appropriate program and looks at the management of transitions to reduce mistaken behavior. The final section considers the benefits in the use of volunteers—especially parents—in managing the daily program.

Chapter 7: *Communicating to Prevent Problems*

Chapter seven introduces skills and strategies for communicating with children in order to reduce the need for mistaken behavior. Seven different communication skills are discussed. Strategies include the use of guidelines (rather than rules), class meetings, and communication techniques with parents.

5

Managing the Classroom

GUIDING QUESTIONS

As you read chapter five, you will discover answers to the following questions:

- **What is the role of learning centers in classroom organization?**
- **How can learning centers be used at the preprimary level?**
- **How can learning centers be used at the primary level?**
- **What is the place of routines in classroom management?**
- **How does the teacher encourage parents to volunteer in the classroom?**

The landmark NAEYC work, *Developmentally Appropriate Practice in Early Childhood Programs Serving Children From Birth Through Age Eight* cited over 550 references to document its recommendations (Bredekamp, 1987). Since then, the literature addressing developmentally appropriate practice (DAP) has grown steadily. As discussed, DAP means that education programs empower the child, at his/her level of development, to construct knowledge through active, personalized learning experiences. A feature of DAP is that due to its emphasis on personally relevant experience, it opens the door to education that is culturally as well as developmentally responsive (Bredekamp, 1987; Derman-Sparks, 1989).

The relevance of DAP to guidance discipline was introduced in the previous two chapters. DAP empowers children to be active, involved, independent learners ("autonomous individuals" in Piaget's terms; "encounterers" in Harlow's—from chapter two). With autonomy, self-esteem is heightened and the need for mistaken behavior is reduced (Essa & Rogers, 1992).

This first chapter of unit two explores management of the physical classroom in ways that are congruent with DAP. A primary focus of the chapter is the use of learning centers. Centers promote the active learning that is at the heart of DAP, both at the preschool and primary grade levels. A second focus is the introduction and use of classroom routines. A premise of the chapter is when children know how to use their physical space, they become confident and productive learners.

USING LEARNING CENTERS TO ORGANIZE THE CLASSROOM

Organization of the classroom is an important element in the prevention of mistaken behavior. Clearly identified **learning centers*** are beneficial in classrooms throughout the age range. Learning centers are distinct areas within the room that provide a variety of related materials for children's use (Gordon & Browne, 1989).

Besides accommodating the natural mode of learning of the child, learning centers break the mold of teacher-controlled, large group instruction on which some preschool-primary teachers still rely. Objections to this mode of instruction is that it imposes "passivity" and conformity on children, restricts the use of critical thinking skills, overextends children's attention spans, and leads to mistaken behavior (Bredekamp, 1987; Brewer, 1992; Katz, 1985; Williams & Kamii, 1986).

Teachers inexperienced with centers sometimes fear that their use in the classroom will result in chaos. The anxiety around "loss of control" may be why some early childhood teachers have centers set up, but utilize them only sparingly. In actuality, even three-year-olds use learning centers productively. Centers in the classroom permit what one teacher calls "play with a purpose." Children aged three to eight are adept at this mode of learning and benefit from being able to select activities of relevance to them. If enough choices are present, center times tend to be busy, positive, and educational (Beatty, 1992; Brewer, 1992; Essa, 1992).

CENTERS IN PRE-PRIMARY CLASSROOMS

In **preprimary** classrooms, traditional centers include art, music, dramatic play/housekeeping, reading, blocks, science, "sensory table" (sand, water, etc.), active play, table activities, and in some classrooms, carpentry (Gordon & Browne, 1989). Modern variations include centers designated for computers,

---

* Other common terms are "learning stations," and "interest centers," each with its own particular meaning. The term "learning center" is used in this text.

Figure 5–1 Even three-year-olds use learning centers productively.

Figure 5–2 Computer or "technology centers" are among the newer types of centers found in early childhood classrooms.

cooking, writing, social/cultural awareness, and dual dramatic play—permanent (housekeeping) and theme-related.

When teachers plan the layout of learning centers, they often use traffic flow patterns and noise factors as organizational criteria. A block center, with play spread out on the floor for instance, should not obstruct flow to a restroom, doorway, or cubbies. Due to similar noise levels, a carpentry center might be placed close to an active play area. Science, reading, and table activities, as more quiet centers, might be grouped together (Brewer, 1992). Planning the layout of learning centers (in classrooms that almost always pose limitations) is an important, ongoing task of the early childhood teacher.

Carpentry and Active Play

For reasons of noise level and safety, teachers sometimes are reluctant to include carpentry and active play centers in a classroom. In the words of an amazed parent upon her first visit to a classroom, young children are "active critters." They need to be able to move in order to learn (Bredekamp, 1987). If for no other reason, carpentry is valuable because it is the only opportunity for some children to hammer and saw until middle school. Girls as well as boys enjoy the use of real tools. Ten ounce "household" hammers, sturdy nails, pine scraps, perhaps a "back saw," and safety glasses are all the materials that are needed. An adult should be present to limit the number of children and monitor for safety—though accidents are less likely than during other active play and are seldom serious.

Anecdote: A kindergarten teacher persuaded a reluctant principal to let her include a carpentry center in the classroom two afternoons a week. Worried about accidents, the principal visited to view the center for himself. The principal arrived just in time to see Anita hit herself on the thumb with a hammer. Anita was about to cry. She saw that if she left the table to go to an adult, another child would take her place. With her thumb in her mouth and a tear on her cheek, Anita continued to pound in the nail.

The aide supervising the table and the principal exchanged smiles. The principal returned to the classroom when he could to visit the carpentry center, but out of interest, not concern.

Like carpentry, an active play center encourages perceptual-motor development. Active play areas are especially important for classrooms in colder climates, where getting bundled and unbundled can take longer than the time outside. While active play is vital on a daily basis, some teachers "close down" active play areas at certain times—circle time, snack, rest. Even in preschools, children quickly comprehend "open" and "closed" signs.

Typically, active play centers feature a multi-use climber of wood or plastic, which can be taken down if necessary, and a rocker. A separate room is advantageous because there is often space to supplement the climber with hoppity-hops, balance beams, trikes, and balls. Even in a classroom with limited space, however, teachers can create an effective active play center:

Anecdote: A Head Start program purchased a mini-exercise trampoline for about thirty dollars. The teacher oriented the preschoolers in its use: only one child at a time; they could only jump so high unless an adult held their hands; they could strap jogger weights to their ankles if they wanted. The trampoline was available during every choice-time all year. After a supervised "training" period, children used it on their own. Several children bounced on the trampoline each day, but wait-times were brief. Few reminders were needed about its use. No injuries occurred. The mini-tramp proved especially helpful for a few very active children in the class. The trampoline became an accepted part of the classroom and was more quiet than the teacher had expected.

Figure 5–3 Carpentry and active play encourage perceptual-motor development.

Independent Activity at the Preprimary Level

Teachers have various names for the times children spend at centers: free play, play time, choice time, work time, center time. At the pre-primary level, two characteristics of center times mark appropriate practice. First, ample time must be allowed, at least forty-five minutes—once during a half-day program, twice during a full day program. Shorter periods prevent children from becoming fully involved (Rogers & Sawyers, 1988). Unfortunately, some teachers use brief play times as "buffer activities" (in between others), a practice that shows misunderstanding of the importance of the center experience (Beatty, 1992; Bredekamp, 1987; Brewer, 1992).

Second, preprimary children need choice both in the centers they select and the activities they do. The High/Scope Model has made famous the "plan, do, and review" sequence, designed to increase intentionality and reflection through the learning experience (Hohmann, Manet & Weikart, 1979). In small groups, children plan what they would like to do during "work time," with the adult and/or child "noting" the choices on paper. Children then "do" independent work times of about an hour, perhaps staying with their choices, perhaps not. Following work time, often during snack, children share what they did, with samples of work encouraged.

Plan, do, and review is just one part of the High/Scope Model. By its implementation of Piagetian thought and a solid research base, High/Scope has done much to legitimize the lasting benefits of child-initiated activity in early childhood (Hechinger, 1986).

A traditional center arrangement, used in some kindergarten classrooms, is for more quiet centers to be open in the morning "when they are fresh" and all centers—including carpentry, music, active play, blocks—during afternoon choice times. This arrangement fails to recognize the active nature of learning for the young child but does allow children self-selection among the open centers.

At the preprimary level, the rotation of groups through centers is not developmentally appropriate. The practice deprives children of the developmental benefits of self-selection and self-direction in learning activities. As Montessori discovered at the beginning of the century, no one knows their level of learning better than the children themselves. For Montessori, the right of child-choice extends through the elementary years, a view still outside of the mainstream in American education.

CENTERS AT THE PRIMARY LEVEL

The use of learning centers in elementary schools remains a progressive idea (Brewer, 1992). After kindergarten, centers included in primary classrooms tend to be few and informally designed. Reading centers are "fixtures," but less common are music, art, and writing centers. More classrooms do have a computer or two, but well stocked computer—or better **technology**—centers are still pretty much in the future. While some classrooms do have informal science areas, centers that encourage three dimensional activity—blocks and other building materials, dramatic play, carpentry, a variety of manipulatives, abundant "sciencing" activities—are still seldom seen.

Earlier in the century, Dewey, Montessori, and Piaget debunked the philosophical separation of mind and body within our schools. Yet, the view of learning as a passive, teacher controlled process, with discipline used to enforce this view, persists. It is almost as if we tell children that upon entering elementary school, they must foresake their bodies for long periods of the day and use only their minds. With such an emphasis, educators abandon the

Figure 5–4 The center most commonly found in primary classrooms is the reading center.

natural and essential integration of movement and thought, so important for healthy development (Wade, 1992; Williams & Kamii, 1986). (That classrooms are overcrowded and resources barely adequate may partially explain, but does not justify, this practice.)

Learning Centers and Integrated Curriculum

Bredekamp (1987), Brewer (1992), and Wolfgang & Wolfgang (1990) argue that DAP means shifting away from the study of isolated academic subjects during defined periods and toward the study of **integrated curriculum** in time blocks. Initiated by Dewey (1902) in laboratory schools at the beginning of the century, integrated curriculum (then called the "project method") has been a part of progressive education, including the nursery school movement, ever since (Brewer, 1992). Still, the changeover has yet to occur in most elementary schools, as Brewer points out:

> The most common approach to curriculum organization in schools in the United States, however, continues to be a subject-matter organization in which learning is segmented into math or science or language arts. For example, you probably remember that in elementary school you had reading first thing in the morning, math right before lunch, and science in the afternoon (p. 135).

Brewer states that in contrast to this fragmentation of the curriculum, a child's learning outside of school is whole and built around personally relevant experiences. She argues that integrating subject matter, as around themes, enables the child to find meaning in learning: "He recognizes that this information is personally useful, not something learned to please an adult, which has no other utility for him" (p. 135).

Myers and Maurer have proposed a model system for learning centers that includes their use in structured instruction as well as play times (1987). The model of Myers and Maurer lends itself to the integrated curriculum. Although these authors directed their approach to the kindergarten, the model applies equally well to the primary grades. The authors assign three different functions to centers depending on instructional intent. The three functions are:

- Self-directing/open-ended
    At each learning center, children select and use materials according to their own interests and abilities.
- Teacher-instructed/exploratory
    The teacher motivates and models exploration of materials at the center according to a preset theme or concept. Children then investigate materials on their own.
- Self-directing/self-correcting
    Children use materials at the center that "have obvious and prescribed uses; the material tells the learner whether a given action is correct or incorrect" (1987, p. 24) i.e. puzzles; object-to-numeral correspondence materials.

The promise of Myers and Maurer's model (1987) is that it enables the use of centers in a wide variety of primary grade activities. Foremost, in terms of integrated curriculum, the model lends itself to the thematic approach. Themes represent a practical application of integrated curriculum—done perhaps in an afternoon time block. In the thematic approach, a topic of interest to the children is selected. A variety of activities, some large group, but many involving the use of centers, are undertaken by the children. The children share the results of their discoveries, and the teacher guides and monitors children's progress (Brewer, 1992; Walmsley, Camp, and Walmsley, 1992).

The case study that follows illustrates the uses of centers suggested by Myers and Maurer through the thematic approach. "Mrs. Ryan" is a composite of a few different Minnesota teachers.

The Theme Approach: A Case Study

Each month, Mrs. Ryan's second grade spent time in the afternoons working with a new theme. For April, the theme was spring. The subtheme for Week One was "signs of spring in the neighborhood." The class was divided into four

Figure 5–5a Non-structured art illustrates the self-direction/open-ended use of learning centers.

Figure 5–5b A stringing demonstration preceded the work of these six year-olds in a teacher-instructed/exploratory activity.

Figure 5–5c The narration with cue to turn the page make this cassette story a self-directing/self-correcting activity at the reading center.

groups by the teacher. (Mrs. Ryan established new groupings for each theme.) The groups named themselves for animals that returned from migration or awoke from hibernation in the springtime: the bears, the hummingbirds, the bugs, and the skunks.

On Monday two parents, a college intern, and Mrs. Ryan took the four groups outside to tour the area around the school looking for signs of spring. They collected samples of everything from insects to new grass to litter. (One parent drew the line at "dog poop.") Each group recorded its observations.

Upon returning, the groups went to four different centers in the classroom. Each group cataloged their findings and pooled their observations. (Use of centers: teacher-instructed/exploratory). Each group reported its findings to the rest of the class.

On Tuesday, the teacher oriented the class to the theme activities for the rest of the week. The four groups would rotate to a new center each day, with large group sharing at the end. Mrs. Ryan and the class decided to assign the groups alphabetically to centers for Tuesday. She made a chart to show the rotation pattern for the rest of the week. The bears were at center one; the bugs at center two; the hummingbirds at center three; and the skunks at center four.

Center one was a self-directed/self-correcting activity in the science center. The children sorted the entire collection of specimens into boxes labeled "plant things," "animal things," "natural things," and "people-made things." A list of sample items was attached to each box. They counted the items in each category. They decided which set of specimens had the "most" and the "least."

Center two was a teacher-directed/exploratory activity in the reading center. The children studied a large collection of books about spring, including reports made by previous classes. They noted favorite parts of the books and shared them. While she monitored all of the goings-on, Mrs. Ryan worked primarily with this group.

Center three was a second teacher-directed/exploratory activity in the writing center. Each of the adult volunteers returned to class on the day their group was at this center. With the adult's help, the children made their own dictionary of words for specimens and other signs of spring, i.e. leaves, litter. They then wrote their "chapter" of the class report on the topic.

Center four was a self-directing/open-ended activity in the art center. Children made story-pictures of things they have done or would like to do when spring comes. They shared the story-pictures with the others in the group. Later, Mrs. Ryan and a few volunteers displayed each story-picture on the class-made bulletin board—the only kind of bulletin board she has in the room.

This is the third year Mrs. Ryan has used the spring theme. The subthemes have changed from year to year, but ones that have worked well include planting seeds, signs of spring at a local city park, hatching eggs, new animals on a farm, and what family members like to do in spring. She comments she is collecting a nice library of the children's reports, which she uses with each theme throughout the year. In the future, Mrs. Ryan hopes to do more with "webbing" (or brainstorming related ideas) with the children to create the subthemes.

Figure 5–6 Assistance with research is a frequent task of the primary grade teacher in the theme approach.

Mrs. Ryan looks at the theme time block as an opportunity to utilize integrated curriculum. Through the use of themes she manages to include content in the following subject areas: science, social studies, math, language arts, music, visual art, health, creative drama, and physical development. She was able to get permission for the large afternoon time blocks for Theme Time by documenting for the principal how she covers outcomes in all nine subject areas. Mrs. Ryan has found Theme Time to be such an effective instructional vehicle that she has been able to free up time for self-directing/open ended activity at centers for a half hour at the end of the day two afternoons a week.

Mrs. Ryan states that the organization of the themes and management of the activities takes "real work." She comments, however, that she sees little mistaken behavior during the theme time block, "because the children are so busy." She believes the children learn so much when they are involved with the themes that the effort is worthwhile. She concluded that when she got volunteers involved the second year to assist with small group activities, "It really helped." Her aim next year is to include the "specialist" teachers in music, art, and perhaps physical education in theme activities.

Independent Activity at the Primary Level

The values of self-directing/open-ended activity play for primary grade children are effectively discussed in the NAEYC Position Statement (Bredekamp, 1987). On a daily basis child-choice manipulative activity is necessary for children through the primary years (Brewer, 1992; Williams & Kamii, 1986)—though teachers feel hard pressed to find this time in their schedules. Certainly, the integrative values of play present a strong argument for this activity (Rogers & Sawyers, 1988). (An often repeated line goes "Through play children learn what cannot be taught.")

The thought, movement, interaction, cooperation, relaxation, and expression that occur during self-directing/open-ended activity improves the satisfaction level of children in the primary classroom. Free for a time from external standards of evaluation, children can experience the gratification of learning for its own sake. With happier children comes a decrease in mistaken behavior. For the professional teacher, the promise of learning centers should outweigh any criticism that self-directed center activity is time spent "off task." There are many reasons to use centers in the classroom. An important one is to assist children to become self-directing, successful learners. Play at learning centers affords this goal.

THE PLACE OF ROUTINES IN EFFECTIVE CLASSROOM MANAGEMENT: A TEACHER'S PERSPECTIVE

Familiarity with the classroom and full use of its many resources help children to become confident, productive learners. Pat Sanford, an experienced

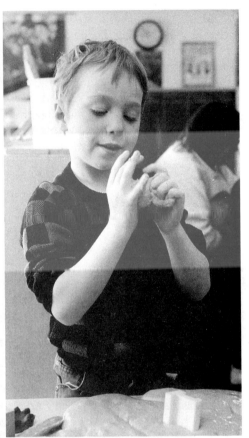

Figure 5–7 The gains possible through self-directing/open-ended activity help children feel positively about themselves in the classroom situation.

kindergarten and primary teacher offered these thoughts about effective use of the classroom.

Pat says that the secret to classroom management lies in getting children used to routines. For example, she shows them just how to store their boots, under their coats with the heels to the wall. This way, they won't get knocked over and mixed up with someone else's. Mittens go inside one sleeve. Then children will always know where they are. She makes sure they know where the restroom is (early on the first day) and how to use it.

Materials go back in boxes and on shelves just where they were. Clearly marked labels with pictures and words help the children decide this. Books are to be read and valued; they go back in the bookcase right-side up, facing out. She dislikes the word, "cubby," so each child has a storage bin and knows how to keep papers and belongings there. The children understand that messes during activities are perfectly OK. They also know that cleaning up afterwards is not an optional chore; it is a part of kindergarten life. After commenting about her management style, Pat adds, "Now, if my home only looked like my classroom. . ."

As a professional, Pat does some things differently than other teachers. Most teachers designate coat hooks and seat locations for children, using printed names to mark the right spots. In Pat's room the children hang their coats and sit at tables wherever they wish:

> Adults like to sit wherever they want; kids should be able to also. Like adults, kids settle in next to someone they're comfortable by. Usually, this is not a problem. If it looks like it might be, I just talk with them privately.

Pat believes that not "institutionalizing" individual space encourages a more comfortable atmosphere. The same goes for the name the children use with their teacher. She makes it clear to the children that she does not want to be called "Teacher" ("Because I am a person"). Some call her "Mrs. Sanford," but most call her, "Pat."

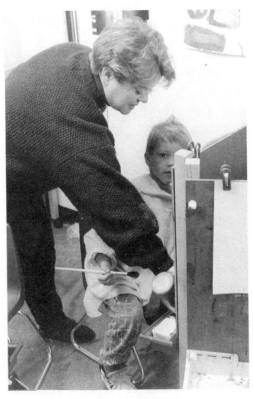

Figure 5–8 Helping children know that it is all right to ask for assistance is a part of Pat's approach to teaching routines.

Although she believes that helping children get used to routines is important to future school success, she brings a sense of humor to her managerial style. For Pat, the mixture of elementary school rituals and early childhood innocence often brings a smile:

Anecdote: One day the author was supervising a student teacher in Pat's classroom. With a grin, Pat sent me over to stand by a boy during the Pledge of Allegiance. With a hand on his heart he said with total confidence, "I pledge Norwegians to the flag. . .

Finally, Pat is definite about her role as a teacher. "My job is not to prepare children for first grade. My job is to help them have the best kindergarten experience it is possible for them to have." Pat attributes the absence of discipline problems in her classroom to helping the children get used to kindergarten routines, "but in a way respectful to each child."

Whether readers agree with all of her ideas about managing the classroom, Pat offers some thoughtful suggestions that teachers of children three to eight would do well to consider.

ENCOURAGING PARENTS TO VOLUNTEER IN THE CLASSROOM

Parents can be involved in several ways in the preschool or primary grade program. They can:

1. Assist children with home assignments;
2. Attend parent-teacher conferences;
3. Go to parent meetings;
4. Participate in home visits by staff;
5. Contribute materials;
6. Follow through with staff recommendations;
7. Chaperone special events;
8. Visit for observation purposes;
9. Make presentations to the class;
10. Volunteer to help on a regular basis;
11. Help to organize special events;
12. Assist other parents to volunteer;
13. Sit on policy boards.

In their parent involvement programs, educators tend to focus on one or a few of these ways and measure success accordingly. Programs with a full range of family services, such as Head Start, might focus on all thirteen. Another method of gauging successful involvement is to first decide which of the ways are appropriate for the particular program, then assess success on a family-by-family basis. For some parents, participation at levels 1–3 might constitute successful participation. For another family, criteria 1–8 might be used.

Figure 5–9 Pat sees her role as not preparing children for first grade, but providing the best possible kindergarten experience for each child.

The present section focuses on those levels of involvement that pertain to the classroom, criteria 7–12. Specifically, the concern is how to help parents feel comfortable enough to volunteer on a regular basis. Previous chapters began the discussion about the importance of parent-teacher partnerships in the guidance approach. Gestwicki (1992) presents the following advantages of encouraging parents to be classroom volunteers:

- Parents gain firsthand experience of a program, of their child's reactions in a classroom, and feelings of satisfaction from making a contribution;
- Children feel special when their parents are involved, feel secure with the tangible evidence of parents and teachers cooperating, and gain directly as parental understanding and skills increase;
- Teachers gain resources to extend learning opportunities, observe parent-child interaction, and can feel supported as parents participate and empathize with them (p. 246).

Roadblocks to Involving Parents

Despite these advantages, teachers sometimes encounter two road blocks: (*a*) other staff are dubious about the merits of using parent volunteers, and (*b*) parents cannot find the time or they are not sure they can contribute (Gestwicki, 1992). In regard to the first situation, few programs and schools have policies forbidding the use of parent volunteers. In this day and age such a practice is ill-advised. As mentioned in chapter one, programs such as Head Start, cooperative nursery schools, and preschool/parent education programs have a rich tradition of including parents in the classroom. In a growing number of school districts, as well, parent volunteers are gaining in acceptance.

The teacher interested in including parents needs to determine what is policy and what simply has never been done. Talking with sympathetic teachers and speaking with the administrator are important first steps. The teacher is more likely to experience success by starting on a small scale and keeping a "low profile," so that the effort does not become a "burning teacher's lounge issue." As Gestwicki suggests, determination on the teacher's part is likely to be the main ingredient for success (1992).

Figure 5–10 Parents volunteer in the classroom in many ways. (Courtesy Richard Faulkner, Family Service Center, Koochiching-Itasca Head Start, Grand Rapids, Minnesota.)

Gradual Encouragement

Brewer (1992) suggests that teachers work carefully with parents and not push them to levels of participation beyond their comfort levels. Ideas for creating the climate for partnership with parents were illustrated in chapter four. The following are suggestions to help parents feel more comfortable about volunteering in the classroom.

1. Send a greeting letter and parent questionnaire (samples provided in appendix). On the questionnaire, have parents check different ways they would be willing to participate in the program. Include choices pertaining to the classroom. Don't ask *if* they would like to volunteer in the classroom. Provide choices of ways to volunteer and ask them to check as many as they would like.

2. Hold an orientation meeting for all parents. Distribute two fliers: (*a*) one that tells about your program, and (*b*) another that gives suggestions and guidelines for parent volunteers (Samples provided in appendix). Go over each flier at the meeting. Stress that you encourage parents to visit and to volunteer. Have a parent volunteer from the previous year share what she did. Mention that you know many parents work outside the home and that it's difficult to get away. Whenever possible, you are open to visits on the parents' time schedule.

3. If the teacher makes home visits, mention volunteering at the home visit. During the first parent-teacher conference, refer to the questionnaire and discuss volunteering in the classroom.

4. Establish with parents when they are welcome. If you choose not to have a general "open house" policy, specify in the flier and at the meeting when parents can visit. Be flexible: parents working outside of the home have limited time availability.

5. Let parents know there are three ways they can volunteer: (*a*) parents can participate on a regular basis (They only need to call if they cannot make it); (*b*) parents can informally visit or initiate a special event, such as a birthday party for a child or a family sharing activity. (It is important that they call you first); and (*c*) parents who can help with field trips, picnics, etc.

6. A brother or sister brought with a parent probably will not be as disruptive as a teacher might think. For some parents, permission to bring a younger sibling is necessary for them to visit at all. Make clear your policy about siblings accompanying the parent.

7. Some parents might like to volunteer, but don't have transportation. Help parents work this out, such as by having two parents "buddy up."

The teacher assumes responsibility for scheduling parents. If s/he is fortunate, s/he will have to limit numbers, so not too many parents volunteer at one time. Teachers who view parent volunteers as a natural extension of parent-teacher partnerships will actively invite parents into the classroom. All stand to gain when parents become members of the teaching team.

Figure 5–11 As this first grader's class is used to visitors, his younger sister does not disrupt the daily program.

SUMMARY

Chapter five began by restating the importance of developmentally appropriate practice in managing the classroom and preventing mistaken behavior. Important in effective classroom management is organization through the use of learning centers and routines.

What is the role of learning centers in classroom organization?

Clearly identified learning centers are a basis of developmentally appropriate classroom management. Learning centers are distinct areas within the room that provide a variety of related materials for children's use. Young children are adept at active learning and benefit from being able to select and complete activities at learning centers.

How can learning centers be used at the preprimary level?

Traditional centers in preprimary classrooms are supplemented by "modern variations," including computer/technology, cooking, social/cultural awareness, writing, and dual dramatic play—permanent, (housekeeping) and theme-related. When teachers plan the layout of learning centers, they often use traffic flow patterns and noise levels as organizational factors. Through the

Figure 5–12 Centers lend themselves both to formal cooperative learning and informal table talk.

large motor and perceptual-motor opportunities they provide, active play and carpentry are two important centers in a pre-primary classroom.

Center-oriented play (whether it is called "work time," "choice time," etc.), with its various alternative terms, is critical in the preprimary program. At least forty-five minute periods—once during a half day program, twice during a full day program—are important. The High/Scope Model has done much to legitimize the benefits of child-selected, child--directed activity in early childhood.

How can learning centers be used at the primary level?

The use of learning centers in elementary schools remains a progressive idea. Centers enable the active learning that such reformers as Dewey, Montessori, and Piaget have advocated and the DAP Position Statement recommends.

Integrated curriculum, through use of the theme approach, is a teaching strategy that relies on the use of learning centers. Myers and Maurer's model for three uses of learning centers fits well with the theme approach and indicates how centers can be used at the primary level. The three uses of learning centers are: self-directing/open-ended, teacher-instructed/exploratory, and self-directing/self-correcting. Children need self-selecting/open-ended activity at centers well into the primary years.

What is the place of routines in effective classroom management?

Familiarity with the classroom and full use of its resources help children to become confident, productive learners. Pat Sanford, an experienced kindergarten and primary grade teacher, believes that the secret to classroom management lies in getting children used to routines. Pat teaches routines beginning on the first day of school, such as the location and use of restrooms layout of the classroom, and the correct bus. She models how to stow outerwear so it will be where the children can find it. She teaches that it is fine to make a mess during activities, but materials need to be returned to the correct box and location.

While Pat states that learning about routines is important, she believes in creating a warm classroom atmosphere, with a minimum of "institutionalization." A sense of humor and respect for each child are important to her. She states that her job is not to prepare children for "next year," but to provide the best possible "present year" for the children in her class.

How does the teacher encourage parents to volunteer in the classroom?

Parents can be involved in programs thirteen or more ways. Teachers need to measure the success of parent involvement by whichever ways are feasible for the individual family. Teachers can overcome the roadblocks to involving parents with a positive attitude and persistence. Seven suggestions were provided for encouraging parents to visit classrooms and become regular volunteers. Parents, children, and teachers all gain when parents become members of the teaching team.

(Courtesy Lin Wahlberg, Early Childhood Family Education, Bemidji, Minnesota.)

FOLLOW-UP ACTIVITIES

Follow-up activities allow the student to interrelate material from the text with "real life" situations. The "observations" imply access to practicum experiences the "interviews" access to teachers and parents. When communicating about the activities, students need to respect the privacy of all participants in the observation or interview as an important professional courtesy.

1. **What is the role of learning centers in classroom organization?**
   a. Observe one or more classrooms for the layout of learning centers. On graph paper draw a layout for a classroom, including learning centers and the location of other items you believe important.
   b. Interview two early childhood teachers about how they locate and use learning centers. What do the teachers agree about; where do they have differing views?
2. **How can learning centers be used at the preprimary level?**
   a. Observe centers in use in a classroom. Watch particularly for one center at which children seem to be getting along. Watch for another center at which children may be having more difficulties. To what do you attribute the differences in the children's reactions?

b. Interview a teacher about one or two of the more active centers in the classroom. Why does the teacher include them? What does s/he believe the children gain from being able to use them?

3. **How can learning centers be used at the primary level?**

a. Observe children who are using a center in one of the three ways described by Myers and Maurer. Which use is it? Why do you think so? In what ways is their behavior productive? What mistaken behavior do you observe? What do you think they are learning?

b. Interview a teacher about his or her use of integrated curriculum, the thematic approach, interdisciplinary units—or whatever term the teacher uses. How does the teacher use centers with interdisciplinary instruction? What does the teacher see as the advantages and drawbacks of interdisciplinary teaching strategy? How does the teacher find the children when involved with theme or unit activities?

4. **What is the place of routines in effective classroom management?**

a. Observe a classroom where there are definite routines. What are the likely effects of the routines on the children? On the teacher? When you teach, would you use routines similarly to what you observed or differently? Why?

b. Interview a teacher about his or her use of routines. How does the teacher believe the use of routine assists with classroom management? Ask the teacher how s/he knows when there is insufficient use of routines in a classroom. When is there an overreliance on routines?

5. **How does the teacher encourage parents to volunteer in the classroom?**

a. Observe a classroom where one or more parents volunteer. Decide the type and level of involvement one or two parents are showing. Document your conclusions.

b. Briefly interview a parent volunteer. What went into the parent's decision to volunteer in the classroom? What part did the teacher play in the parent's decision to volunteer?

SUGGESTED RESOURCES

Beaty, J.J. (1992). *Preschool: Appropriate Practices*. Fort Worth, TX: Harcourt Brace Jovanovich College Publishers.

Brewer, J.A. (1992). *Introduction to Early Childhood Education: Preschool Through Primary Grades*. Boston: Allyn and Bacon.

Essa, E. and Rogers, P.R. (1992). *An Early Childhood Curriculum: From Developmental Model to Application*. Albany, NY: Delmar Publishers Inc.

Hechinger, F.M. (1986). *Better Start: New Choices for Early Learning*. New York: Walker and Company.

Katz, L. (1985). Video: "Curriculum for Preschool and Kindergarten: A Discussion with Lillian Katz." Washington, DC: National Association for the Education of Young Children.

Myers, B.K. and Maurer, K. (1987). "Teaching With Less Talking: Learning Centers in the Kindergarten. *Young Children, 42*(5), pp. 20-27.

Walmsey, B.B., Camp, A.M., and Walmsley, S.A. (1992), *Teaching Kindergarten: A Developmentally Appropriate Approach*. Portsmouth, NH: Heinemann Educational Books.

Williams, C.K. and Kamii, C. (1986). "How Do Children Learn by Handling Objects?" *Young Children, 41*(8), pp. 23-26.

REFERENCES

Beaty, J.J. (1992). *Preschool: Appropriate Practices*. Fort Worth, TX: Harcourt Brace Jovanovich College Publishers.

Bredekamp, S. (ed.), (1987). *Developmentally Appropriate Practice in Early Childhood Programs Serving Children from Birth Through Age 8*. Washington, DC: National Association for the Education of Young Children.

Brewer, J.A. (1992). *Introduction to Early Childhood Education: Preschool Through Primary Grades*. Boston: Allyn and Bacon.

Derman-Sparks, L. (1989). *Anti-Bias Curriculum: Tools for Empowering Young Children*. Washington, DC: National Association for the Education of Young Children.

Dewey, J. (1902). *The Child and the Curriculum*. Chicago: The University of Chicago Press.

Essa, E. (1992). *Introduction to Early Childhood Education*. Albany, NY: Delmar Publishers Inc.

Essa, E. and Rogers, P.R. (1992). *An Early Childhood Curriculum: From Developmental Model to Application*. Albany, NY: Delmar Publishers Inc.

Gestwicki, C. (1992). *Home, School, Community Relations*. Albany, NY: Delmar Publishers Inc.

Gordon, A.M. and Browne, K.W. (1989). *Beginnings and Beyond: Foundations in Early Childhood Education*. Albany, NY: Delmar Publishers Inc.

Hechinger, F.M. (1986). *Better Start: New Choices for Early Learning*. New York: Walker and Company.

Hohmann, M., Banet, B. and Weikart, D.P. (1979). *Young Children in Action*. Ypsilanti, MI: The High/Scope Press.

Katz, L. (1985). Video: "Curriculum for Preschool and Kindergarten: A Discussion with Lillian Katz." Washington, DC: National Association for the Education of Young Children.

Myers, B.K. and Maurer, K. (1987). "Teaching With Less Talking: Learning Centers in the Kindergarten." *Young Children, 42*(5), pp. 20-27.

Rogers, C.S. and Sawyers, J.K. (1988). *Play in the Lives of Children*. Washington, DC: National Association for the Education of Young Children.

Wade, M.G. (1992). "Motor Skills, Play, and Child Development: An Introduction." *Early Report, 19*(2) (Winter, 1992), pp. 1-2.

Walmsley, B.B., Camp, A.M., and Walmsley, S.A. (1992). *Teaching Kindergarten: A Developmentally Appropriate Approach*. Portsmouth, NH: Heinemann Educational Books.

Williams, C.K. and Kamii, C. (1986). "How Do Children Learn by Handling Objects?" *Young Children, 41*(8), pp. 23-26.

Wolfgang, C.H. and Wolfgang, M.E. (1992). *School for Young Children: Developmentally Appropriate Practices*. Boston: Allyn and Bacon.

6

Managing the
Daily Program

GUIDING QUESTIONS

As you read chapter six, you will discover answers to the following
questions:

- **How does the teacher balance reliability and novelty in the
  daily program?**
- **What is the appropriate mix of active and quiet times?**
- **What part do large group activities play in the developmentally appropriate program?**
- **How does managing transitions effectively reduce mistaken
  behavior?**
- **How can the teacher make use of parents and other classroom
  volunteers?**

Unit two addresses the teacher's role in reducing the need for mistaken behavior. Three components of prevention explored in the unit are: managing the
classroom, managing the daily program, and communicating to prevent
problems. Chapter six addresses **managing the daily program**, including
the schedule, types of activities, transitions between activities, and the use of
volunteers.

THE DAILY PROGRAM

In the daily program children need both a sense of reliability and the promise
of novelty. Too little of the former results in a lack of predictability and

anxiety. Too little of the latter results in tedium (Brewer, 1992). A set schedule that children are familiar with provides a useful baseline for both the informal **teachable moment**, the gerbil having babies, the planned special event, or a visit from Smokey the Bear.

A schedule provides security (Gordon & Browne, 1989). There is much in life that is beyond children's control, from the time they get up in the morning to the time they go to bed. Some choices, like which of two sets of clothes to wear, are good for children and add to their self-esteem. Other choices, such as whether to go to school or not, children are not in a position to make.

When they cannot decide a matter for themselves, children benefit from understanding about a decision that is made for them. Understanding reasons helps children find reliability in the relationship with the teacher and in the classroom environment—necessary basic needs for personal growth.

The daily schedule is one of those decisions that children don't make on their own, but need to rely on. When unscheduled events enable positive results—celebration, delight, wonderment, enlightenment—they add immeasurably to the everyday program. An unpredictable program, however—whether it is just inconsistent or overloaded with spontaneous teachable moments—makes children feel anxious and insecure. The teacher maintains a healthy balance in the schedule by monitoring the feeling level of the class—anxious, bored, interested, involved—and responding. By reading children's feelings, and discussing

Figure 6–1 When unscheduled events enable positive results, they add to the everyday program.

reasons with them, the teacher may vary from the schedule. Returning to it allows children the security of knowing what is expected of them.

Three Sample Schedules

Three sample schedules follow that model developmentally appropriate programming; make full use of the classroom; and provide a daily program through which interesting experiences can happen. Some use of volunteers, as in the teaching team concept will facilitate some small group activities. Schedules such as these attempt to balance the novel and the predictable so that children are involved, but not overloaded—making mistaken behavior less likely. As Walmsley, Camp, and Walmsley note, flexibility in the schedule is a prerequisite for a developmentally appropriate program (1992). Discussion of key specifics from the schedules follows throughout the chapter.

Table 6.1
Prekindergarten Schedule

(Six hour schedule, as in some Head Start programs. Half day and full day programs can be adapted.)

Time	Activity
8:15– 8:30	Arrival. Teacher greets each child. Informal child-choice activity until all children arrive.
8:30– 9:00	Breakfast in family groups of 8-10, each with an adult. At tables, teachers preview events; planning by children for center time.
9:00–10:15	Center time. (Self-directed/open-ended activity at centers). All centers open. Clean up.
10:15–10:35	Snack in family groups. Review of "special things" done during choice-time.
10:35–11:00	Active play, inside or out.
11:00–11:15	Large group: music, story, movement activity, occasional guest.
11:15–11:45	Small group activities—art, cooking, creative drama, walk outside.
11:45– 1:00	Lunch in family groups. Rest.
1:00– 2:00	Center time. (Self-directed/open-ended activity at centers). All centers open. Clean up.
2:00– 2:30	Class meeting: songs, story, review of day. Get ready to go home.

Table 6.2
Kindergarten Schedule

(Full day schedule. Half day schedule can be adapted.)

Time	Activity
8:30– 9:00	Arrival. Teacher greets each child. Breakfast for some children. Informal child-choice activity as children arrive.
9:00– 9:20	Morning class meeting. Attendance, practical time and weather questions. Quick preview of day.
9:20– 9:30	Large group lead-in to small group activities through use of discussion, story, song, object, or picture. (Teacher instructed/ exploratory activity, with introductory instruction in large group.)
9:30–10:10	Small group follow-up such as with story-pictures, "sciencing," cooking activity.
10:10–10:30	Snack time.
10:30–11:30	Center time. Self-directed/open-ended activity at selected centers. Clean-up.
11:45–12:30	Lunch and child-choice activity inside, or active play outside (depending on weather).
12:30– 1:00	Story. Reading, relaxing, rest.
1:00– 1:45	Special Activity (gym, art, music, library, computer).
1:45– 2:30	Self-directed/open-ended activity; All centers open. Clean up. Occasional special event during part of this time.
2:30– 3:00	Afternoon circle time: songs, movement activities, finger plays, review of day. Get ready to go home.

Table 6.3
Primary Schedule

Time	Activity
8:30– 9:00	Arrival. Teacher greets each child. Breakfast for some children. Informal child-choice activity as children arrive.
9:00– 9:20	Morning class meeting. Discussion of important events and issues—brought up by either children or teacher. Preview of language arts time block. Assignment of small groups to centers.
9:20–10:20	Integrated language arts time block with small groups rotating through centers.
10:20–10:30	Break, restroom, snack (bring your own).

Table 6.3 (continued)
Primary Schedule

Time	Activity
10:30–10:50	Active large group, inside—movement to music, obstacle course, etc.; or outside.
10:50–11:30	Monday: Super Silent reading Tuesday: Art specialist Wednesday: Super Silent writing Thursday: Choice of SSR or SSW Friday: Child-directed/open ended.
11:20–11:30	Teacher-read story,
11:30–12:20	Lunch and recess.
12:20– 1:00	Integrated math and science time block. Large group orientation, small groups in centers.
1:00– 2:00	Large and small groups work on themes. (See Mrs. Ryan Case Study)
2:00– 2:10	Break, restroom, movement activity.
2:10– 2:50	Monday: Continue work on themes; self-directing/open-ended activities Tuesday Music specialist Wednesday: Continue work on themes; self-directing/open-ended activities Thursday: Physical education specialist Friday: Continue work on themes; self-directed/open-ended activities.
2:50– 3:15	Afternoon class meeting. Happenings of the day and future events discussed. Preparations to go home.

Tracking the Daily Schedule

Teachers use various methods to acquaint children with the daily schedule. One is the **day clock**. Until age seven or eight, children have trouble reading a two-handed clock (Elkind, 1976). The teacher can effectively use a one-handed "clock," however, to help the class follow the daily schedule. If each time block has an illustration and a name, children have contextual clues in order to read it—and, they can help to move the hand.

Time concepts that have personal meaning for young children—snack, rest, choice time—provide the building blocks for the gradual mastery of chronology. The teacher can use the clock during a morning meeting time to introduce the events of the day. A "special event" wedge could be placed over a usual time-block to indicate a change in the schedule.

MIXING ACTIVE AND QUIET TIMES

In the words of that awestruck parent (previous chapter), young children are "active critters." They learn most effectively through movement of large and small muscles (Wade, 1992). Much of the daily program should include activity at a **busy** level, with occasional excursions into the **boisterous** and the **bucolic**. The center approach, discussed in the previous chapter, defines busy activity. **Table talk** (Johnson, 1988) and movement at and among centers are common in classrooms functioning at the busy level.

Boisterous activity is known to all—jumping on a mini-tramp, climbing on a climber, dancing to "The Pop Corn Rock," running, riding a trike, playing "Ninja Turtles." Bucolic activity (defined "pastoral, peaceful") includes attending in large groups, doing "seatwork," reading a book, watching a video, resting.

Traditionally at the elementary level, educators have made "bucolic" the goal, with activity at the busy level occasionally acceptable, and boisterous activity only under special circumstances. The problem is that bucolic activity often lapses into **passivity** (Katz, 1985). Children become bored and restless, and mistaken behavior results.

When children have difficulty in a program, adults often use common, sometimes trendy tags to describe their behavior: "immature," "hyper," "antsy," "active but alert," "strong willed," "attention-deficit disordered." Sometimes these behavior patterns have a physiological or psychological basis that needs

Figure 6–2 In the guidance classroom, the normal activity level is busy.

to be diagnosed and remediated. But often the labels result from a mismatch of the program and the child—the program tending toward the bucolic level, and children needing to be actively engaged, **busy**. Rather than suppress the developmentally appropriate activeness of the young, teachers do better to guide it and empower children through it (Wade, 1992).

Rest and Relaxation

Though "busy" sets the tone of the developmentally appropriate classroom (Bredekamp, 1987; Brewer, 1992), neither children nor teachers can function all day at the busy level. For some years, books by such authors as Clare Cherry (*Think of Something Quiet*, 1981) and albums by such musicians as Hap Palmer (*Sea Gulls*, 1978) and Greg and Steve (*Quiet Places*, 1986) have been helpful in promoting relaxation in the classroom. With modern family life-styles and the pressures of school, children, like adults, become tense and anxious. Cherry (1981) and Honig (1986) have pointed out that children do not always have the ability to relax on their own.

The traditional naps in preschool, the rest periods or naps in kindergarten, and quiet periods in elementary grades all—when done nonpunitively—serve to restore a sense of equilibrium for children and teachers. Stories too, when done on a daily basis in a relaxed atmosphere, have regenerating values. The **relaxation materials** mentioned above go a step further, however, by providing activities to specifically reduce stress in young children. A few topics in the Cherry text, for instance, are:

- creating wholesome environments;
- responding to stress;
- developing inner awareness;
- learning to relax muscles (pp. v-vii).

In full day preschool programs, nap times can be challenging. Children have different rest needs and show differing behaviors when adjusting to nap time (Saifer, 1990). When children of different ages share the same room for rest, problems can be compounded. The following table provides suggestions for helping staff "troubleshoot" problems:

Table 6.4
Troubleshooting Preschool Nap Problems

Problem	Suggestion
Many have trouble settling down.	Review: (a) Activity level prior to nap—relaxing, quiet? (b) Method of creating mood—story, music relaxation activity used? (c) Environment—comfortable temperature, low lighting, enough space? (d) Role of adults—present, speaking quietly, lying with children, rubbing backs?

Table 6.4 (continued)
Troubleshooting Preschool Nap Problems

Problem	Suggestion
Children rest, but many ready to rise too early.	Assess length of nap time. Consider shortening.
Older children don't sleep; ready to rise before others.	Move children to different room or separate area. Allow to read books on mats. Allow to rise early and do quiet activities.
Individual child doesn't sleep; ready to rise. Doesn't seem tired.	Check with parent about priorities. If willing, try solution for older children above; note how child responds.
Individual child doesn't sleep; ready to rise. Does seem tired.	Separate from others. Adult rubs back, lies by child. At another time talk with child about problem. Talk with parent about child.
Individual child not ready to rise with others.	Let child sleep. Monitor health of child. If pattern continues, talk with parent.

Adults help children to nap when they create a conducive mood and setting. Maintaining a firm, friendly, and quiet response style is important. Staff who take a problem-solving approach to rest almost always improve the situation (Saifer, 1992), often within a day or two.

Anecdote: A day care center had in one group preschoolers from age three to five and part-time kindergarten children who arrived from school each day at noon. The kindergarten kids felt they were "too old" for naps, and the younger children were affected each day by their arrival. "Rest" was proving difficult.

One day a teacher aide had one kindergarten child rub the back of his younger brother to help the three-year-old get settled. The preschool staff got to talking about this and decided to try something new. They had each kindergarten child rub the back of a selected preschooler. After the preschooler fell asleep, the kindergartners lay down on their mats behind a long book shelf. On their mats the "k" kids looked at books or listened to relaxing music. In just a few days rest time at the center changed completely.

Active Play

For teachers to use *boisterous* level activity productively, three ideas are important.

1. The teacher should not rely on occasional active play times or physical education periods as sufficient to meet children's needs. At the preprimary level, include an active play center that is open during at least one child-choice time per day. Throughout the age span, movement-to-music during large group activities refreshes children and renews their ability to concentrate.

   Replicating a common practice in Asia, some schools in northern Minnesota begin the day with movement to music. Pieces by Steve and Greg, Hap Palmer, and various "aerobics for kids," artists are piped into classrooms over the loudspeakers. Teachers as well as the children move to the music.

2. Effective activities involve children without the need to compete or take turns. Young children run for the sake of running, and skip for the sake of skipping. The rules and complexities of competitive games tend to confuse young children and cause hurt feelings (Hendrick, 1992). Moreover, the wait times between turns in organized games are often frustrating and limit the opportunity for physical activity that is the main reason for the activity to begin with. When all participate, informally and enjoyably, everybody wins.

Anecdote: A Head Start teacher became tired of the staple active game in her class, Duck, Duck, Grey Duck. A large portion of the game was spent in squatting down. Once the children began running, the teacher noticed most did not want to stop. The inability of some children to catch the others took away from everybody's fun. The teacher ended the game. Instead, she adapted Red Light, Green Light for her group by requiring different ways to move each time the "green light" showed and declaring the whole class winners as soon as the last child crossed the finish line. The game became the new favorite of the children, especially when the teacher taped a red light to her front and a green light to her back, jumped around, and enthusiastically called out directions.

Teachers who take the guidance approach need to consider the balance of active and quiet times in the daily programs. Distinct from traditional practices, the general noise level of classrooms should be **busy**, with planned periods of **boisterous** and **bucolic**.

Figure 6–3 Children play actively without the need for adult direction, even under less than ideal conditions. (Courtesy Michael Crowley, Family Service Center, Koochiching-Itasca Head Start, Grand Rapids, Minnesota)

THE PLACE OF LARGE GROUPS

A hallmark of effective programs is that they accommodate the range of developmental responses that any group of children will show. A productive *center*, such as a reading center, does this by providing a variety of materials from picture books to "early readers" to elementary science texts. Productive *materials*, such as blocks and clay, do this by allowing children to construct whatever they will, from a simple stack to a castle, from a simple clay ball to a bird sitting on its nest of eggs. Productive *activities* also are developmentally inclusive. In the area of art, for instance, the teacher avoids dittoes and craft projects, but instead motivates children to work creatively with the materials provided, so that each child can succeed at his or her level.

Likewise, productive **grouping patterns**—large groups, small groups, individual activities—encourage children to function effectively at their various levels of development. A problem with overreliance on large group, teacher-directed activities is that they easily exceed most children's developmental levels and attention spans (Brewer, 1992). Very few preschoolers, only some kindergarteners, and many—but not all—primary grade children learn effectively by sitting, listening, and following directions (Bredekamp, 1987; McAfee, 1986).

An argument for frequent large groups is that young children need to get used to sitting and listening in order to succeed at school. However, the physiology of preprimary children prevents them from sitting for long periods comfortably. To the comment that young children must learn to sit and listen, the response is that young children are not developmentally ready; they will become more ready as they get older (Brewer, 1992). In fact, even though the development of primary grade children means that they attend longer, the DAP research indicates that even primary grade children learn more effectively when they are doing and interacting (Bredekamp, 1987; Brewer, 1992; Williams & Kamii, 1986).

Anecdote: On a sunny spring afternoon, a first grade class went to the library. While there, they silently read/looked at books, then heard the librarian read quite a long story. When they arrived back at the classroom, a parent who was scheduled to read a book that morning arrived and asked if he could read then. The teacher felt this was important and agreed. She and the student teacher sat with the children and worked hard to keep them focused on the story.

The next scheduled activity was another large group; the student teacher was to do a lesson with a puppet named Charlie on friendship. After three tries at starting the lesson, the student teacher whispered to the teacher. Then, the Puppet announced, "Boys and girls, Charlie thinks that it is hard to listen when you have to sit so long. When I call your name it is time to get ready to go outside." An afternoon's pent up energy expressed itself in a bedlam of activity. After a half hour outdoors, the teacher and student teacher again had "happy campers." The class came in and worked industriously on their daily journals.

Throughout this age span, children learn best when they engage in many independent activities, frequent small groups, and *occasional* large groups that are friendly, participatory, relevant to the children's experiences, and concise (McAfee, 1986). Brewer (1992) and McAfee (1986) recommend that teachers review standard large group practices for such criteria. From this perspective the chapter examines: **taking attendance, calendar and the weather, show and tell, stories**, and **large group instruction**. To challenge these traditions of early childhood education is a bit controversial. Teachers would do well, however, to reflect about the meaning of these activities for the children as well as themselves.

Figure 6–4 Primary grade children, like younger children, learn more effectively when they are doing and interacting. (Courtesy Michael Crowley, Family Service Center, Koochiching-Itasca Head Start, Grand Rapids, Minnesota)

Taking Attendance

Attendance can be done efficiently if children "register" immediately when they arrive. One way of doing this is to have laminated "mushrooms" with each child's name, a child-made design, and the child's photo. After learning their names, the children take their own mushrooms from slots in one tagboard sheet and put them in the slots with their names on a second sheet. At a morning class meeting, the teacher quickly reviews the charts with the class, and those missing and present are noted. (Even three-year-olds quickly recognize their names.)

Another alternative, which many teachers enjoy, is to sing an attendance song that mentions each present child by name. (Such songs often have made-up words to familiar tunes.) Songs make taking attendance more participatory, an objective for successful large groups. Teachers who use greeting songs seem to overcome two minor difficulties with them: (a) with a large class, long verses take a lot of time; (b) some children get embarrassed and may not want their names sung. Short verses and a matter-of-fact approach with individual children make this method of greeting successful.

Calendar and the Weather

Calendar and weather activities often become rituals rather than learning experiences (McAfee, 1986). Until middle childhood, children experience **time**

confusion, which means they have difficulty understanding adult time concepts (Elkind, 1976). A first grade teacher was amused to discover this when she asked her students two time questions: what season the month of November is in and how old they thought she was. (She got answers that included "salty" and "about 13.") Weather concepts also are more abstract to children than we may realize. Two cloudy days following two partly cloudy days simply is not an every day topic of conversation for five-year-olds.

In a morning **class meeting**, an alternative is to ask four or five questions that encourage children to think about time and weather concepts in terms that have personal meaning for them. Sample questions are these:

* Who can remember what you had for supper last night?
* Who knows what you will do after school today?
* Who can remember three things you saw on the way to school this morning?
* Was it hot or cold when you came to school today? How could you tell?
* It is windy today. Who saw the wind push something?
* It is raining today. Who hopes it is still raining after school today? Why (or why not)?

These questions relate directly to the children's experience. If children know that all interpretations of questions are welcome (and not just one answer that the teacher has in mind), they will participate readily. Through participation, the children gain in observation powers, thinking skills, and communication abilities (McAfee, 1986). They will have a foundation in personal experience that will help them master adult weather and time concepts as they progress through the primary grades.

The author recognizes that many teachers would not want to give up especially calendar activities. They value the introduction of numerals and time concepts the activity allows. The suggestion here is that young children may not understand as much of the activity as the teacher might think. A compromise is to do the calendar concisely and move on to activities that have more intrinsic interest for the audience.

Show and Tell

Show and tell often is criticized as "bring and brag" (Brewer, 1992). The thought behind show and tell seems to be that if children bring in familiar objects, they will feel comfortable showing them in a large group and so use communication skills. One problem with show and tell is that it is materialistic. Children expect one another to bring in interesting items. Then they judge each child on the basis of the items shown (Brewer, 1992). A second problem is that the child may not have a lot to say about the item. The teacher then has to become an interviewer, and the rest of the group may tune out. Problems of attentiveness are likely to increase if all in the group share (Saifer, 1992) and after a few months of following the same routine (McAfee, 1986).

Teachers handle problems with show and tell in various ways. Most directly, some teachers have ended the practice. They spark discussions in the circle time instead that lead to a fuller sharing of thoughts and feelings. Open-ended questions that children can personally relate to are a superior medium for developing communications skills. The kinds of questions mentioned under the calendar and weather heading are examples. A few others are:

- Who can tell us about a time when you went swimming?
- Who can share about when you were in a snowball fight?
- Who knows about an interesting pet that someone owns?

Such questions lead well into themes and whole language activities that may follow the large group. They arouse interest and focus on *ideas* rather than *things*.

For teachers who do not wish to end show and tell altogether, Saifer (1990) provides ideas for dealing with "bored children during show and tell." Saifer's ideas include:

- Do show and tell in small groups (such as during center time, for those who are interested);
- Schedule show and tell on a rotating basis with only some children sharing each day;
- Directly encourage other children to ask questions; stand behind the child to direct the group's attention;
- "Have children share family experiences, a picture they made, or what they did earlier in the day at school. Sharing themselves rather than things, helps children who have no item to share; develops the children's ability to review; and makes for more personal, meaningful sharing" (Saifer, 1990, p. 22).

Using Stories with Children

The traditional method of delivering stories is the large group. When doing stories in a large group, to preserve lines of sight, teachers frequently sit on low chairs. Children sit on rug samples or other markers. This reduces crowding and the frequent complaint that "I can't see." The technique is efficient, but results in a separation between adult and children. An alternative in story delivery is the small group. With children on the adult's lap or all lying on stomachs around a book, an important closeness results, which the Mc-Crackens term the lap technique (McCracken & McCracken, 1987). Ideally, the lap technique begins early in the child's life at home. To encourage an appreciation of books and reading, the lap technique is an important method to use, but difficult to accomplish in the large group.

Of course, a role remains for stories in large group settings (McCracken & McCracken, 1987). Perhaps it is helpful to think of two different purposes for using stories in large groups: first is to entertain and encourage appreciation, second is to inform and encourage personal expression. By focusing on the particular intention of the story experience, the teacher can reduce mistaken behavior.

Reading for Entertainment. Teachers who wish to entertain and encourage appreciation want to reduce disruptions. The story experience is meant to be relaxing. Usual times when the teacher reads to foster enjoyment are after vigorous activity, for a calming effect; and to set a relaxed mood for an activity to come, such as lunch, nap, or going home. Adults can use various methods to encourage a relaxing setting. Three suggestions are these:

1. Use giant picture books. Then all can see the important details. Or, use filmstrips, but not necessarily with the sound cassette. Provide the narration yourself to personalize the story experience.
2. Allow children to read their own books while you read. Many children can attend to two things at once, and this will help to keep them occupied. The practice sounds unorthodox but is in line with the outcome of appreciation for reading and books. In one classroom the individual readers stay with their own books until the teacher gets to a "good part." Then they look up and follow the teacher's story.
3. Occasionally tell stories rather than read them. This takes fortitude the first few times, but children adjust quickly to this "radio way of learning." Similarly, some stories have no illustrations; ask children to close their eyes and see the pictures in their minds. Having children spread out and lie down adds to the success of this experience—and makes the technique useful especially at rest time.

Reading to Encourage Personal Expression. Teachers also use stories to inform and encourage personal expression. For this purpose, some interaction between children and the adult is expected. The teacher uses an *inclusive technique*, which means that if a child makes a comment that doesn't seem to relate, the teacher includes it in the discussion and then gently steers the discussion back to the book.

Often teachers use the informing/expression function as a lead-in for related expressive activity such as creative drama, journaling, story pictures, or just a free-flowing discussion. Effective follow-up depends upon the teacher evoking a topic to which the children can relate. Often the most effective follow-up is in small groups.

Anecdote: After a snow fall, a kindergarten teacher was reading about Peter in the classic, *A Snowy Day*, when Clarise raised her hand: "Teacher, me and Cleo went sliding and she got snow down her pants!" (General laughter.)

Teacher: "That must have been cold. What did she do?"
Clarise: "She went inside but Paul and me kept sliding. It was fun."

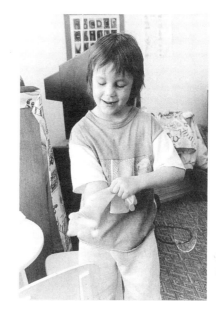

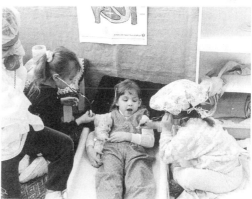

Figure 6–5 Stimulated by a teacher in surgical garb, children follow-up large group discussion with hospital play, complete with doctors, patients, and even infants.

Teacher: "Paul and you stayed outside so you could keep having fun. Thanks for sharing, Clarise, did anyone else go sliding last weekend?"

After several children shared, the teacher commented, "You had lots of good times sliding and skiing. Now let's see what's going to happen to Peter."

At the end of the book, the teacher announced: "It sounds as if you like to do lots of fun things in the snow. Right now, when I tell you to, I would like each table group to take their seats. Use the materials that are laid out and make story pictures of your favorite thing to do when it snows." She dismissed the class by table groups, and each group chatted about snow adventures as they made their story pictures.

When they use stories to spark follow-up small group or independent activity, teachers encourage active learning and a full appreciation by the child of the literature they have shared.

Large Group Instruction

Teaching in large groups seems normal because it is the way most teachers themselves were educated, kindergarten (or first grade) through college. In traditional large group instruction, the teacher transmits information and then solicits repetition or application of the information from "volunteers" who "ensure" group understanding.

The basic criticism of this "didactic method" is that children are "over taught and under practiced" (McCracken & McCracken, 1987). They absorb the information but don't have the opportunity to construct their own knowledge from it. They are not fully able to "own" the learning, make sense of it, value it. Caught in an artifically passive conception of what a learner is, children may "tune out" or feel confused, ill at ease, sometimes embarrassed, at times hostile. With some children, chronic mistaken behavior results.

Contrasted with the didactic instructional approach, the DAP position is that learning is **interactive**. The teacher provides opportunities for the child to integrate learning through expression in creative endeavor—art, music, play, creative drama, construction, and discussion (Bredekamp, 1987). Large groups work well for orienting children to an interactive learning experience (establishing an **anticipatory set**). The child then moves to a follow-up activity, either alone or in a small group. Using large groups to establish an anticipatory set *is* developmentally appropriate.

Whenever a large group is to be the sole vehicle for instruction, however, the teacher needs to proceed with caution (Bredekamp, 1987; McAfee, 1986). Successful large group experiences tend to include a series of short activities—a concise presentation or demonstration, a brief story, a movement activity or

Figure 6–6 Large groups work well to orient children to interactive experiences on an individual basis or in small follow-up groups.

song, class business—each of which is less than five minutes. A quick pace to the large group, followed by a crisp transition, reduces the amount of passivity. To reiterate an earlier statement, for large groups to be a part of an interactive learning program, they should be friendly, participatory, relevant to children's experiences, and concise.

MANAGING TRANSITIONS

Transitions, changes from one activity to the next, can be disruptive occasions (Saifer, 1990). One classic transition "dilemma" occurs between individual activity and large group. A conventional approach is to get most of the children into the circle and then call out, "We're waiting for Ryan and Sonya." Such an approach embarrasses the targeted children and may make others in the circle wonder who is going to get "nagged" next.

Instead, the professional teacher will use alternative strategies that get children to the group on time but do not undercut self-esteem. Here are some basic strategies worth trying. Some are more appropriate for preprimary class-rooms; others pertain throughout the age range.

1. Give a notice five minutes before the transition. Some children—like adults—get so involved that they may need an additional "two minute" notice.
2. Model enthusiasm for the clean-up process. Make the process a game with comments like, "I need some strong kids over here who can carry lots of blocks. Who is strong enough?" Participate in the clean-up.
3. "Give generous encouragement to the children who are conscientious about cleaning up" (Saifer, 1990, p. 32). Ignore or use matter-of-fact comments to children who are slow in making the transition. Avoid labels like "lazy," singling out, and prolonged debates.
4. Sing a clean-up song with the children. Make up words and put them to a familiar tune. Children capture moods more easily than adults. Songs, or even popular pieces of recorded music, both identify the transition and get children into the mood.
5. Make up and sing a song in the large group naming children who are there. (To your own tune:)

   We're happy to see you, see you, see you.
   We're happy to see you, Cathy, at circle time today.

Be sure to include all of the children, including the late-comers when they arrive so that no one feels left out. The song is likely both to speed up the transition and serve as a **buffer activity**, using time

Figure 6–7 Recognize that even after a five minute notice, children sometimes will need a bit longer to finish.

while waiting. (One of the fringe benefits of teaching young children is they don't care if you can't carry a tune, just if you don't sing.)

6. With enthusiasm start the large group before all have arrived. The magnetism of an exciting large group will attract the rest of the children. No comment about anyone who is late is needed.

Waiting. A primary consideration in managing transitions is the reduction of time children spend **waiting**. Young children live totally in the here and now (Elkind, 1976). Although most do it better as they get older, children under seven or eight years don't wait well. Strategies the teacher uses to cut down on waiting times prevent many problems.

Anecdote: A student teacher was in charge of "art and writing time" in a kindergarten class. Her projects were all open-ended and creative (and so developmentally appropriate). She ran into problems, though, with the wait time before the children could do the projects. First, she had the children sit at the tables while she discussed the project with them. Then she handed out the materials to each table. The problem was all of the children grabbed for the materials right away, and this method ended in mini-chaos.

Her next attempt was to have the materials all out on the tables when the children came in from recess. This time they began using the materials before she could introduce the project, so the theme was lost.

Finally, she used a two-step approach. She set out the materials on the tables but had the children sit at the large group circle when they came in. She discussed the project with them at the circle. Then she dismissed them to their tables a few at a time by the color of clothing they wore: "All wearing purple or yellow may get up and slowly walk to their tables." The student teacher did not interrupt the flow by challenging children who had interesting interpretations of purple or yellow; the purpose was to get them to the tables efficiently without a stampede or hurt feelings.

Waiting and young children don't mix. Strategies for avoiding the "dead time" in between activities are worth developing and implementing.

Buffer Activities. Buffer activities keep children occupied during a transition. A song in a large group before everyone arrives is an example. At the primary level, a teacher often has alternative activities for children who finish first. Such activities range from "working quietly at your desk" to use of selected learning centers. Although these types of buffer activities are useful, they should not be so attractive that they encourage hurried completion of the

main lesson. Such a pattern discourages thorough work habits and discrimi-
nates against children who work slowly or find the task difficult. Activities
used as buffers should be available at another time of day as well for all to
enjoy. With thought, the teacher can use buffer activities to reduce significant
amounts of mistaken behavior:

Anecdote: Children at a Head Start center were having problems each day
just before lunch. The schedule called for them to come in from
outdoor play, line up to use the restroom and wash hands. During
this time, the lead teacher prepared the tables for lunch and the
assistant teacher monitored the lines. Waiting in line with nothing
to do was difficult for many of the children. Pushing and fights
were becoming more frequent.

The teaching team reviewed the situation and tried a new
arrangement. The teacher brought in a few children early. They
washed their hands first and helped the teacher set the tables and
bring in the food on carts. The rest of the children sat at the
reading center near the restroom and sink where they looked at
books together. During this buffer, the assistant teacher had small
clusters of children use the facilities and rotate back to their books
until lunch. The waiting in line was eliminated and with it the
mistaken behavior.

A first step in creating a successful buffer activity is awareness that
mistaken behavior can be situationally caused, such as by prolonging the time
that children are waiting. With this awareness, the second step follows:
adapting the program to better accommodate the children's development.

Lines. The use of lines pose transition perils at whatever age level. In many
preschools, formal lines are seldom used. Out-of-building excursions are safest
when the ratio of adults to children is about 1:4 and lines are not needed. This
ratio is so important, especially on busy streets, that staff should do their
utmost to recruit additional volunteers for these occasions. An unsafe alternative is the old-time use of ropes with loops that each child holds. Besides the
"chain gang" appearance, anyone who has seen one child stumble and all lose
their balance knows this is one piece of equipment that should be retired.

Preschools located in public school buildings sometimes experience difficulty
with movement of the group through halls. The concept of two-by-two lines is
not a natural one for three- and four-year-olds. School administrators should
not expect the same "hall expertise" of preschoolers that they expect of third
graders. Discussions with administrators about their expectations are
important even before preschools locate in school buildings.

At the elementary school level, teachers learn quickly that more is needed
than simply stating, "Everyone line up at the door." Instead, teachers need

Figure 6–8 A video of a previous class event keeps these guys entertained until the rest of the class is ready for large group.

"creative alternatives," orderly methods for lining up, all of which take under a minute. The methods should *not* violate the principle of unconditional positive regard—"Millie, you've been quiet; you can line up first today." This practice results in hurt feelings among the others who have been quiet and weren't selected. "Chance-based" criteria, such as "Everyone whose first name begins with a C or K may quietly line up," are more appropriate. Chance-based criteria reduce the appearance of favoritism from the line-up procedure and get the job done efficiently.

A common point of contention is who will be the "leader" (and sometimes "trailer") when lines form. Some programs have a Very Important Kid or Star of the Week who leads the lines for a designated period. Another method is to have a large chart with each child's name. A marker, moved each day, indicates who will lead. (Perhaps the child who led the previous day could be the "caboose".) Other markers could be placed on the chart to identify other "classroom helpers." This practice makes selection systematic and visible and eliminates "I was first!" "No, it's my turn!" controversies.

Here are two other suggestions about line procedures, one perhaps controversial, the other, "common sense." In agreement with the ideas of anti-bias curriculum (Derman-Sparks, 1989), the author recommends lines that do not pair girls and boys. This practice needlessly exaggerates differences between the sexes in an era when cross-gender cooperation needs to be encouraged. Healthy cross-gender interactions become more difficult in programs that institutionalize gender differences (Derman-Sparks, 1986).

Instead, the teacher should work to create an atmosphere in which gender is accepted as just another element in who each child is. As *Anti-Bias Curriculum* points out, teachers have more say about reducing sexism in the classroom environment than they might think (Derman-Sparks, 1986). (See further chapter ten, "Liberation Teaching.") Comfortable cross-gender relations are in keeping with a guidance approach and should be reflected in line-up procedures as well as all other parts of the program.

The common-sense suggestion is in relation to helping children wait and move in lines cooperatively. Whenever a teacher can make such time an enjoyable experience, s/he is showing skill at preventing mistaken behavior. Having finger plays and songs ready for when children in line must wait is sound preventive practice. Simple songs that use the children's names pass the time quickly.

Similarly, when children walk in lines, stimulating their imaginations can work wonders.

Anecdote: A particular kindergarten teacher used the children's imaginations to move her class efficiently. On one day she whispered: "Today, we are the elephant mommies and daddies. We need to tiptoe quietly so we don't wake up the sleeping baby elephants. Let's very quietly tiptoe down the hall." When the principal came out of his office to compliment the class, one of the children told him, "Ssh, you'll wake up the babies."

PARENTS AND OTHER CLASSROOM VOLUNTEERS

A premise of the chapter is that the shift away from large groups toward small group and individual activities promotes a developmentally appropriate program. Moving to the **multi-dimensional** classroom, though, does pose some new challenges for the teacher. In the multi-dimensional classroom, the teacher is a manager of the daily program as well as lead teacher. The **teaching team** concept, discussed in chapter four, is not an absolute requirement for the multi-dimensional classroom, but it does make the teacher's tasks easier.

The teacher has two sources of adults to comprise the teaching team, paid staff and volunteers. In the preschool classroom, typical paid staff members are assistant teachers and aides. In the elementary classroom paid staff are aides, special education personnel, team teaching partners, and specialists. Volunteers in either setting are likely to be "foster grandparents" (from federal or state-sponsored programs for retired citizens), college students, older students from the school system, private citizens, and parents.

Depending on the skills and comfort level of the teaching team members, staff and volunteers perform a variety of functions in the classroom. The goal

Figure 6–9 Classroom volunteers often include foster grandparents, college interns, students from older grades, and parents.

of the teacher is to have volunteers working with individual children, reading stories, leading small groups, being in charge of centers, and presenting on occasion to the full group. Children gain from the role modelling, encouragement, support, and teaching that caring adults can provide.

Anecdote: In a kindergarten with an effective volunteer program, five parents visit the class once a week at center time. (One attends each day.) They usually help with the same center each week, where an index card provides them with instructions. Occasionally, Mona (the teacher) will ask a parent to go to a different center or help with a particular project, like making cookies with small groups. Several other parents have come to share a hobby, interest, or item of family heritage with the class. Many parents have come in on their child's birthday and on monthly class field trips. Parents know they are welcome, and some have brought younger brothers or sisters when they have visited.

Mona is an exception in her school, and it has taken a few years for her to develop the program. Some parents each year have chosen not to participate. Not all teachers approve, though more are including parents than in prior years. It has taken extra work, but Mona believes firmly that involving parents in the classroom is worthwhile.

Working with Parents in the Classroom

A first step in working with parents is to help them feel welcome. At whatever point a parent enters, s/he should be greeted by the teacher and usually introduced to the children. Taking time to briefly orient the parent is important. A "parent's nook," though not always possible in the classroom, provides a great home base. A bulletin board, check-out library, pamphlets and fliers, a collection of newsletters, and a place the parent can leave belongings all might be included. One teacher set up a nook behind a tall book stand in the reading center. When not used by the teacher at story time, a rocking chair was kept in the "nook."

In addition to parent helpers with parties and field trips, parents who share knowledge or skills with a class are important "special events" volunteers. One teacher asked three families per month to share a favorite dish, the vocation of a family member, a family interest (including the interest of an older brother or sister), and/or a bit of family heritage. The social studies program for the year was taken care of on this basis. Parents working in nontraditional gender roles are a particularly important resource. A male nurse, a woman firefighter or police officer, an in-home working dad all raise children's consciousness levels and horizons.

Figure 6–10 The busyness of developmentally appropriate classrooms draws parents into activities.

On the first visits for parents who may become regulars, the teacher encourages the parent to walk around, interact, and observe, but not take on undue responsibility (Gestwicki, 1992). The teacher is aware that the busyness of the developmentally appropriate classrooms will draw the parent in. Sitting and talking with a group as they work, reading a book to children, and helping a child get a coat on closely resemble parenting tasks—tasks that parents generally find nonthreatening in a home or classroom.

Some children feel strong emotions when parents enter the room or leave for the day. Teachers often cite this drawback for not encouraging parent involvement (Gestwiki, 1992). The teacher addresses this possibility in discussions and handouts, reassuring the parent that the teacher will handle any problems, as the one in charge (Gestwicki, 1992). Allowing the child to sit with the parent shows sensitivity to the child's feelings. Reassurance and diversion to activities are standard at the time of separation. As children adjust to frequent visitations by parents, their own included, need for their parents' undivided attention subsides.

When a few parents have begun to volunteer regularly, the teacher may want to meet with them after school. "Old hands" might be invited to attend as they can share suggestions and sometimes educate about DAP as well as the teacher. (An important example is educating parents to let children do their own artwork.) If a meeting proves difficult and a parent needs extra guidance, the teacher needs to find a way to provide it (Gestwicki, 1992). The unusual circumstance of asking a parent to come in less is made the rarer by open and frequent communication.

The teacher will know when a volunteer is a true "regular" when ongoing communication becomes unnecessary. Teachers then can begin to rely on the skills of the volunteer by assigning a center and providing a "work card," as Mona did in the anecdote. Gestwicki sums up the process of helping parents become productive in the classroom by stating:

> As teachers invite parents to participate in classroom learning activities, they need to concentrate on their skills for working with adults. Teachers need to be able to relax and enjoy the contribution of others to their classrooms and not feel threatened by any attention transferred from themselves to a visiting adult. It is important to remember that as more specific information is given to parents, parents will feel more comfortable knowing what is expected of them (p. 259).

The most important reason for involving parents in the classroom, of course, is that it encourages them to be more active in their children's education

Figure 6–11 The most important reason for involving parents is that it encourages them to become more active in their children's education.

(Gestwicki, 1992). Each year as a result of parent involvement, families become more interested in their children's success at school—and the children respond (Greenberg, 1989). This reason is enough, but annually as well some parents become interested in teaching careers themselves, as a result of a successful volunteering experience.

> Parents like feeling that they're making a valuable contribution to a classroom. Many parents will try to find the time for a visit if they feel truly needed and wanted. A note of appreciation from the teacher and children afterwards, pictures of the event displayed on a bulletin board, a mention of the event as a classroom highlight in the next newsletter—all these convey to parents that their time was well spent (Gestwicki, 1992, p. 260).

SUMMARY

How does the teacher balance reliability and novelty in the daily program?

Programs that lack consistency are unpredictable and cause anxiety for children. Programs that never change or incorporate the teachable moment result in tedium. The schedule provides a base line of predictability for the children about the program. When unscheduled events enable positive results for children, they add to the everyday program. The teacher maintains the balance between predictability and novelty by reading children's feelings and discussing reasons for changes with them. Developmentally appropriate schedules for prekindergarten, kindergarten, and the primary grades provide reliability, but still allow for novelty.

What is the appropriate mix of active and quiet times?

In the developmentally appropriate classroom, much of the daily program is at a **busy** level with occasional excursions into the **boisterous** and the **bucolic**. Teachers sometimes stigmatize a child who does not fit the sedentary activity level of their classrooms. Rather than suppress the innate activeness of the young, teachers do better to empower children through programs that are more active and allow for a better developmental match.

Though "busy" sets the tone for the classroom, children and teachers also need periods of rest and relaxation. Relaxation activities and a thoughtful, problem-solving approach to rest times rejuvenate spirits in children and adults alike.

Three ideas boost the benefits of active play for children and the program. First, the teacher needs to supplement formal active play times with opportunities for boisterous activity during other periods of the day, such as choice-time and music. Second, throughout the age span movement-to-music during large group activities refreshes children and renews their ability to concentrate. Third, effective boisterous activities avoid formal rules, competition, and taking turns. Children run for the sake of running; they do not need, or benefit from, the incentive of winning. Further, they can only run and be active when they are not waiting for a turn.

What part do large group activities play in the developmentally appropriate program?

A problem with overreliance on large groups is that they easily exceed children's developmental levels and attention spans. For this reason, large groups should be used selectively and not as a matter of institutional routine. Teachers who want to use large groups effectively do well to review traditional large group practices: taking attendance, calendar and the weather, show and tell, reading, and large group instruction. A developmentally appropriate use of large groups is to establish an **anticipatory set** for interactive follow-up activities done either independently or in small groups. For large groups to be a part of an interactive learning program, they should be friendly, participatory, relevant to children's experiences, and concise.

How does managing transitions reduce mistaken behavior?

Transitions, changes from one activity to the next, can be disruptive occasions. The professional teacher develops and implements strategies for transitions that get the job done, but do not undercut self-esteem. A primary consideration in managing transitions is the reduction of time children spend waiting. One strategy to reduce the "dead time" during waits is through buffer

Figure 6–12 Movement activities fit the criteria for developmentally appropriate large group experiences.

activities. When lines prove necessary, teachers need to plan strategies for lining up and waiting in lines that support each member of the group and capture children's imaginations.

How can the teacher make use of parents and other classroom volunteers?

In the **multi-dimensional classroom**, the teacher is a manager of the daily program as well as lead teacher. The use of other staff and volunteers, as a **teaching team**, contributes to the success of the program. Depending on the skills and comfort level of the teaching team members, staff and volunteers perform a variety of functions in the classroom. A first step in working with parents in the classroom is to help them feel welcome. The teacher helps the volunteer to find tasks s/he is comfortable with, such as fastening coats, that a parent might do at home.

Leadership by the teacher at "trouble points" such as separations adds to the parent's comfort about volunteering. The teacher maintains ongoing communication with the parent, but recognizes when the parent has become a regular and needs less support. The most important reason for involving parents in the classroom is that the experience encourages them to become more active in their child's education. The parent stands to benefit in other ways as well. The teacher who involves parents and other adults in the classroom has an added role to perform and additonal tasks to do. Because the entire program stands to gain, the extra effort is worthwhile.

FOLLOW-UP ACTIVITIES

Follow-up activities allow the student to interrelate material from the text with "real life" situations. The "observations" imply access to practicum experiences, the "interviews" access to teachers. When communicating about the activities, students need to respect the privacy of all participants in the observation or interview, as an important professional courtesy.

1. **How does the teacher balance reliability and novelty in the daily program?**
   a. Observe an instance of the "teachable moment" when a teacher deviated from the schedule to provide the children with a special experience. How did the teacher manage the change of routine? What did you notice about the children's behavior before, during, and after the special event?
   b. Talk with a teacher about the daily schedule s/he uses. What parts of the schedule is the teacher pleased with? If the teacher were going to modify the schedule, what parts would s/he change? Why?

2. **What is the appropriate mix of active and quiet times?**
   a. Observe three activities, one each at the bucolic, busy, and boisterous levels. Note typical interactions in the classroom at each level. Did you notice instances of mistaken behavior? At which levels? How was the mistaken behavior similar at the various levels? How was it different?
   b. Interview a teacher about how s/he conducts a rest time, a busy activity, and a vigorous activity. What potential problems is the teacher alert to in each kind of activity? How does s/he work to prevent the difficulties from arising?

3. **What part do large group activities play in the developmentally appropriate program?**
   a. Observe children in a large group activity. If most children are positively involved, what about the large group seems to be holding their attention? If several children look distracted, or are distracting others, what do you think are the reasons?
   b. Interview a teacher about large group activities. How does the teacher plan large groups to hold children's attention? While teaching, what techniques does the teacher use to hold children's attention?

4. **How does managing transitions reduce mistaken behavior?**
   a. Observe a transition to or from a large group activity. How does the teacher prepare the children? How does the teacher manage the physical movement of the children? How does the teacher get the new activity started?
   b. Interview a teacher about how s/he handles transition situations. Ask about what s/he does when some, but not all, children have finished an old activity, and are ready to begin the new activity.

What suggestions does the teacher have for when s/he and the class have to wait for an event; when s/he and the class have to walk in a line?

5. **How can the teacher make use of parents and other classroom volunteers?**
   a. Observe a teacher working with staff or volunteers in the classroom. What is typical in how the teacher communicates with the other adults? How much of the teacher's attention is directed to working with the other adults? How much to working with the other children?
   b. Interview a teacher about having other adults in the classroom, staff and volunteers. What benefits does the teacher see in the arrangement? If there are difficulties, what are they? What would the teacher recommend about working through some difficulties that might come up?

SUGGESTED RESOURCES

Cherry, C. (1981). *Think of Something Quiet.* Belmont, CA: David S. Lake Publisher.

Derman-Sparks, L. (1989). *Anti-Bias Curriculum: Tools for Empowering Young Children.* Washington, DC: National Association for the Education of Young Children.

Honig, A.S. (1986). "Research in Review. Stress and Coping in Children." J.B. McCracken (ed.), *Reducing Stress in Young Children's Lives* (pp. 142-167). Washington, DC: National Association for the Education of Young Children.

McAfee, O.D. (1986). "Research Report. Circle Time: Getting Past 'Two Little Pumpkins.'" J.B. McCracken (ed.), *Reducing Stress in Young Children's Lives*, (pp. 99-104). Washington, DC: National Association for the Education of Young Children.

Palmer, H. (1978). *Sea Gulls.* Topanga, CA: Hap-Pal Music. (Music)

Saifer, S. (1990). *Practical Solutions to Practically Every Problem: The Early Childhood Teacher's Manual.* St. Paul, MN: Redleaf Press.

Scelsa, G. and Millang, S. (1983). *Quiet Moments with Steve and Greg.* Los Angeles, CA: Youngheart Records. (Music)

REFERENCES

Bredekamp, S. (ed.) (1987). *Developmentally Appropriate Practice in Early Childhood Programs Serving Children From Birth Through Age 8.* Washington, DC: National Association for the Education of Young Children.

Brewer, J.A. (1992). *Introduction to Early Childhood Education: Preschool Through Primary Grades*. Boston: Allyn and Bacon.

Cherry, C. (1981). *Think of Something Quiet*. Belmont, CA: David S. Lake Publisher.

Derman-Sparks, L. (1989). *Anti-Bias Curriculum: Tools for Empowering Young Children*. Washington, DC: National Association for the Education of Young Children.

Elkind, D. (1976). *Child Development and Early Childhood Education: A Piagetian Perspective*. New York: Oxford University Press.

Gestwicki, C. (1992). *Home, School, Community Relations*. Albany, NY: Delmar Publishers Inc.

Gordon, A.M. and Browne, K.W. (1989). *Beginnings and Beyond: Foundations in Early Childhood Education*. Albany, NY: Delmar Publishers, Inc.

Greenberg, P. (1989). "Parents as Partners in Young Children's Development and Education: A New American Fad? Why Does It Matter?" *Young Children, 44*(4), pp. 61-75.

Hendrick, J.A. (1992). *Whole Child*. Columbus, OH: Merrill Publishing Company.

Honig, A.S. (1986). "Research in Review. Stress and Coping in Children." J.B. McCracken (ed.), *Reducing Stress in Young Children's Lives* (pp. 142-167). Washington, DC: National Association for the Education of Young Children.

Johnson, M. (1992). *Teaching Kindergarten and First Grade Kids to Write*. Hill City, MN: Crescent Publishing, Inc.

McAfee, O.D. (1986). "Research Report. Circle Time: Getting Past 'Two Little Pumpkins.'" J.B. McCracken (ed.), *Reducing Stress in Young Children's Lives*, (pp. 99-104). Washington, DC: National Association for the Education of Young Children.

McCracken, R.A. and McCracken, M.J. (1987). *Reading Is Only the Tiger's Tale*. Winnipeg, Canada: Perguis Publishers Limited.

Palmer, H. (1978). *Sea Gulls*. Topanga, CA: Hap-Pal Music. (Music)

Saifer, S. (1990). *Practical Solutions to Practically Every Problem: The Early Childhood Teacher's Manual*. St. Paul, MN: Redleaf Press.

Scelsa, G. and Millang, S. (1983). *Quiet Moments With Steve and Greg*. Los Angeles, CA: Youngheart Records. (Music)

Wade, M.G. (1992). "Motor Skills, Play, and Child Development: An Introduction." *Early Report, 19*(2), pp. 1-2.

Walmsley, B.B., Camp, A.M., Walmsley, S.A. (1992). Teaching Kindergarten: *A Developmentally Appropriate Approach*. Portsmouth, NH: Heinemann Educational Books.

Williams, C.K. and Kamii, C. (1986). "How Do Children Learn by Handling Objects?" *Young Children, 41*(8), pp. 23-26.

7

Communicating to Prevent Problems

GUIDING QUESTIONS

As you read chapter seven, you will discover answers to the following questions:

- **How does a supportive atmosphere prevent mistaken behavior?**
- **Why are guidelines, not rules, important in a guidance approach?**
- **What are seven communication skills that assist the teacher to prevent mistaken behavior?**
- **How do class meetings help to prevent mistaken behavior?**
- **How does the teacher communicate with parents to prevent problems?**

Two causes of mistaken behavior are a mismatch between the child and the educational program and miscommunication between the child and teacher. Previous chapters in the unit discussed reducing the need for mistaken behavior by the use of developmentally appropriate programming. Chapter seven discusses how the teacher uses communication skills to prevent classroom problems. As the final chapter in the unit, chapter seven continues the premise of guidance discipline that "prevention is the best medicine." Both through the program implemented and the communication skills used, the teacher reduces the need for mistaken behavior.

Figure 7–1 Both through the program and the communication skills used, the teacher reduces the need for mistaken behavior.

A SUPPORTIVE ATMOSPHERE

It goes without saying that educators want children, as they mature, to be able to say no to vandalism, cigarettes, alcohol, drugs, and premature sex. The ability to make ethical decisions takes not just self-control, but individual strength, the product of positive self-esteem. By educating about necessary guidelines for behavior without belittling personalities, the teacher assists in the development of self-control *and* self-esteem. Children gain in these qualities to the extent that they can go to the teacher as an advisor knowing that they won't be demeaned.

Occasionally, teachers of young children find that their "graduates" come back to visit—to receive a hug, a bit of affirmation, or advice. Whenever an older child faced with a problem can talk with a present or past teacher and be helped, the preventive aspect of guidance discipline has been affirmed.

Building a supportive atmosphere in the classroom begins in the first few days. The teacher establishes leadership by acquainting the class with routines and guidelines. Children benefit from knowing what is expected of them and what the limits of acceptable behavior are. The teacher is clear, firm, and friendly in this communication effort. When they blur the distinction between "firm" and "strict," friendliness drops out of the formula and teachers work against their own best intentions. In this matter, the guidance approach differs from traditional discipline.

Conventional thought about discipline holds that the teacher is *strict* at the beginning of the school year, in order to "take charge of the classroom" (Canter, 1988). Then, with the teacher's "right to teach" established, s/he eases up in demeanor. From the guidance perspective, there are pitfalls in this position. The teacher may fixate on the assertion of will and lose faith in more positive teaching practices. Children and teacher alike get used to the teacher in the role of disciplinarian. S/he becomes a disciplinarian as part of a permanent teaching style. This unfortunate situation is epitomized by the proverbial teacher who meant only "not to smile until Christmas"—and didn't smile for forty years (Gartrell, 1987).

Even if the strict teacher gradually does "lighten up," children suffer from negative encounters in the interim. Working with limited experience to develop feelings of initiative and belonging, children who have conflicts early in their school careers may receive lasting damage to self-esteem (Greenberg, 1988). It is important to note that a "law and order" environment in the classroom affects even "model children" who do not normally "get in trouble."

Anecdote: Early in September, a parent who was also a health professional noticed her first grader seemed bothered by something. Shirley asked her daugher what was the matter. The first grader, an early reader, had seen a word on the chalkboard and asked what it was: "D-E-T-E-N-T-I-O-N." Shirley explained, and her daughter then asked several other questions:

"Where is detention?"
"Do the children get to go home?"
"Why do Jarrod and Paula go there?"
"Are they bad children?"
"Will the teacher put me there?"

Shirley commented later that she saw concern in her daugher's face that she had never seen during kindergarten. Shirley went in and talked with the teacher who said, "The children need to know that I am here to teach, and they are here to learn. I will not let individual children keep this from happening."

Shirley wondered about a classroom where the first words children learned to read were the names of friends being punished. She monitored her daughter's feelings closely and talked with the teacher several more times that year. The following spring she worked with the principal to place her daughter with a second grade teacher whom Shirley knew to be more positive.

Firm and Friendly

No matter how anxious a teacher is about beginning the year, children are more anxious. In the first days, the teacher starts a course for children's education that makes it either a welcome event, or an event arousing ambivalence and negative feelings.

Anecdote: During the first week of kindergarten, two teachers responded to a similar situation differently. Trying to acquaint their groups with desired routines, each teacher instructed children to put away the materials they were using and come to the circle for large group.

Teacher one reminded Juan, who was building a road, to put away the blocks; she then got the group in a circle. She was set to begin when she noticed that Juan was still quietly building. From her place at the head of the group, the teacher said loudly, "Get over here, young man. In this classroom, children listen to the teacher." After waiting for Juan to join the group, she explained the daily schedule to the children.

When *teacher two* was about to begin the large group, she noticed that Darnell—to whom she had just spoken—was still building with Legos. The teacher walked to Darnell, smiled, and held out her hand to him. She said quietly, "You can finish your building after circle time. We need you to join us now." Back in the large group, she introduced the children to the daily schedule.

The teacher in room two was showing leadership no less than the teacher in room one. She reacted differently, though, to "the old war plan" that the teacher must "be tough from the beginning." Teacher two recognized that children in the first days of school can become overloaded and that they readily identify with materials that seem "safe." Teacher two did not equivocate with a guideline for her classroom, but took a guidance approach by educating children to the guideline. She used guidance measures so that Darnell (and the rest of the class) would not develop doubts about themselves, but would learn classroom routines.

GUIDELINES, NOT RULES

The writings of Glasser (1977), Canter (1976), and more recently Curwin and Mendler (1988) emphasize the importance of establishing expectations with children. Standards for behavior, understood by all, are important in any education setting. Insufficient attention has been given, however, to differences between rules and *guidelines*. In making the case for guidelines as a part of the guidance approach, this section looks anew at the conventional use of rules.

Figure 7–2 In the first days of school, children identify with materials that are familar and seem safe.

Rules tend to be stated in negative terms: "No running in the classroom"; "No gum chewing in school." Frequently, punishments are predetermined for the transgression of a rule:

- No talking out of turn or your name goes on the board;
- No unfriendly words or you sit in the time-out chair;
- No homework completed or you stay after school.

The conventional thinking about rules with known consequences is that they convey clear conditions of citizenship and teach children about governance by law in adult society (Dreikurs & Cassel, 1972). There are two difficulties with this view.

First, rules with defined consequences institutionalize the use of punishment in the education system. The negative phrasing of rules conveys that teachers expect children to break them. Spelled out consequences underscore this perception. Reason, cooperation, and caring become secondary when educators enforce preset standards that may or may not fit the complexities of actual situations. The teacher who reacts with an automatic response often shows less than full understanding of the event. S/he is then functioning as a technician. If teachers choose "to make an exception" and not enforce a predetermined punishment, their leadership comes into question.

A second problem lies in the effects of punishment itself. Punishment tends to reduce human interaction from the educational to the moralistic. The factor of developmental egocentrism in young children makes this issue critical. Developmental egocentrism means the younger the age, the less the child understands about social expectations (Elkind, 1976). Because of lack of experience and development, young children have difficulty understanding that when they are punished for breaking a rule, the punishment is the result of their *actions*. They tend instead to internalize the shame associated with the punishment and to feel that they are being punished because they are "bad children." Diminished self-esteem results (Clewett, 1988; Greenberg, 1988). The child has been influenced away from feelings of initiative, belonging and industry, and toward shame and self doubt. (Elkind, 1987).

Logical Consequences

With his writings, Dreikurs raised discipline practice to a level above the reliance on punishment (Dreikurs, 1968; Dreikurs & Cassel, 1972). Dreikurs suggested that misbehavior has **logical consequences**, responses taken by adults that "fit" a child's mistaken act. Logical consequences differ from punishment because the redress imposed is a logical extension of the misbehavior itself. For example, if a preschooler marks on a table, s/he cleans it off. If a second grader neglects doing homework, s/he completes it before going out at recess. (This consequence contrasts with the punishment of having to report to detention whether the child finished the assignment during the day or not.)

The use of logical consequences fits a guidance approach if two conditions are met: (*a*) the consequence is logical to the child as well as the adult; and (*b*) the consequence is *not* set out beforehand.

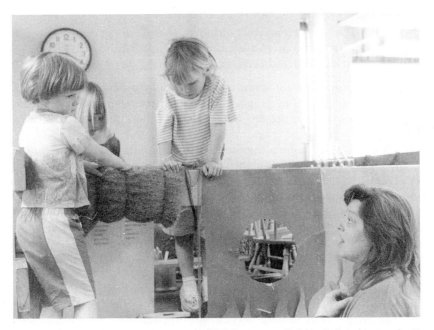

Figure 7–3 A logical consequence of climbing on a divider is to choose between staying on the floor in the same area or moving to the "real climber".

In reference to the first condition, note the difference between these statements:

> "You get a sponge and wipe that mark off the table right now."

> "It's OK, your marker just went off the paper. Let's get a sponge and clean it off."

An adult may have thought the first statement was a "logical consequence," but it probably sounded like punishment to the child.

In reference to the second condition, a primary grade child may have legitimate reasons for not completing homework, such as baby-sitting for a sibling during a family emergency. In a guidance approach a teacher uses professional judgment to evaluate an event before deciding upon a logical consequence. The teacher acting as a professional recognizes that every situation is different.

In a foremost current interpretation of Dreikurs' theories, Linda Albert (1989) handles very carefully the use of logical consequences. The method is included more as a last resort than the "first line of defense," as it was treated in the past (Charles, 1989). Dreikurs maintained that his approach to discipline was a democratic one. In the new interpretation of his work, emphasis is placed on communication *before* problems arise—an effective use of democratic leadership. Albert's work is in line with the guidance approach and is titled well: *Cooperative Discipline: How to Manage Your Classroom and Promote Self-Esteem* (1989).

Using Guidelines

Standards are needed in the classroom in order to increase understanding about the requirements of social living. Like rules, guidelines do this. Unlike rules, guidelines sustain the supportive atmosphere of the guidance approach.

Guidelines tell what productive behavior is, not admonish against mistaken behavior. As a method within the guidance approach, guidelines teach what productive behavior is. As such they lend a supportive tone to the classroom environment. Contrast the following guidelines with conventional classroom rules that the reader may be familiar with:

- Use words to solve problems;
- Friendly touches only;
- Sometimes we need to stop, look, and listen;
- We walk inside except at special times;
- We all help to take care of *our* room;
- We appreciate each other, ourselves too;
- It is OK to make mistakes—just try to learn from them.

Teachers at various levels work with guidelines in different ways. In fact, the National Association for the Education of Young Children document on DAP (Bredekamp, 1987) recommends that standards not be used formally with children under four:

Adults know that three-year-olds do not usually understand or remember the rules. Guidance reasons that are specific to a real situation and that are demonstrated repeatedly are more likely to impress young children (p. 40).

Teachers of three-year-olds keep guidelines in mind ("guidance reasons") as reference points to make communication consistent across situations. Though not on a formal basis, teachers of threes model and reinforce guidelines in their work. "Use words, not biting" is an example.

A difference in the use of guidelines in preschool, kindergarten, and primary grades is the number of guidelines they use. Teachers often comment that there should not be too many rules. This recommendation applies as well for guidelines. The exact number of guidelines depends on the teacher and the group, but usual practice is 2–3 guidelines in pre-kindergarten classes; 3–4 in kindergarten; and 4–6 in the primary grades. These figures are arbitrary, however. Pat Sanford, the kindergarten teacher mentioned in chapter six, uses three: "Be kind," "Be safe," and "Be smart."

Commonly, teachers who use guidelines meet with children at the beginning of the year to establish the list. Because they have a clearer idea about guidelines than the class, an honest approach is for teachers to present their list for discussion. Even if the class does not actually formulate them, children develop ownership of guidelines by discussing them—why they are important; why we might not always remember to use them; what procedure is followed when a mistake is made.

In a helpful passage from *Teacher and Child* (1972) Ginott suggests the spirit in which guidelines should be used. He points out that the major obstacle to learning is fear of failure and humiliation. He states:

> To motivate learning, one teacher encouraged his class to discuss the meaning of failure in their lives. The children talked about their fear of failure and the pain of humiliation. As a result of this discussion, the children and the teacher put together a set of motivating mottos to guide life and learning in the classroom. The list was displayed prominently on the front wall.
>
> 1. In this class it is permissible to make mistakes.
> 2. An error is not a terror.
> 3. Goofs are lessons.
> 4. You may err, but don't embrace your error. Don't dwell on it, and don't excuse it.
> 5. Mistakes are for correcting.
> 6. Value your correction, not your error.
> 7. Don't let failure go to your head (pp. 187-188).

While the wording suggests an older grade level, "motivating mottos" certainly fits with the use of guidelines as a part of guidance discipline.

Class meetings are often used to introduce and reinforce guidelines. But, do class meetings work with younger children? Hendrick (1992) discusses "teaching the principles of democracy in the early years" (p. 51). She comments that one part of the process is "learning to trust the group" (p. 52). Hendrick states: "Even four-year-olds can participate successfully in making simple group decisions that solve social problems" (p. 52). She goes on to say:

> Together, for example, they might plan ways to stop children from running through the room. They might also discuss which special outside activity to do—would they rather take a snack and ride their trikes around the block or get out the wading pool for a swim? As children move on to kindergarten and first grade, opportunities of greater magnitude arise (pp. 52-53).

Class meetings to discuss guidelines, and problems in relation to them, is a common occurrence in a guidance classroom, even in the preschool.

A first reason for using guidelines is that they supportively educate children to standards of behavior. *A second reason is that guidelines allow teachers a range of choices and so empower them to be professionals.* Rules with set punishments force teachers to act as technicians. They do not encourage teachers to be professionals who can use their store of experience to help children settle problems wisely. In contrast to rules, guidelines create neither hierarchies of authority that young children feel compelled to challenge nor lines of morality that children feel pressed to cross. Guidelines contribute to an environment where mistaken behavior is seen as the result of a problem that a child needs help to solve. Note the difference in the teachers' roles in the following anecdotes:

Anecdote: (Teacher working with rules.) At recess on a rainy day, second graders Clarence and Rubey first argued, then fought over a "friendship bracelet." Mrs. Cleary came into the room, separated the children, and declared, "You know the rule in here about fighting. You both will go to the principal's office."

The principal asked Mrs. Cleary what the punishment was for fighting. Mrs. Cleary explained it was detention and sitting out the class's next popcorn party. When the two children returned, they were made fun of by others in the class. The two looked miserable as they sat in detention. Rubey did not attend school the next day when the class party was scheduled.

Anecdote: (Teacher working with guidelines.) At recess on a rainy day, a second grade teacher, Mrs. Drewry, entered her room to find two children fighting. She separated the children and had them each cool down at their desks. She then asked Cosby and Marla to "a private meeting." In turn, each spoke. Marla said she brought some cookies to eat at recess and Cosby tried to take them. Cosby said he didn't either. The teacher said she wanted to hear how they would keep from fighting next time. Marla told Cosby he should bring his own stuff to eat. Cosby said his mom wouldn't let him.

The teacher paused and said to Cosby: "Our guideline says 'snacks are OK at recess.' If you want Marla to share, you need to ask with words, but Marla doesn't have to. Cosby, I've got an idea; how about if you save an apple or roll from breakfast in the lunch room. Then, you'd have something to eat at recess." Cosby shrugged and Marla looked relieved. The teacher ended the meeting by stating firmly, "Remember, in this class we use words to solve problems." Mrs. Drewry made a mental note to talk with the kitchen staff the next morning.

When young children have disputes, they gain if they are helped to talk through the difficulty. To the complaint that the teacher should not be a "referee," the response is that the adult is teaching **conflict resolution skills**, the ability to solve problems with words. Perhaps there is no more important life skill as we approach the twenty-first century.

COMMUNICATION SKILLS

Seven communication skills follow. Each is helpful in creating and maintaining a supportive classroom atmosphere. The first, the use of **encouragement**, was

Figure 7–4 When young children have disputes, they gain if they are helped to talk through the difficulty.

introduced in chapter three. The other six relate to **encouragement** and apply to situations with an individual child, the entire class, or both. They are: **listening to life experiences, contact talk, the compliment sandwich, humor, touch, and discussing inclusively**.

Encouragement, More than Praise

A basic difference between encouragement and praise is that encouragement focuses on the efforts of the child; praise highlights the achievements (Hitz & Driscoll, 1988). With the process-orientation young children bring to activities, encouragement is important if only for this reason. As developed in chapter three, however, encouragement is preferable to praise for other reasons as well.

A typical example of praise is, "Children, see what a good worker Joshua is." Writers such as Dreikurs (1972), Ginott (1972), and Hitz & Driscoll (1988) have several problems with comments like this:

1. The statement is made more to elicit conformity from the group than to recognize the individual child.
2. Others in the group who were working as hard as Joshua feel slighted that they were not praised.
3. Class members feel resentment toward Joshua for being praised.
4. All in the class are reinforced toward dependency on the teacher for evaluation of their efforts, rather than being taught to evaluate their efforts for themselves.
5. The class is uneasy about whom the teacher will single out next and what s/he will say.
6. Joshua experiences mixed emotions: pride at being praised, embarrassment at being publicly recognized, worry about how others will react, uncertainty about exactly what he did that was "right," and concern about what the teacher will say to him next time.

Encouragement happens in two primary ways, publicly directed to the entire group, privately directed to the individual. A teacher says to her kindergarten class, "You are working very hard on your journals today. Many special story pictures are being made. I am proud of you all." Strengths in group-focused encouragement are:

1. The group has received clear feedback and knows their efforts are being recognized.
2. The teacher has not made a value judgment about "the class personality," but has given a **self-report**: She has described the event being recognized and given an **I message** or personal response to it.
3. No children feel the ambivalence of being singled out.
4. The teacher has avoided institutionalizing "winners" and "losers," in-groups and out-groups. S/he has eliminated the negative social dynamic of differential treatment.

5. The group feels a positive group spirit, a sense that "we are in this together and we are succeeding."
6. While being supportive of their work, the teacher has left room for children to evaluate their efforts for themselves (Ginott, 1972). S/he is empowering a sense of competence in the members of the class.

Many of the same benefits apply to encouragement given personally to an individual child. Note this teacher's response to Julia when the four-year-old mentions she is building a castle: "You *are* building a castle, Julia. There are towers and walls and windows and doors. I am impressed."

In all likelihood from this one comment, Julia knows what it is in her work that the teacher has noticed. Because the comment was in private, Julia sees that encouragement really was meant for her. Julia was allowed to draw her own conclusions about her building ability, without undue expectations on her for the next time. Julia feels that she and her work are appreciated by the teacher. She feels positively about building again.

Stickers and Smiley Faces. A few "non-traditional" comments about stickers and smiley faces add to the discussion of encouragement and praise. Stickers and smiley faces constitute praise: They reward achievement rather than effort. They are easily interpreted by young children as judgments about personality. They give the impression of differential treatment as children tend to compare who gets how many, how often. Stickers and smiley faces build up dependency on the teacher. They demean the intrinsic worth of the learning activity. (If it's developmentally appropriate, no external reward should be necessary.)

Personal encouragement instead, either spoken or written, is more appropriate for young children. The notation to a first grader, "You got all your m's on the line," offers information that is both specific and reinforcing. (Written encouragement even to kindergarteners is a sure inducement to "early reading.") Such feedback is of more value than a smiley face, a Sesame Street sticker, or a stock phrase like "good work," or "excellent." As the teacher's comment to Julia suggests, a specific statement of encouragement goes a long way with a young child.

Encouragement—What to Say. When they are beginning to use encouragement, teachers sometimes find it difficult to know just what to say. Especially with art, clay, and building projects that are "pre-representational," they can find themselves at a loss for words. A strategy here is to say something that elicits a response from the child; the support comes from the interaction. Two **starter sentences** some teachers use are:

You are really working hard on that . . .(picture, construction, puzzle, etc.)
>   **or,**
You are really using lots of . . .(colors, blocks, clay, ideas, writing, etc.)

These starter statements tell the child that the teacher is interested and wants to hear more. Listening is a big part of the act of encouragement. The support has registered when the child says something like, "Yep, that's a picture of my baby brother. You can't see him cause he's hidin' under the covers."

The teacher is developing skill in the use of encouragement when s/he can pick out details in the child's or group's efforts and positively acknowledge them. **In fact, the ability to notice and comment positively about details ends the "loss for words" problem**. Encouraging statements are simple, but have real effect:

- You have all the puzzle pieces in but one.
- You've printed your whole name.
- Everyone worked hard to clean the room today.
- We're almost ready for the story.
- You got eight of the ten problems correct.
- You slid down the slide all by yourself.
- You didn't get upset even once today.

Though such statements may address achievements, they implicitly recognize the effort behind the deed.

When Praise is Appropriate. Praise is not always inappropriate, though it does need to be given with care. As mentioned in chapter three, on occasion there is solid rationale for having the class recognize an individual child. One reason is to acknowledge achievement after a child has struggled publicly and persevered. The class can appreciate in any child a hard fought victory.

A second example is the practice in some classrooms of recognizing a "Star of the Week" or "Very Important Kid." If using this practice, the teacher needs to ensure that children know they will all have a turn. (One way to designate turns is the chart with each child's name and a movable marker. The children might be listed in order of age, with the youngest child the first Very Important Kid.) When praise is done carefully in select situations, both the individual and the group benefit. The child receives a boost in self-esteem, and the class a boost in empathy levels toward individual members.

Listening to Life Experiences

The educational values that support developmentally appropriate practice and guidance discipline denote a teacher who cares about children. The teacher recognizes that young children who are unhappy at school cannot easily express anxieties in words. In many children the symptoms of anxiety manifest themselves in "unwell" conditions. Symptoms range from the twice-a-year stomach ache to actual ulcers, from occasional headaches to hypertension and depressive reactions. The causes of **school anxiety** can be related to specific situations, such as the morning bus ride or the afternoon "power test," or be more pervasive—a general feeling of being disliked. Teachers who understand that school can be a source of trauma are alert to the strong need for support that some children feel.

Children also show the toils of troubles from outside the school situation, of course, and this matter is discussed in chapters eight and nine. Pertinent here is the reality that children learn effectively only when they are not beset by personal worries. Teachers often watch for the moods of children upon arrival in order to reduce problems that might arise later in the day.

Anecdote: In a first grade class the children each drew in their own way three faces—happy, sad, and angry—on large paper plates. With help, they labeled each face and attached dials to their "face plates." When children came in each morning, they set the dials according to their moods. The teacher and an aide made a point of noticing each child's setting and talked with those children who might need an adult to listen. The class talked about how sometimes they weren't feeling in any particular mood. They decided they could put their dials in between faces on these days. (One said that between sad and angry, though, "was the worsetest.")

An increasing problem in our schools is that teachers must be social workers as well as educators (Boyer, 1992). Children's lives have grown more complex. In previous times, a grandma, grandpa, aunt, or uncle would provide support when parents could not. With the proliferation of one- and two-parent nuclear families, that "other" caring adult more and more is the teacher. In the presence of serious problems, the teacher collaborates to the extent possible with parents, colleagues, and other professionals. For less serious problems, sometimes a listening ear and words of encouragement are all that is needed.

Anecdote: When a third grade teacher witnessed Jesse tear up his arithmetic and say, "I hate this damn stuff," he reacted with a friendly hand on the shoulder and some kind words. The teacher might have reacted differently except for a talk he had with Jesse earlier that morning:

"Hi, Jess, you're not smiling today." When Jesse looked down and shook his head, the teacher added, "Something you'd like to talk about?"

Jesse said no, then fighting back tears shared, "Bumpers got hit by a car. We thought he was gonna be OK, but we took him to the vet. The vet took X-rays and said his whole back end was broken. We had to put him to sleep."

The teacher said, "Oh, Jesse, I'm so sorry. I know what Bumpers meant to you."

Figure 7–5 Sometimes a listening ear and a few words of encouragement are all that is needed.

> Jesse ended the conversation with, "I got to say good-by to him, and I got to keep a little bit of his fur." The boy went to his desk and a few other children who had heard went over to talk with him. The teacher knew it would be a long day for a child who had lost his best friend.

A few caring words by a teacher mean a lot to a child. Young children who know that their teacher likes and respects them tend not to show serious mistaken behavior (Albert, 1989). A teacher need not "reach" each child, each day. Still, **contact talks** with those who need them is an investment in a positively functioning class.

Contact Talk

Contact talk is a variation of the practice of "quality time," adapted for the classroom. Teachers seldom have more than a minute or two to make personal contacts. The point is that even a very short time matters to children; it tells them they are valued so much that their busy teacher takes time to talk with them.

On the surface, contact talk sounds similar to the tactic of "catch them being good," but the two are different. The "catch them" practice tends to involve a one-way conversation with the teacher giving praise. Honest recognition of productive behavior **is** essential with children, but this is only part of the reason for contact talk.

With contact talk, the teacher has the motive of getting to know a child. The teacher initiates, or allows the child to initiate, a conversation. S/he follows as the child defines the course of the conversation. For the time that the teacher can give, s/he is a "good listener." Children are generally eager to have contact talks with adults. The teacher's role is pivotal, as s/he decides whether or not the conversation will happen.

A clear example of a contact talk at the primary grade level was illustrated in a previous section of the chapter. The teacher who gave permission to Jesse to talk about his dog was using contact talk. Given class sizes, primary teachers must work hard to find time for frequent contact talks. At the pre-primary level, contact talks should happen on a continuous basis. Teachers of three- to five-year-olds can hardly escape them, and of course shouldn't.

Anecdote: Mavis bounded in the door of Head Start, ran a circle around the teacher, and announced, "Me gots new shoes, teacher!"

Looking down at Mavis' pulled up pants, the teacher exclaimed, "Oh, Mavis, those are sure some colorful sneakers."

Indignant, Mavis replied, "Not sneakers. 'Letic shoes!"

Grinning broadly, the teacher corrected herself, "I'll bet you can sure run fast in those athletic shoes." With a nod over her shoulder, Mavis galloped out the door to the playground.

As time is precious during the day, the teacher must look for opportunities for a contact talk to occur. Some likely moments in the daily program are:

- before other children arrive,
- during a choice time,
- at recess (inside or out),
- at lunch,
- during a break in the day,
- after a self-directing activity has begun,
- after school.

The advantage of preschools in staffing arrangements—hopefully with an adult-to-child ratio of 1:10—means that contact talks can more easily occur. In the supportive prekindergarten classroom, a reasonable goal is *at least* one contact talk with each child every day.

Contact talks are more difficult on a regular basis at the elementary school level. A system that allows every child to be reached is critical. Here is where use of the **teaching team** can help. If the teacher can bring other adults into the classroom, more contact talks can occur. With only one adult in the room, a teacher might only be able to have a few conversations a day—still better than none at all. Teachers who work to increase the number of contact talks tend to be rewarded:

Anecdote: In his first year of teaching, Clay felt hampered because he was only able to relate to his thirty third graders as "students." He decided to try an after school program that he called "Get to Know Our City." He got approval from the principal and sent home letters with permission forms. One day each week, he took a carload (five) of the third graders to visit interesting places.

By the end of the school year, all children had gone with him at least once. Most had gone a few times. Clay found the experience helped him gain new understanding about the children, and they about him. (The entire class learned more about the city.) It especially helped his relations with a few children he had mainly known before as "strong willed."

Anecdote: For a workshop assignment, Gayle, a kindergarten teacher, made a chart of the children's names set against a four week calendar. Daily, the teacher made a point of having two minute personal conversations with at least five children and noted these conversations on the chart. With alternate day programming, Gayle was able to have at least one contact talk with each child every two weeks—and with most children more than one.

After the month, Gayle decided to continue the practice. The teacher discovered she was becoming more receptive to the children, especially those who were less outgoing. She found she was not only getting to know the children better, but they were also getting to know her. Gayle felt there was a change of atmosphere in the classroom.

The value of contact talks is that as teachers and children get to know each other, trust builds, and the need for mistaken behavior lessens. There is evidence that teachers tend to talk most with children who are talkative and from backgrounds similar to their own (Mattick, 1981; Derman-Sparks, 1988). A chart seems mechanistic, but ensures that all of the children (and the teacher) receive the benefits of contact talks.

The Compliment Sandwich

Some years ago, Dr. Julie Jochum came across the idea of the **compliment sandwich**. She developed the concept as a feedback technique for teacher

Figure 7–6 The value of contact talk is that as teachers and children get to know each other, trust builds, and the need for mistaken behavior lessens.

education majors when journaling with children (Jochum, 1991). As adapted from Jochum's usage, the compliment sandwich provides a focused way of giving **encouragement**. The technique is useful with children or adults, for the purpose of preventing or resolving problems. (The technique even works with family members, though sometimes a "triple decker" is needed.)

The compliment sandwich has three parts: *Two* statements of encouragement; *one* suggestion, recommendation, request or question. The two encouragements recognize effort, progress, or interim achievement. (They are the two pieces of "bread.") The peanut butter in the middle guides the child toward further progress. The ratio is important as some research has shown that two positives per negative is the barest minimum for a child to feel supported (Kirkhart & Kirkhart, 1967). In other words, three pieces of bread ("triple-decker encouragement") is desirable. If the teacher considers adding a second request or recommendation, s/he makes a new sandwich.

What do compliment sandwiches sound like? The reader can tell very quickly what is and is not a compliment sandwich. Let us "overhear" two second grade teachers, one during language arts, the other during math time.

Language arts: You are being careless again. Look at how those sentences wander over the page. You forgot your periods. This is messy work. You will need to do it again.

Math: You have seven of the problems just right. This is a hard assignment and you are really staying with it. Use your chips again and see if you can get different answers for the other three.

By using the compliment sandwich—as opposed to "character assassination"—the second teacher was probably helping to prevent math anxiety. The technique is self-explanatory—for whatever change the teacher requests, s/he recognizes two or more indicators of progress or effort. The math teacher's use of the skill was in an academic situation. The compliment sandwich also can be used with more general classroom situations. Here are some examples of compliment sandwiches, first with a group and then with an individual child:

Preprimary: You children have put away the blocks and the books. We just have the table toys to finish and then we can go outside.

Jamie, you have your coat hung up and your boots off; you just need to put them under your coat and you're all set.

Primary: You read lots of books in the library today and you sat very quietly for the story. Coming back through the hall, though, was a little too noisy. Who has ideas for how to make the walk back more quiet?

Sondra, you stayed in your seat and didn't have any problems with your neighbors. I'm proud of you. Now, how can we help you to remember to use that "inside voice?"

The encouragement that is a part of the compliment sandwich reassures children that the teacher is on their side. (It is always easier to improve when the coach is pulling for you.) With serious mistaken behavior, the compliment sandwich also helps to remind the *teacher* of this fact. In meetings with parents, the compliment sandwich helps establish a spirit of cooperation, that the parent and teacher are working together for the child.

Humor

The sensitive use of **humor** affirms positive relations with children and affords a friendly atmosphere in the classroom. An attraction of teaching young children is the delightful unpredictability in their responses. Teachers who find themselves refreshed by the reactions of young learners know why they are practicing at this age level. The ability to use humor with a class adds to the "positives" of the profession.

Different kinds of situations are apt to make teachers smile. One such occasion is when teachers hear their own words echoed by children:

Anecdote: A teacher was at first amazed, then amused when a four-year-old made the following request: "I am having a difficult morning, so I need kindness." The teacher remembered making a similar comment earlier in the week.

The fact that children interpret words quite literally can be a source of enjoyment for adults and children alike:

Anecdote: It began raining heavily outside the windows of a kindergarten class. The teacher exclaimed, "Why, it's raining cats and dogs out there."

The children looked out of the windows intently. Then one child turned to the teacher and said with a smile, "Teacher, it's raining elephants even."

A classroom atmosphere in which humorous moments are enjoyed by all is a positive atmosphere. Teachers who see humor even in trying moments can defuse problems effectively (Ginott, 1972). Curwin and Mendler suggest the use of mildly self-effacing humor as a remedy for power struggles (1988). This use of humor can be challenging for a teacher, but has its rewards.

Anecdote: In front of the class a fearless third grader said to his male teacher, "Boy, Mr. D., you sure are hairy."

The teacher, who had forgotten to shave, said, "You're right, Willie. I couldn't find my razor today, so I hit my whiskers in with a hammer and bit them off inside. Guess I missed some." The class, including Willie, shook their heads and laughed. The moment was quickly forgotten as Mr. D. got a project started.

Humor helps in sustaining positive teacher-child relations. But, humor also can be used against children, by a teacher who needs to control through humiliation. Dr. John Halcrow, an education professor in human relations, has this to say about the use of humor:

We need humor in the classroom, but let's be careful about it. Humor can be a two-edged sword. Some rules for humor: Never use it as a weapon, nor to chastise or correct. Never make a student the butt of a joke, and remember not to take yourself too seriously.

We need fun, hope, even frivolity in the classroom. If we put too much focus on the mechanics of what we're teaching, we kill the joy. Work students hard, then let them play with what they've learned. Let them talk to each other, try out their ideas and correct their own errors along the way (1988).

Touch

Along with humor, another practice that conveys warmth in relations is the use of **touch**. One point of separation of young children from some teachers is that children are tactile beings, needing physical closeness, while some teachers are

Figure 7–7 A practice that conveys warmth in relations is the use of touch.

uncomfortable with this need. Adult discomfort is usually the result of an attitude that children must be weened from an "immature" habit, or of concern about the possible suggestion of sexual abuse. In either case the discomfort is unfortunate.

Physical closeness accomplishes what no words can in forming healthy attachments with children (Curwin & Mendler, 1988). As Hendrick points out, children "require the reassurance and comfort of being patted, rocked, held, and hugged from time to time (p. 103, 1992)." Hendrick goes on to say:

> Research as well as experience supports the value of close physical contact. Montagu (1986) has reviewed numerous studies illustrating the beneficial effect of being touched and the relationship of tactile experience to healthy physical and emotional development. Investigations documenting the link between touching and the development of attachment confirm those findings (p. 103, 1992).

Curwin and Mendler recommend the use of hugs and touching in communicating with children. They decry the fallacy of prohibition against touch because of sexual misunderstanding, but seem to assume that this proscription pertains only to teachers of "older students" (p. 16, 1988). Yet, Hendrick points out that recent "sensationalized court cases" have made early childhood teachers as well "uneasy about touching or cuddling youngsters lest they, too, be accused" (pp. 102-103, 1992). The article, "Vanishing Breed: Men in Child Care

Programs" (Robinson, 1988) points out that male teachers of young children are particularly susceptible to such suspicions.

Given the value of nurturing touches for children, physical closeness should not be deleted from the teacher's repertoire. Rather, as Hendrick points out, educators need to maintain written policies that allow open visitation by parents; require clear understanding among all staff regarding physical closeness; and mandate thorough background checks for prospective employees. The rationale for the guideline "friendly touches only" needs to be fully communicated to children, parents, and staff. Such actions are important for the inviolability of this important teaching technique.

Anecdote: A teacher worked to develop a sense of belonging in her class. She decided to concentrate on arrivals and departures. Stationing herself by the door, every day she greeted each child with a smile and a friendly comment. Fairly quickly, she got so she could tell who needed a contact talk or a hug on the lap to get started. Although the teacher did not like having to prepare for the day earlier, she believed the greetings helped the day go better.

She also paid attention to the end-of-day farewells, and adopted the practice of hugging or shaking hands with the children as they left the room. The children had their choice, though before long almost all elected the hug.

Discussing Inclusively

In group discussions as well as conversations with individuals, the teacher listens. S/he does not discard comments that seem out of context. On the surface what sounds like inattentiveness may indeed be careful listening and hard thought—but from a perspective different than the teacher's.

Anecdote: With the coming of spring, a kindergarten class had finished a dinosaur unit and was well into hatching chicken eggs. In a discussion the class talked about how baby chickens know to peck for food. The teacher asked if anyone knew what the word, "instinct" meant. One child raised her hand and announced, "That's like dinosaurs 'cause they're not alive any more." The teacher started to call on another child, then turned to the first child and thanked her for the comment. With an impressed smile, the teacher explained to the class the difference between "instinct" and "extinct."

The teacher here knew that the kindergarten class would not gain a full understanding of the terms from her brief explanation. (Some may even have heard the word "extinct" as "eggstinct.") But, she never could have anticipated the association made by the child. The teacher might have passed over the remark as having no connection to the present discussion—in fact she almost did. Instead, the teacher's open-ended expectation of progress was rewarded, due to her willingness to listen. The teacher was **discussing inclusively**.

What can the teacher do, however, when children really do *not* listen? The conventional practice has been to call on a child who is "chatting" or day dreaming to force renewed focus. The implication of the guidance approach is that the teacher **needs to make the discussion interesting so that children will want to participate**. On average, by the time children have begun kindergarten, they have watched nine months to a year of television, including perhaps a month of Sesame Street. From television—as well as the family—they have acquired a host of receptive experiences to work through and share.

The days are gone when teachers could force compliance to didactic instructional methods, focused on retrieval of a series of "right answers." Children no longer come from the "children are seen and not heard/think before you speak" home environments that prepared them for the traditional classrooms of the past.

Children learn willingly when ideas are interesting to them. They fail to learn, in significant ways, if content and delivery have no relevance (Wing, 1992). When "discussions" come down to a right answer that children may not know, many develop defensive strategies—playing "dumb," making jokes, acting belligerent—in order to escape the embarrassment of public correction (Holt, 1972). Discussions that accommodate a diversity of ideas and opinions mean that the teacher has mastered the skill of discussing inclusively.

THE CLASS MEETING

Glasser is credited with popularizing the use of **class meetings** (1969). In Glasser's model, class meetings are held to identify problems and work toward solutions. The meetings center around behavior issues, curriculum matters, or concerns of students. Glasser is adamant that the class meeting occurs without blame or faultfinding by participants. Honest opinions stated and respected are the keys that make the method work. When children know they have a say in how the program goes and how it can be made better, they feel like they belong and want to contribute.

In an update of the writing of Glasser and others on building "a sense of togetherness" within the class, Charles (1989) states:

> To foster a sense of togetherness, the teacher should continually talk with the class about what they will accomplish *as a group*, how they will deal with the problems they encounter as a group, how they will work together to get the best achievement possible for every individual in the group. In order to bring this

about, responsibilities are given and shared, students are encouraged to speak of their concerns while the class attempts to find remedies, and the teacher takes special steps, when necessary, to incorporate every student into the ongoing work of the class (1989, p. 142).

Teachers in early childhood use class meetings to establish a sense of belonging, conduct class business, and to solve problems that arise. Whatever the purpose, during class meetings guidelines such as these apply:

- Anyone can talk;
- Take turns;
- Be honest;
- Be kind.

The teacher might also have personal guidelines for class meetings, such as: "Maintain a positive group focus;" "Individual situations require private remedies;" "Class meetings are to solve problems, not create them." In general, there are two types of class meetings: scheduled and unscheduled.

Scheduled Class Meetings

A common time for scheduled class meetings is each morning after the children have arrived. The **morning meeting** was introduced in the last chapter and

Figure 7–8 Teachers use class meetings to establish a sense of belonging, conduct class business, and to solve problems that arise.

might include attendance, class business, orientation to the day and a high interest discussion. As mentioned in chapter six, personally relevant time and weather questions can spark the discussion; or, the teacher can ask other questions that tie in with a theme, area of study, or special event.

In early childhood, special event discussions usually relate to members of the group, such as a trip to the hospital, a missing tooth, or perhaps the death of a pet. Special event discussions should be handled with sensitivity. If they directly involve a class member, the teacher may wish to discuss the circumstances with the child and parent before "going public."

A second time common for scheduled class meetings is just before going home. The purposes of the meeting are to review the day and discuss coming events. Children might share something they learned or enjoyed doing, or someone "new" that they did something with. When a teacher or child experiences a problem, the end of the day meeting is one time to discuss it (Greenberg, 1992). The teacher, or a child, may want to bring up the mess in the restroom or inappropriate behavior involving members of the group. If an afternoon meeting becomes too involved, the teacher asks the class to think about it overnight so that "we can discuss it in the morning when we are fresh." The teacher works to end class meetings on a positive note.

Unscheduled Class Meetings

Usually, the teacher calls unscheduled class meetings to address mistaken behaviors that cannot wait. Examples are when an activity gets out of hand, or a word like "dorky" is "catching on" and "driving a teacher bananas."

From the work of Glasser (1969), discussion skills that the teacher models and teaches during class meetings are the following:

1. The dignity of individuals is protected;
2. Situations are described, not judged;
3. Feelings are stated as "I" messages;
4. Suggestions for solutions are appreciated;
5. A course of action is decided, tried and reviewed.

Class meetings that focus on problems provide an excellent opportunity for learning human relations and conflict resolution abilities. Some of the most important learning that the class and teacher will do occurs during class meetings:

Anecdote: In Vicki's kindergarten class, Gary wet his pants. A volunteer took Gary to the nurse's office where extra clothes were kept. Vicki overheard some of the children talking about Gary and decided it was time for a class meeting. She explained to them what had happened. She then told a story about when she was a little girl, she wet her pants too and felt very embarrassed. She said people sometimes have accidents, even adults, and it's important that we be friendly so they don't feel badly.

The children began to share similar experiences they remembered. When Gary came back to the room, another child smiled at him and said, "It's OK, Gary; last time I wet my pants too."

Other children said, "Me too." Looking greatly relieved, Gary took his seat. The class got back to business.

Class Meetings and Circle Times

Class meetings transcend the academic curriculum and deal with life in the classroom. Circle times, in contrast, tend to emphasize the traditional academic pursuits of early childhood: singing, finger plays, stories, creative movement, visits from guests, theme-related discussions, and "anticipatory set" activities. Class meetings on occasion flow into circle times and vice versa. Whatever type of large group, the teacher should remain vigilant to attention spans and interest levels.

Circle times go back to Froebel's first kindergarten programs in Germany. For Froebel, the circle represented the non-beginning/non-end of the universe and the unity of humankind with God. Whether or not modern teachers work from this symbolism, the circle suggests the equality and worth of each individual and lends itself to the community spirit of the class meeting. Class meetings that are cooperative in tone can be held successfully even with classes of preschoolers (Greenberg, 1992; Hendrick, 1992). Such meetings are a staple in the guidance approach to discipline.

COMMUNICATING WITH PARENTS TO PREVENT PROBLEMS

The responsibility for opening lines of communication with parents lies with the teacher. Parents depend on teachers, even those younger than themselves, to initiate contacts and maintain relations. Most parents respect and appreciate even beginning teachers who enjoy working with young children and take pride in their programs. This section provides suggestions for maintaining ongoing communications with parents, in order to prevent problems.

Previous chapters offered ideas for establishing productive parent-teacher relations. To summarize, some of the key ideas are:

1. Send welcome letters to children and parents before school starts. If possible, make home visits.
2. Begin the program on a staggered schedule when possible. Make a point of inviting parents in during the first few days.

Figure 7–9
Causes of Problems in the Classroom

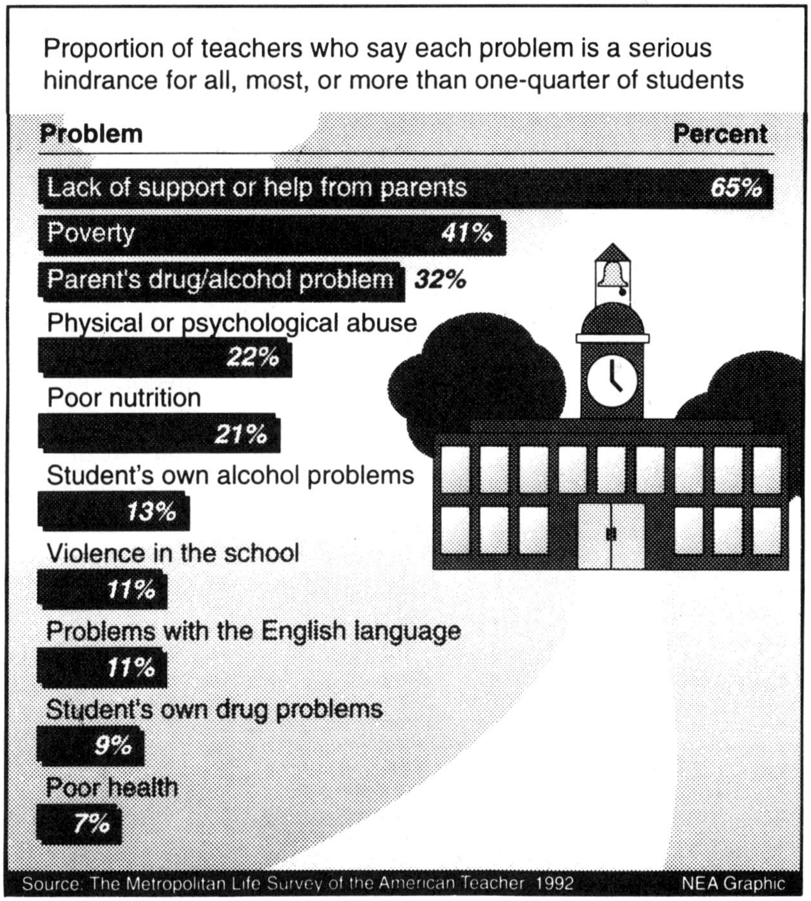

Proportion of teachers who say each problem is a serious hindrance for all, most, or more than one-quarter of students

Problem	Percent
Lack of support or help from parents	65%
Poverty	41%
Parent's drug/alcohol problem	32%
Physical or psychological abuse	22%
Poor nutrition	21%
Student's own alcohol problems	13%
Violence in the school	11%
Problems with the English language	11%
Student's own drug problems	9%
Poor health	7%

Source: The Metropolitan Life Survey of the American Teacher 1992   NEA Graphic

Figure 7–9 Though not social workers, early childhood teachers work with parents to increase their involvement in the education of the child.

3. Call each family on the evening of the first day. Check with the parent about any problems the teacher might help to resolve.
4. Hold an orientation meeting on two occasions during the first week or two, inviting parents to attend either. Go over a pamphlet about the program that explains policies and highlights opportunities. Feature an open classroom policy. Spark discussion about the program. Ask parents to complete an optional survey.
5. Hold parent conferences during the first month. Use the conferences to get to know each parent, referring to the survey if appropriate.

6. Invite parents to be involved in the program. Make sure parents know they are welcome to volunteer in the classroom. Help them feel welcome and useful when they visit.

7. Assist parents to find tasks in the classroom that they are comfortable doing, so that they will return.

The above suggestions give direction to building relations with parents. Discussion now focuses on three of the most basic types of communication: (a) written notes; (b) telephone calls; and (c) parent-teacher conferences, helpful in maintaining positive teacher-parent relations.

Notes Home

Some parents associate notes home with criticisms of children's behavior. In the guidance approach, notes home are neither for the purpose of punishment nor correction. The reason is straightforward: notes do not allow for discussion. The written message is, as it were, cast in stone. The parent has a limited range of responses which frequently come down to doing nothing, becoming upset with the child, and/or feeling "dumped on" by the school.

When personal notes go home discussing a child, the teacher uses **encouragement**. The note takes the form of either an occasional, unsolicited "happygram" or of a statement of progress, perhaps as follow-up to a conference. (In the latter case, the logical format is the **compliment sandwich**.) Because children may wonder about the content of personal notes from the teacher, s/he does well to read them to the child beforehand. If the tone of the note is encouraging, most children will take pride in seeing that it is delivered. (If the matter is serious, it probably is best handled not by a note but by a conference.)

A suggestion is that the teacher send a happygram or two home with each child during the first month, reading the note to the child beforehand. Such notes give the child a "real idea" about what the teacher thinks; lets the parent know that the teacher is "on the child's side;" and helps children feel positively about carrying notes home in general. (Those early happygrams actually may improve the rate of note delivery for the rest of the year.)

Regarding routine notes about events, the teacher needs to be aware of three factors: (a) delivery rates, especially when a return is requested, are seldom 100 percent; (b) with a single written notice, some parents will forget; and (c) some parents are nonreaders. The teacher can use newsletter items and repeat notes to remediate factors (a) and (b). If s/he knows that illiteracy is a factor, the teacher can either telephone or have the message delivered personally.

Phone Calls

Phone calls allow for personal conversation, but not for physical proximity and face-to-face contact. For this reason, unless the teacher knows the parent, the author recommends that the phone be used in a similar fashion as notes home. In other words, under normal circumstances a teacher should not attempt a serious conference on the phone. Phone conversations are helpful in underscoring the need for special conferences. They are also excellent for personally "delivering" of happygrams, following-up conferences and inviting parent participation in special events.

When requesting a conference with a parent over the phone, the use of a compliment sandwich is important. If the teacher is upset at a behavior, the "compliments" help the teacher put the behavior in perspective. For the parent, they convey the message that "my child is not a total problem because the teacher sees at least some 'good' in him." Note the difference between these two calls home regarding Jeremy, a four- and a half-year-old.

Call One: Jeremy was a total monster today. He hit two children, bit one, and threw a book at me. We will have to talk about his behavior tomorrow because I've had it. How is eight o'clock?

Call Two: Jeremy has been working hard on his behavior, but he had a rough day today. He had conflicts with three children this morning. After that he settled down, and the rest of the day went better. He's making progress, but I think we need to talk. What time would be good for you tomorrow?

Phone calls are well suited to giving positive feedback, such as after a conference. If the teacher wants to communicate more directly than with a note, a call like this would mean a lot to a parent:

I just wanted to let you know how Jeremy did this week. No hitting or kicking at all. He only got upset once, but he used words. He was also playing more with the other children. I'm really pleased. How are things going for him at home?

Parent-Teacher Conferences

Conferences provide the most direct link between teacher and parent, and much has been written in recent years about them. Gestwicki devotes a chapter to conferences in her text, *Parent, Teacher, Community Relations* (1992). Some others who have written about conferences are Bjorklund and Burger (1987); Bullock (1986); Koulouras et al. (1986); and Readdick et al. (1984). The 1992 article, "Effective Techniques for Involving 'Difficult' Parents," (Boutte et al., 1992) is especially useful. The present chapter provides information about routine, regular conferences. Chapters eight and nine discuss conferences to remediate problem situations.

Gestwicki suggests there are three phases to successful conferences: **preparation**, **conduct**, and **evaluation** (1992). In preparing, the teacher needs to make sure the parent knows the reasons for the conference. A statement about conferences might be included in a pamphlet about the program (Appendix C) and repeated in a notice home. Time options are helpful for the parent, including both night and daytime slots if possible. An informal private setting,

Figure 7–10a Phone calls and confer- ences are two important ways to communi- cate with parents.

Figure 7–10b Serious discussions occur best in the face-to-face setting of the conference.

in which parent and teacher can sit side by side at a table, is preferable to conversing over a desk (Charles, 1989). Likewise, adequate time is preferable to the "get them in; get them out" atmosphere common in some K–12 settings.

The teacher should have a folder for each child with samples of the child's work over time. Dated observational notes are helpful. A form to record notes from the conference, in preparation for a later written summary, rounds out preparation (Gestwicki, 1992).

There is considerable agreement about the **conduct** of the conference. The teacher begins with a positive "I statement" about the child, such as: "I really enjoy having Claire May in class. She works so hard and has such a sense of humor." The teacher goes over materials she has prepared, and invites parent discussion about them. S/he asks about items the parent would like to discuss. S/he paraphrases comments the parent makes and uses **reflective listening**, which means repeating back the thoughts and feelings the parent is expressing (Gestwicki, 1992). The compliment sandwich is another useful communication technique. If a follow-up plan comes out of the conference, the teacher writes it out and sends it to the parent for approval. The teacher ends the conference on a positive note (Gestwicki, 1992).

Gestwicki includes a list of pitfalls to avoid during conferences:

- Technical terms and jargon. Use terms parents can understand.
- Playing the "expert." Describe events and trends rather than make broad judgments.
- Negative evaluations of a child's capabilities. (Use compliment sandwiches.)
- Unprofessional comments: talking about others; becoming too personal; taking sides. Respect the principle of confidentiality.
- Giving advice. Offer alternative suggestions "that have worked for other parents," for the parent to consider.
- Trying to solve all problems on the spot. Decide instead on a cooperative plan of action that will be reviewed (Gestwicki, p. 221, 1992).

Gestwicki concludes her discussion of conferences with this important paragraph:

It should be remembered that nonattendance at a conference does not necessarily indicate disinterest in the child or the school. Instead, it may be a reflection of different cultural or socioeconomic values, of extreme pressures or stress [on the] family or work demands. A teacher's response to nonattendance is to review the possible explanations. . . see if different scheduling or educational action will help, persist in invitations and efforts, and understand that other methods of reaching a parent will have to be used in the meantime (p. 222).

Following the conference, the teacher reviews notes and completes a brief summary, perhaps on a prepared form. S/he files the form for herself and when a cooperative plan has been decided upon, sends a copy to the parent. The teacher also reflects in personal terms about the success of the conference and notes possible changes in approach for conferences to come (Gestwicki, 1992).

SUMMARY

Chapter seven continued the premise of guidance discipline that "prevention is the best medicine." The chapter examined how the teacher uses communication skills to prevent classroom problems.

How does a supportive atmosphere prevent mistaken behavior?

A supportive atmosphere allows the teacher to set and maintain guidelines at the same time as reinforcing self-esteem. The combination of self-control and self-esteem empowers children to make intelligent, ethical decisions.

Teachers need to establish their leadership at the beginning of the year, but as leaders who are democratic. They educate children to the routines of the classroom, but do so in ways that make school an interesting rather than anxiety-producing place.

Why are guidelines, not rules, important in a guidance approach?

Rules tend to be stated in negative terms and have preset consequences. Rules institutionalize the use of punishments, reduce the role of the teacher to a technician, and fail to respond adequately to the complexities of situations. Guidelines educate children toward productive behavior and positive self-esteem. Guidelines allow the teacher the range of choices appropriate for a professional. Guidelines mean that the teacher works to solve problems and mediate disputes. The teacher so teaches conflict resolution skills, crucial as we approach the twenty-first century.

What are seven communication skills that assist the teacher to prevent mistaken behavior?

Encouragement—more than praise. Praise rewards achievements, is public, is used often to manipulate the group, and fails to distinguish between personality and deeds. Encouragement recognizes effort and progress, does not single out individuals, gives specific feedback, and reinforces the supportive climate of the classroom.

Listening to life experiences. The teacher can often help a child through small problems with just a listening ear. S/he can work with other adults to help with the bigger problems. These kinds of activities are important, because a troubled child cannot learn effectively and tends to show mistaken behavior.

Contact talk. Contact talk is quality time adapted for the classroom. More than "catch them being good," contact talk is a brief conversation a teacher has with a child to get to know the child better. The teacher sets up opportunities for contact talks to occur and ensures that s/he has a contact talk with every child on a regular basis.

Compliment sandwich. The compliment sandwich has three parts: two statements of encouragement; one suggestion or request. The encouragement reminds the child, the teacher, (and the parent) that they are on the same team. It is easier for others to accept suggestions for change when they know that the teacher is on their side.

Humor. The sensitive use of humor affirms positive relations with children and affords a friendly atmosphere in the classroom. The ability to use humor, in harmony with the class, adds to the positives of the profession.

Touch. Children need the reassurance of warm physical contact for healthy physical and emotional development. Teachers need to communicate policies clearly to counteract public anxieties about sexual abuse. The values of touch outweigh the concerns, both for the individual child and the entire class.

Discussing inclusively. In group situations, as well as with individuals, the teacher listens. S/he goes beyond a preoccupation with "right or wrong" answers and who is and who is not listening. Instead, the teacher focuses on including all perspectives into group decisions and works hard to make discussions interesting.

How do class meetings help to prevent mistaken behavior?

Class meetings are held to maintain a sense of community and to solve classroom problems. Scheduled class meetings occur most often at the beginning and end of the day. The teacher calls unscheduled meetings when events cannot wait. Guidelines for class meetings for both children and the teacher help to make class meetings positive and productive experiences.

How does the teacher communicate with parents to prevent problems?

The responsibility for maintaining lines of communication lies with the teacher. Seven actions for building relations were reviewed. Three basic types of communication were highlighted: notes home, telephone calls, and conferences. Notes and telephone calls are used best to deliver "happygrams" and compliment sandwiches, to provide necessary information to the parent, and to set up conferences.

Conferences have three phases: preparation, conduct, and evaluation. In preparing, the teacher makes sure the parent knows the reason and the time and place for the conference. During the conference, the teacher attempts to put the parent at ease and shares specific information about the child. After the conference, the teacher reviews notes, completes a brief summary, and follows-up with the child and the family.

FOLLOW-UP ACTIVITIES

Follow-up activities allow the student to interrelate material from the text with "real life" situations. The "observations" imply access to practicum experiences, the "interviews" access to teachers. When communicating about the activities, students need to respect the privacy of all participants in the observation or interview, as an important professional courtesy.

1. **How does a supportive atmosphere prevent mistaken behavior?**
    a. Observe a classroom in which you believe a supportive atmosphere is present. What do you see that documents your view? What kinds of mistaken behavior do you observe? Do you hypothesize the causes to be from within the classroom or elsewhere?
    b. Interview a teacher who maintains what you believe to be a supportive classroom atmosphere. What would the teacher like the

(Courtesy of Lin Wahlberg, Early Childhood Family Education, Bemidji, Minnesota.)

children's attitudes to be: (1) toward themselves as learners; (2) toward the classroom; (3) toward the teacher?

2. **Why are guidelines, not rules, important in a guidance approach?**
   a. Whether s/he uses the term "rules" or "guidelines," observe how a teacher uses standards in the classroom. Is the use of standards closer to that of "rules" or "guidelines"? Document your conclusion.
   b. Interview a teacher about how s/he uses standards with young children. (The use of the term "guidelines" is new, so s/he may use the term rules.) What considerations about the children's development does the teacher make in creating and using the standards?

3. **What are seven communication skills that assist the teacher to prevent mistaken behavior?**
   a. Observe a teacher using two of the communication skills. What were the situations? What did the teacher say or do? How did the children react? What did you learn from the observation about the communication skills?

b. Interview a teacher about any of the communication skills that the teacher uses. What does the teacher like about each technique? What suggestions does the teacher have for each technique's use?

4. **How do class meetings help to prevent mistaken behavior?**
   a. Observe a class meeting in which an issue or problem facing the class is discussed. What role did the teacher play? How involved were the children in the discussion? What were the benefits of the meeting for the children? For the teacher? What were any difficulties in the procedure that you observed?
   b. Interview a teacher who uses class meetings (though s/he may not use this term). In the teacher's view what contributes to a successful class meeting? What are some drawbacks the teacher finds in conducting "business meetings" about issues or problems with the class?

5. **How does the teacher communicate with parents to prevent problems?**
   a. With a teacher and parent's permission, sit in on a teacher-parent conference. What did the teacher say and do that you thought was productive? How did the teacher's approach compare or contrast with the recommendations for conferences in the chapter?
   b. Interview a teacher about an instance where a conference was held to resolve a problem a child was having. What steps did the teacher take to ensure (*a*) the conference was positive; (*b*) a plan was worked out; (*c*) follow-up to the plan occurred. Based on the teacher's experience, what suggestions does s/he have about using conferences to help children resolve difficulties.

SUGGESTED RESOURCES

Albert, L. (1989). *A Teacher's Guide to Cooperative Discipline*. Circle Pines, MN: Guidance Service.

Bjorklund, G. and Burger, C. (1987). "Making Conferences Work for Parents, Teachers, and Children." *Young Children, 42*(2), pp. 26-31.

Boutte, G.S., Keepler, D.L., Tyler, V.S. and Terry, B.Z. "Effective Techniques for Involving 'Difficult' Parents," *Young Children, 47*(3), pp. 19-22.

Boyer, E.L. (1991). *Ready to Learn: A Mandate for the Nation*. Princeton, NJ: The Carnegie Foundation for the Advancement of Teaching.

Bullock, J. (1986). "Teacher/Parent Conferences: Learning from Each Other." *Day Care and Early Education, 14*(2), pp. 17-19.

Hitz, R. and Driscoll, A. (1988). "Praise or Encouragement New Insights into Praise: Implications for Early Childhood Teachers." *Young Children, 43*(4), pp. 6-13.

Holt, J. (1967). *How Children Fail*. New York: Pitman.

Robinson, B.E. (1988). "Vanishing Breed: Men in Child Care Programs." *Young Children, 43*(6), pp. 54-57.

REFERENCES

Albert, L. (1989). *A Teacher's Guide to Cooperative Discipline*. Circle Pines, MN: American Guidance Service.

Bjorklund, G. and Burger, C. (1987). "Making Conferences Work for Parents, Teachers, and Children." *Young Children, 42*(2), pp. 26-31.

Boutte, G.S., Keepler, D.L., Tyler, V.S. and Terry, B.Z. "Effective Techniques for Involving 'Difficult' Parents," *Young Children, 47*(3), pp. 19-22.

Boyer, E.L. (1991). *Ready to Learn: A Mandate for the Nation*. Princeton, NJ: The Carnegie Foundation for the Advancement of Teaching.

Bredekamp, S. (ed.) (1987). *Developmentally Appropriate Practice in Early Childhood Programs Serving Children From Birth Through Age 8*. Washington, DC: National Association for the Education of Young Children.

Bullock, J. (1986). "Teacher/Parent Conferences: Learning from Each Other." *Day Care and Early Education, 14*(2), pp. 17-19.

Cantor, L. (1976). *Assertive Discipline: A Take-Charge Approach for Today's Educator*. Seal Beach, CA: Canter and Associates.

Canter, L. (1988). "Viewpoint 1: Assertive Discipline and the Search for the Perfect Classroom," *Young Children, 43*(2), p. 24.

Charles, C.M. (1989). *Building Classroom Discipline*. New York: Longman, Inc.

Clewett, A.S. (1988). "Guidance and Discipline: Teaching Young Children Appropriate Behavior." *Young Children, 43*(4), pp. 26-36.

Curwin, R.L. and Mendler, A.N. (1988). *Discipline with Dignity*. Alexandria, VA: Association for Supervision and Curriculum Development.

Derman-Sparks, L. (1989). *Anti-Bias Curriculum: Tools for Empowering Young Children*. Washington, DC: National Association for the Education of Young Children.

Dewey, J. (1902). *The Child and the Curriculum*. Chicago: The University of Chicago Press.

Dreikurs, R. (1968). *Psychology in the Classroom* (2d ed.). New York: Harper and Row.

Dreikurs, R. and Cassel, P. (1972). *Discipline Without Tears*. New York: Hawthorn Books, Inc.

Elkind, D. (1976). *Child Development and Education: A Piagetian Perspective*. New York: Oxford University Press.

Elkind, D. (1988). *The Hurried Child*. Reading, MA: Addison-Wesley Publishing Company, Inc.

Elkind, D. (1987). *Miseducation: Preschoolers at Risk*. New York: Alfred A. Knopf.

Gartrell, D.J. (1987). "Assertive Discipline: Unhealthy to Children and Other Living Things." *Young Children, 42*(2), pp. 10-11.

Gestwicki, C. (1992). *Home, School and Community Relations: A Guide to Working with Parents*. Albany, NY: Delmar Publishers, Inc.

Ginott, H. (1972). *Teacher and Child.* New York: Avon Books.

Glasser, W. (1969). *Schools Without Failure.* New York: Harper and Row.

Greenberg, P. (1988). "Ideas that Work with Young Children. Avoiding 'Me Against You' Discipline." *Young Children, 44*(1), pp. 24-33.

Greenberg, P. (1989). "Ideas that Work with Young Children. Parents as Partners in Young Children's Development and Education: A New American Fad? Why Does it Matter?" *Young Children, 44*(4), pp. 61-75.

Greenberg, P. (1992). "How to Institute Some Simple Democratic Practices Pertaining to Respect, Rights, Responsibilities in Your Classroom Without Losing Your Leadership Position," *Young Children, 47*(5), pp. 10-21.

Halcrow, J. (1988). "Laughter in the Classroom." Professional Education Document. Bemidji, MN: Bemidji State University.

Hendrick, J. (1992). "Where Does It All Begin? Teaching the Principles of Democracy in the Early Years," *Young Children, 47*(3), pp. 51-53.

Hitz, R. and Driscoll, A. (1988). "Praise or Encouragement? New Insights Into Praise: Implications for Early Childhood Teachers." *Young Children, 43*(4), pp. 6-13.

Holt, J. (1967). *How Children Fail.* New York: Pitman.

Jochum, J. (1991). "Responding to Writing and to the Writer." *Intervention, 26*(3), pp. 152-157.

Kirkhart, R. and Kirkhart, E. (1967). "The Bruised Self: Mending in Early Years," in Yamamoto, K., *The Child and His Image: Self Concept in the Early Years.* Boston: Houghton Mifflin Company.

Koulouras, K. Porter, M.L. and Senter, S. (1986). "Making the Most of Parent Conferences." *Child Care Information Exchange, 50*, pp. 3-6.

Maslow, A.H. (1962). *Toward A Psychology of Being.* Princeton, NJ: D. Van Nostrend Co, Inc.

Mattick, I. (1981). "The Teacher's Role in Helping Young Children Develop Language Competence," in Cazden, C.B. (ed.). *Language in Early Childhood.* Washington, DC: National Association for the Education of Young Children.

Readdick, C., Golbeck, S., Klein, E. and Cartwright, C. (1984). "The Child-Parent-Teacher Conference." *Young Children, 39*(5), pp. 67-73.

Robinson, B.E. (1988). "Vanishing Breed: Men in Child Care Programs." *Young Children, 43*(6), pp. 54-57.

Williams, C.K and Kamii, C. (1986). "How do Children Learn by Handling Objects?" *Young Children, 42*(1), pp. 23-26.

Wing, L.A. (1992). "The Interesting Questions Approach to Learning," *Childhood Education, 69*(2), pp. 78-81.

Unit Three

Solving Problems
in the Classroom

Unit Three Chapter Summary

Chapter 8: *Finding Solutions for Mistaken Behavior*

Chapter eight presents conflict resolution strategies for addressing mistaken behavior—especially at levels one and two. Strategies include: applying the concept mistaken behavior; making the decision to intervene; using quick intervention techniques; responding to behaviors reported by children; and intervening when follow-up is needed. A question answered is "Why take the time to find solutions?" The final section makes suggestions for enlisting the assistance of parents.

Chapter 9: *Guidance in the Tough Times*

Chapter nine offers information to help prospective and practicing teachers cope with and remediate strong needs (level three) mistaken behavior. Conditions that make intervention necessary are examined. Methods of crisis management and of handling feelings of anger are discussed. Strategies for working with level three strong needs mistaken behavior are presented. The chapter concludes with considerations for when teachers and parents disagree.

Chapter 10: *Liberation Teaching*

Chapter ten defines liberation teaching. The chapter links liberation teaching and anti-bias curriculum. A section explains why liberation teaching is important for a guidance approach to discipline. The chapter concludes with application of the concept to relations with parents.

8

Finding Solutions for Mistaken Behavior

GUIDING QUESTIONS

As you read chapter eight, you will discover answers to the following questions:

- **How do teachers apply the concept of mistaken behavior?**
- **What goes into the decision to intervene?**
- **What are four quick intervention strategies?**
- **How does the teacher respond to mistaken behaviors reported by children?**
- **What are strategies to use when interventions require follow-up?**
- **Why take the time to find solutions?**
- **How does the teacher gain assistance from parents?**

Chapter eight introduces the basic theme of unit three: **Rather than punish children for having problems, guidance discipline teaches children to solve them**. The chapter emphasizes a problem-solving approach with level one, experimentation mistaken behavior, and level two, socially influenced mistaken behavior. Level three mistaken behavior, strong needs, is mentioned, but is given full treatment in chapter nine.

MISTAKEN BEHAVIOR: APPLYING THE CONCEPT

Ability to understand the level of a child's mistaken behavior helps with intervention decisions. When teachers perceive the motives at work, they can respond effectively. Yet, intervention usually cannot wait for the teacher to make a "formal diagnosis." The teacher has to act on the basis of a quick judgment. Often s/he will be right and regardless will learn from the experience. Reflection about the level after the event assists the teacher to work with the child in the future. For these reasons, a return to the three levels of mistaken behavior begins the discussion of resolving classroom problems.

Level One Mistaken Behavior

Children show level one, **experimentation level** mistaken behavior, in the course of interactions with others and the environment. The mistaken behavior might be the result of a spontaneous situation or an intentional act. (The child is acting out of involvement or curiosity.) In either case, the behavior is an attempt to learn about the limits and realities of daily life. Examples are:

- a child who "uncharacteristically" uses an expletive and watches for a reaction;
- a child who is not finished with an activity and does not want to put materials away;
- two children who quarrel over a material;
- a child who randomly marks on a table;
- a preschooler who wanders from a playground;
- third graders who giggle at a photo from *National Geographic*;
- a second grader who forgets to do an assignment;
- a kindergartener who talks to a neighbor after large group has begun.

Experimentation level mistaken behavior is common and should be expected by teachers even in appropriate educational programming. Unless there is danger of actual harm or serious disruption, teachers generally "soft pedal" their reactions. They may remind about guidelines or assist to solve a problem, but they recognize that children are meeting a need to learn through their behavior—mistakes as well as achievements. Teachers support the dynamic for development that leads to level one mistaken behavior even while they teach children skills to manage their behavior more effectively (Gartrell, 1987).

The irony with the experimentation level is that this mistaken behavior should not always be prevented. Mistakes in social living are a natural part of the total learning of children. An environment that allows children to learn from their mistakes helps them to build personal resources. Classrooms intolerant of the natural mistakes of childhood undermine their ability to learn healthy lessons from life (Ginott, 1972; Greenberg, 1988).

Especially if the level one behavior involves "testing," the teacher acts as a leader and reinforces a guideline. Still, when a teacher overreacts to level one mistaken behavior, the child feels hurt and may sense power in the act. Innocent behaviors become socially reinforced and more calculated. Unless the child is secure, stifled emotional needs become a factor, and s/he may act out, showing mistaken behavior even at level three.

Figure 8–1 A carpet square as a "hat" is not what the teacher had in mind. No one is being bothered by this level one mistaken behavior, however, and the teacher is proceeding with the activity.

Level Two Mistaken Behavior

Level two, socially influenced mistaken behavior, is learned behavior. Children show level two mistaken behavior when they are reinforced by significant others toward a particular behavior. Socially influenced mistaken behavior shows itself in distinct ways, such as:

- preschoolers who hear a word used to make fun of another and repeat it: "Blimpo," "Poopy-butt";
- a kindergarten child used to roughhousing at home who wrestles and "plays guns" at school;
- a first grader who hears explicit language and uses it as an older person would;
- second graders who shun another child, following the model of others;
- third graders who "act up" to get their names written on the board as "the 'in' thing to do."

The influence by the other can be intentional or unintentional, but the result is the same, the child behaves as a result of that influence. Common authority sources that reinforce level two behavior are:

- parents
- other family members

- friends of the family
- children who are neighbors
- classmates

Unfortunately, educators too can model inappropriate attitudes and reinforce level two mistaken behaviors.

Anecdote: Angelina loved to draw with markers. An only child, she used markers frequently at home, and her parents enjoyed her pictures. During art time at Thanksgiving, the teacher showed the children how to make a turkey, using their hands as an outline and three "Thanksgiving colors." Angelina had seen a "real turkey" on Sesame Street. She drew the turkey from memory using a variety of bright colors. The teacher noticed Angelina's turkey and told her in front of her table group that she hadn't followed directions and that her picture was messy. After the teacher was done, her seat mates told Angelina, "You can't draw," and "Yeah, you don't know how to make a turkey." Angelina went home from school a sad little girl.

The teacher in the anecdote caused level two mistaken behavior in Angelina's classmates. She also interpreted creative behavior on the child's part as unacceptable, instead reinforcing conformity and diminishing self-esteem.

In a guidance approach, when teachers encounter level two mistaken behavior, they make a determination as to whether the behavior is unique to one child, a habit such as inappropriate language, or more collective in nature, "contagious" name calling. When an individual child makes a level two mistake, the teacher intervenes either at the point of the mistaken behavior or later. S/he has a **guidance talk** with the child in which s/he reinforces a guideline and teaches an alternate acceptable action. The teacher does not judge the child or the source of the behavior, but establishes with the child that the behavior is not acceptable "in our classroom." **Encouragement** and the **compliment sandwich** are helpful as a follow-up.

With socially influenced mistaken behavior in the group context, the teacher holds **class meetings**. S/he involves children in discussion about the relevant guideline, requesting their suggestions for solutions to the problem. The class develops a plan for eliminating the mistaken behavior and implements it (Hendrick, 1992a). Using encouragement and compliment sandwiches to follow-up, the teacher discusses progress with the class in the elimination of the difficulty.

Level Three Mistaken Behavior

Level three, strong needs mistaken behavior, is serious. The primary difference between level three and level one or two mistaken behavior is the strong emotional content of level three reactions. All children (and even teachers) are entitled to a "level three day" now and then—due to health or psychological circumstances When a child continues to act atypically ("strangely") or in an extreme fashion, the teacher should suspect trouble in the child's life and the presence of strong unmet needs. In acting out as a result of those needs, the child shows level three behavior.

Typically, level three mistaken behavior shows itself in these kinds of ways:

- a child who loses control and acts out over minor-seeming frustrations;
- a child who noticeably changes social patterns, such as from sociable to withdrawn;
- a child who displays a pattern of nonparticipation, inattentiveness, sadness (depression);
- a child who exhibits fear or hostile reactions to adults or other children;
- a child who is continuously active and cannot concentrate;
- a child who lies, takes things, or manipulates others toward level two mistaken behavior;
- a child who shows inappropriate interest in or knowledge about sexuality;
- a child who is noticeably competitive, by showing a need to do things perfectly or to dominate peers and adults.

Individual guidance talks and class meetings reduce mistaken behavior at the first two levels. These methods are only components of a more comprehensive approach that is necessary with children showing level three. Discussed in the next chapter, the comprehensive approach includes:

1. non-punitive intervention at the point of crisis;
2. effort to increase understanding about the child and the situation;
3. a plan of action developed with parents, the child, and others concerned;
4. work at building a relationship with the child;
5. implementation and review of the plan.

Teachers cannot always solve the problems that cause strong needs mistaken behavior. By being proactive and non-punitive, however, the teacher can make life easier for the child, the rest of the class, and him or herself. See further chapter nine.

THE DECISION TO INTERVENE

In response to a basic question about the role of the early childhood teacher, s/he **is** a friend to children—but as an adult and a child must be friends, with the adult as leader and guide. Writers about discipline from Glasser (1969) to

Figure 8–2 By being proactive and nonpunitive, the teacher makes life easier for the child.

Canter (1976) to Hendrick (1992) share the view that children need to know the limits of acceptable behavior.

The teacher acts with firmness if guidelines protecting safety or well-being are endangered. Guidance discipline rests upon the authority of the teacher to protect the learning environment for all. There is security for children in clear limits reinforced in consistent ways (Hendrick, 1992). Still, it is important to note that punitive discipline practiced with consistency is still punitive discipline. Teachers need to appreciate the difference between firmness and harshness (Clewett, 1988; Gartrell, 1987; Greenberg, 1988).

As well, firmness as an *overriding* personal characteristic limits other important personality dimensions, such as flexibility. The professional teacher is sometimes permissive and sometimes firm, depending on judgments about the situation. (From this perspective, the saying "Don't smile until Christmas" is better expressed perhaps as "Don't smile in this situation.") If children know when the teacher will smile and when s/he will be firm, **consistency** has been achieved.

Working to Understand the Situation

Kounin's concept of **withitness** (synonymous with "eyes in the back of the head") is an important teaching skill (1977). Yet, in a guidance approach teachers recognize that the judgments they make are more appropriately thought of as **hypotheses**. Teachers must react, quickly and firmly, to situations, but the professional teacher does not hold judgments as infallible. Instead, s/he attempts to learn from the situation.

Anecdote: In a Head Start classroom, a four-year-old named Sharisse was playing with Kiko, also four, at the water table. After a few minutes, Sharisse stormed over to the teacher and said, "Kiko spilt water on me." She had a spot of water on her overalls. Upset, the teacher walked over to the water table. Kiko turned around. His shirt and pants were soaked and he was crying silently. The teacher got down to Kiko's level and asked what happened. After listening to him, she figured out that Kiko had dropped a bottle and it splashed up on Sharisse. Sharisse then dumped a bowl of water on his front.

The teacher helped Kiko get a change of clothes. She then talked with Sharisse and Kiko together. Kiko had been having a rough week with frequent displays of mistaken behavior. The teacher felt fortunate that she had gotten additional facts.

In this situation the teacher was able to collect information that helped her modify her original hypothesis. Anytime a teacher can act less like a police officer on the street and more like a judge, s/he is in a better position to make informed decisions. Withitness is an important skill, but even for "gifted" teachers, the skill takes continuous effort.

Daily, teachers of young children respond to the situations they encounter. In addition to a judgment about the level of mistaken behavior, the teacher makes three key decisions:

1. whether the situation involves one or two children or a number of children;
2. whether or not to intervene;
3. the degree of firmness of the intervention.

1. The Number of Children Involved.

A first decision is whether one or two children are involved, or whether several are. With only a few children, **child guidance** responses are called for; with several, **group management** responses are needed. Child guidance responses involve intervention in the least obtrusive way possible to bring the child's behavior within guidelines. Then, the teacher uses **guidance talks** which guide toward alternative behavior.

Group management responses address the entire group and avoid calling attention to individuals. Communication techniques discussed later in the

chapter along with class meetings, encouragement, and compliment sandwiches are responses useful for group management.

2. Whether or Not to Intervene.

A second decision is whether or not to intervene. In cases of serious mistaken
behavior, the teacher has no choice; s/he must enter the situation. In other
cases, the decision is not so clear. Three situations that require thought about
whether to intervene are **marginal mistaken behaviors**, **"bossy" behaviors**, and **arguments**.

Marginal mistaken behaviors. Teachers have different comfort levels with
mild mistaken behaviors. One teacher intervenes; another does not. As there
is no one way to use guidance discipline, this human difference is to be expected.

An important question to ask is if the behavior is bothersome only to the
teacher and not particularly to the group. When this is the case, care should be
taken in the intervention decision. Unless the intervention is matter-of-fact
and nonthreatening, the intervention may constitute more of a disruption than
the mistaken behavior itself. In such a case, the degree of firmness is mis-
matched with the situation.

Anecdote: During rest time in a day care center, a teacher witnessed the
following event. A four-year-old, Missy, who "never misbehaved,"
reached out and tugged a neighbor's hair. Then, she rolled over
and pretended she was asleep. The neighbor, a three-year-old, sat
up, rubbed his head, and complained. He then lay back down and
closed his eyes. The teacher *did not* wade through the sleeping
bodies and scold Missy. Instead, she smiled at this unusual event
and commented later to a colleague that she thought Missy was
finally feeling comfortable at the center.

The day care teacher decided that Missy's level one mistaken behavior did
not warrant intervention. To do so would have embarrassed a child with high
personal standards and disrupted a group of sleeping preschoolers. The
teacher did make a point of watching Missy's behaviors more closely and
involving Missy in more activities.

Marginal mistaken behaviors are the sort that some teachers might react to
one day but not the next. **Consistency** in teacher-response is needed both by
the child and group. As mentioned, consistency provides reliability in the environment and facilitates trust between child and teacher. In determining
whether to intervene, the teacher references behavior to the guidelines that
have been established, the specifics of the situation, and the personalities of the
children involved. While referencing to guidelines helps with consistency, the

teacher ultimately must rely on his or her professional judgment. Reflection after the event helps the teacher decide if adjustments are necessary for "next time."

Bossiness. Many teachers experience negative feelings about the marginal mistaken behavior of bossiness. A democratic society depends on citizens with leadership abilities. When young children show beginning leadership behaviors, they do so with the developmental egocentrism that they show in all behaviors. As a sense of fair play is strong in most teachers, they need to check tendencies to come down quickly on bossiness.

Anecdote: At choice-time four kindergarten girls were playing cards. The game went like this: Lisa, who frequently organized play situations, stacked and dealt the cards. All four children picked up their hands and giggled, then put them back in the deck. Lisa again stacked the cards again and re-dealt.

The teacher, who was watching, fought a tendency first to teach the children a "real game" and second to have each girl get a turn stacking and dealing. As it was, none of the other children pressed to have a turn, and the game went on for over half an hour.

Figure 8–3 Teachers positively acknowledge and encourage "beginning leadership."

Children learn about leadership and group participation from experience with peers. Teachers may need to remind a child to give others a chance; this is understandable. At the same time, they should positively acknowledge and encourage instances of "beginning leadership." The children provide an indication of how leadership is showing itself. If others willingly associate with the leading child, intervention should be minimal. If other children shy away, the child probably needs guidance. Teachers frequently can help a child feel less need to dominate by building a personal relationship and helping the child feel accepted by the group.

Arguments. Teachers generally feel a need to intervene when children quarrel. In the guidance approach, the teacher uses "withitness skills" to analyze the situation and takes any of several possible courses of action, as table 0.1 suggests.

Table 8.1
Troubleshooting Classroom Arguments

Situation	Teacher Response
Reasonable chance children can work out difficulty.	Monitors, but may not intervene. If needed, coaches children to practice conflict resolution skills.
Argument would prove too disruptive to a focused group activity.	Teacher intervenes. Redirects to class activity. States if children cannot settle, s/he will help them do so later. Teacher follow-up.
Argument becoming heated. Children don't seem able to resolve on own.	Teacher mediates. May use **talk and listen chairs**. Has each talk in turn until problem is resolved.
One child reports argument to teacher; wants assistance.	Teacher avoids taking sides. Determines whether #1, #2, or #3 above applies. Responds accordingly.
One or both have lost control; children are yelling or fighting.	Teacher intervenes. Separates children for **cooling down time**. Works for reconciliation when tempers have cooled.

When there is a danger of harm or serious disruption, teachers intervene. Wichert (1991) suggests that teachers judge situations for the level of intervention needed: high adult intervention, minimal adult intervention, or allowing children to take charge. The teacher works to help children build skills so that they can resolve conflicts on their own.

Anecdote: Head Start teachers, Tammy and Connie, had a stock phrase whenever children had a disagreement: "We have a problem. How can we solve this problem?" At the beginning of the year, they helped children settle arguments on a daily basis with the phrase. As the year went on, the two needed to use it less and less. The reason was that other staff (including a teenage assistant) and the children themselves began to say: "We have a problem. How can we solve this problem?"

Children who learn to solve problems with words are gaining a life skill of lasting value (Wichert, 1991). *Meditation skills* can be learned by prekindergarten children no less than by third graders.

3. Firmness of Intervention

A third decision is about the level of firmness to use if intervention is necessary. Matching firmness to the seriousness of the mistaken behavior is a practice usually taken for granted. Part of practicing "withitness" should be conscious thought about the degree of firmness to be used.

As Ginott points out, "Children are dependent on their teachers, and dependency breeds hostility. To reduce hostility a teacher deliberately provides children with opportunities to experience independence" (Ginott, p.76, 1972). The teacher avoids communication that pits her authority against children (Greenberg, 1988). Instead, s/he **invites, requests**, or **commands choices**. The teacher does so in factual non-demeaning ways, because children "resist a teacher less when his communications convey respect and safeguard self-esteem" (Ginott, p. 77, 1972).

Putting choices to children illustrates how to use degrees of firmness in teacher responses. A first degree is **inviting cooperation**:

"I need some strong helpers to put the blocks away." For some teachers, a mild invitation in situations like this is all that is needed. For others (and in other situations for all teachers) increased firmness is needed. A second degree is **requesting cooperation**:

"As soon as the blocks are picked up, we can go outside."

or

"The blocks need to be picked up before we can go out." (Suggesting a reward after a task has been done is known as the "Premack Principle").

When requesting cooperation, the tone of voice as well as the words convey a matter-of-fact determination that the task be done.

The third degree of firmness is **commanding cooperation**:

"Children, I am bothered that the books are still on the floor. You need to put the books away so you don't miss some of your recess."

When commanding choices, the teacher often includes an **"I" message** to underscore the seriousness of the situation. Notice use of the "I" message, factual report, and firm direction in the teacher's statement. The teacher has avoided the "me-against-you" pitfall evident in the contrasting statement,

"Either you pick up the book now, or I will keep you in at recess." Commanding choices respects the autonomy of the learner by giving the responsibility for choice to the child.

When putting choices to children at any degree of firmness, an objective is to make the **in-choice** attractive. (The "in-choice" is the one the teacher hopes the child will make.) The teacher must be prepared, though, for the occasional selection of the "out-choice." Children generally do not feel the need to rebel in classes where positive regard is present. If a child does select the "out-choice," however, the teacher accepts the choice, figures out how to re-include the child, and works on phrasing for next time.

Offering choices is basic in the guidance approach, but the skill takes practice. Sometimes, beginning teachers offer a choice that is too open-ended, or where choosing really is not warranted. Take the offer: "Do you want to wash your hands for lunch?" Children will need to know what the teacher wants them to do in order to cooperate. Sometimes a task gets done with minimum fuss if, instead of a choice, a friendly request is given: "It's time to wash hands for lunch now."

QUICK INTERVENTION STRATEGIES

Unlike marginal mistaken behaviors, teachers often agree about classroom situations that require intervention. When teacher-time is limited, the resolution of problems frequently becomes more difficult. Nonetheless, the objective is still to solve the problem, and effective techniques for resolving problems quickly are among the most important for teachers to learn. With quick and effective intervention, little problems tend not to become big ones, and the spread of mistaken behavior to other children—socially influenced mistaken behavior—is prevented. The quick intervention strategies to be considered include: **humor, nonverbal techniques, brevity,** and **being direct.**

Humor as Problem-Solver

Just as good-natured humor prevents mistaken behavior, so it diffuses problems that do occur. The ability to see humor in a difficult situation relieves tension. When not at the expense of a child, humor compliments well the firmness teachers show, and helps children and teachers alike put mistaken behavior in perspective.

Anecdote: In a child care center, the preschoolers were making a foot print mural. An assistant at one end of a five foot strip of butcher paper helped children step into a bin of red paint and pointed them in the right direction. The teacher at the other end assisted as the children stepped into a bin of soapy water and onto an absorbent towel.

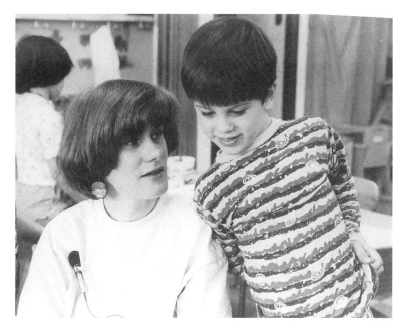

Figure 8–4 With quick intervention, little problems tend not to become big ones.

Two children waiting in line began to push and the assistant went back to mediate. A three-year-old decided not to wait for the assistant's help. She stepped into the paint, walked onto the paper, and took an abrupt left turn. The teacher at the receiving end was busy with another child and looked up to see red tracks leading to the restroom, just as the door closed. The two adults looked at each other, grinned and shook their heads. The assistant stayed with the waiting line while the teacher, still smiling, retrieved the three-year-old.

Anecdote: A teacher in an elementary school classroom was also the part-time principal. The children knew that when she was out of the room, silence was to reign. On one occasion when Mrs. Kling returned, she was dissatisfied with the noise level and demanded, "Order, please!"

From the back of the room a reply was heard: "Ham and eggs!" The young man (whose voice sounded a lot like the author's) was greatly relieved at the teacher's response: She laughed with gusto.

It is the teacher's choice to use humor in a difficult situation. For some, humor comes easily and helps all to function comfortably in the classroom. For others humor takes work; it requires that the teacher look freshly at events when "the pressure is on." Young children, because they look freshly at all situations, make humor an obvious tool to use. The challenge is for teachers not to take themselves too seriously and to remember that they and the children are in the same boat.

Nonverbal Techniques

The advantage of nonverbal techniques is that they remind about guidelines without undue embarrassment. Charles comments that nonverbal techniques typically include eye contact, physical proximity, body carriage, gestures, and facial expression (1989). Smiles and a friendly facial expression are, of course, the basic nonverbal technique. Also important, **physical proximity** is useful both in prevention and intervention with young children. In the active, developmentally appropriate classroom, the teacher is constantly moving about and interacting. Locating by children who have a problem is frequently enough to refocus attention. The skillful teacher often does so without disrupting the flow of the lesson.

Body Language. Frederich Jones is known for his writing about body language as a method in positive classroom discipline (1987). For purposes of intervention, Jones' nonverbal techniques apply mainly to children in the *primary grades and up*. Preprimary children are so involved in situations that they tend to be oblivious to all but the most direct nonverbal techniques—physical proximity and physical contact. A second proviso about nonverbal techniques is that eye contact and some touches, such as a pat on the head, may be appropriate with European American children, but not with children of some other cultural backgrounds. Knowledge of the social expectations of the families one works with is important.

As they progress through the primary grades, children become attuned to the teacher's use of body language. Appropriate with this age group, a multistep strategy for addressing mistaken behavior follows, based on the work of Jones (1987). Although the final steps involve words, the words are carefully chosen and follow from the nonverbal foundation.

Step one: Eye contact
             The power of eye contact, the age old stare, is remembered
             from school days by most adults. Generally making eye
             contact involves less embarrassment than if the teacher calls
             out or writes down the child's name.

Step two: Eye contact with firm gestures
             A slow shake of the head with a gesture such as the palm up
             or an index finger pointed up at about shoulder height reinforces the message of the stare.

Step three: Physical proximity

Mistaken behavior occurs most often away from the teacher. An important finding of Jones was that nearness of the teacher to children, is effective at reestablishing limits.

Step four: Proximity with general reminder

Having moved close to children, the teacher makes a general reminder such as "I need everyone's attention for this." (A quick glance at the children makes this step more emphatic.)

Step five: Proximity with direct comment

After establishing proximity, the teacher makes eye contact and firmly requests the behavior expected. (The teacher protects self-esteem by speaking in low but determined tones.) A follow-up conference might be warranted.

Jones has contributed to quick and effective intervention practices with his emphasis on body language. According to Jones, body carriage even more than spoken words tell children about the teacher's sureness of professional calling and comfort level with the group (1987). The basic element of body language, of course, is facial expression. About facial expression, important for all teachers of young children, Charles (1989) says this:

Figure 8–5 A caring expression communicates acceptance and support for a child in need.

Like carriage, facial expression communicates much to students. It can show enthusiasm, seriousness, enjoyment, and appreciation, all of which tend to encourage good behavior; or it can reveal boredom, annoyance, and resignation, which may tend to encourage misbehavior. Perhaps more than anything else, facial expression, through winks, smiles, and contortions, can demonstrate a sense of humor, the trait that students say they like most in teachers (p. 93).

Brevity

Among writers about teacher-child relations, none discusses the use of language more constructively (or elegantly) than Ginott (1972). Ginott states:

> Teachers like parents, need a high degree of competence in communication. An enlightened teacher shows sensitivity to semantics. He knows that the substance learned by a child often depends on the style used by the teacher (1972, p. 98).

About the use of language during intervention, Ginott speaks of the importance of **brevity**. Young children have difficulty understanding lengthy explanations. Concise statements by the teacher that address the situation and motivate toward change are the objective.

Anecdote: When Justin spoke to a neighbor for the third time during a class discussion, the teacher moved over to him and did **not** state: "Justin, you certainly have had a lot to say today. Your mouth and your ears can't work at the same time. When you're talking, others can't hear either and this makes it difficult for the class to have important discussions. Do you think it is possible for you to sit quietly for the rest of group? You can talk all you want to the other children when you're out on the playground. Now, I don't want to hear another word out of you. Do you understand? I am certainly glad that you do."

Establishing proximity, the teacher **did** say (quietly but firmly), "Justin, only one person talks at a time. You have good ideas to share, but you need to raise your hand."

The brief use of encouragement while reinforcing a guideline captures well Ginott's sense of the positive power of words.

Being Direct

Confrontation as an intervention technique must be used with care. The line between earned authority and forced authority is crucial in the guidance classroom. This is why the use of humor and nonverbal strategies anchor nonpunitive intervention. Ginott provides many useful suggestions for confronting mistaken behavior. The matching of firmness to the behavior by using choices (previous section) is a key concept. Another set of ideas offer a sound guidance strategy when mistaken behavior is more serious. Ginott's trio of ideas are these (1972):

- **Describe without labeling;**
- **Express displeasure without insult;**
- **Correct by direction.**

Describe Without Labeling. The teacher accepts the individual, but need not accept the individual's mistaken behavior. In a paraphrase of other Ginott words: address the situation, do not attack personality. The teacher describes what s/he sees that is unacceptable, but does so without labeling personalities, because "labeling is disabling" (1972). *Example*: "Stefan, you have a right to be upset, but there is no hitting in our classroom. Hitting hurts."

Express Displeasure Without Insult. Anger leads to mistaken behavior, in children and adults. For this reason, even obedience discipline models maintain that "teachers should never act out of anger." As Ginott points out, anger is an emotion that all teachers feel; they either manage it or are controlled by it (1972). Since they assist children to express emotions in acceptable ways, professional teachers need to model the management of anger themselves. The careful use of displeasure, to show that you mean business but will not harm, is a necessary teaching skill. Ginott advocates the use of "I" messages, to report feelings without condemnation. Example: "I am really bothered that you two are fighting. You will sit down in different places. We will use words to talk as soon as both of you and I have cooled down."

Correct By Direction. This statement echoes another guidance basic: "Don't just tell children what not to do; tell them what to do instead." Direct children to alternate, acceptable behaviors. The difference is between intervention that is punitive and educational. Young children are still learning "what to do instead" and have a need for and a right to this guidance. Example: "Voshon, I cannot let you hit anyone, and I will not let anyone hit you. You need to use words to tell him how you feel. He doesn't know until you tell him."

Using the Ideas Together. The describe-express-direct intervention techniques recommended by Ginott need to be used with care. They are guidance-oriented only when they address mistaken behaviors and at the same time support self-esteem. It is important to note that the teacher expresses displeasure only when s/he feels bothered by events and needs to get personal feelings "on the table." **Describe** and **direct** are sufficient to move many behaviors back within guidelines, and tend to sustain a more supportive classroom atmosphere. Notice the difference in the following figures.

Table 8.2
Examples of Describe-Direct Intervention

* Many outside voices are being used. Inside voices only please.
* It sounds like the battle of the Sumo wrestlers over here. Solve the problem or separate please.

Table 8.3
Examples of Describe-Express-Direct Intervention

* It is difficult to listen to one child when many are using outside voices. I am bothered by the noise. Inside voices please.
* You two are arguing like cats and dogs. I am really upset about this. You choose; solve the problem or do things separately. Which will it be?

BEHAVIORS REPORTED BY OTHER CHILDREN

"Tattling" bothers most teachers. They would prefer that children "attend to their own affairs" and solve their own problems. In some classrooms children are punished for tattling. In others, a child who chronically tattles acquires a label such as "tattle tale" or "busy body."

Child-report (an alternate term to tattling) is difficult to deal with because the motives of children are not always what they seem. The reason for a child-report may be that the child has a legitimate concern, wants attention, or seeks to manipulate the teacher. From a guidance perspective there are two reasons why teachers should remain open in the occurrence of child-report.

First, there are times when a teacher wants a child to report, for instance when:

- another child has strayed from the playground;
- children are fighting and one has been hurt;
- a child has been injured in an accident;
- a child is having a seizure or is otherwise ill;
- others are acting inappropriately toward a child.

Children should be encouraged to report such incidents. The well-being of children and the professional integrity of the teacher are supported by children acting as "concerned citizens."

Second, a report by a child is a request for a response by the teacher. Children need positive contact with teachers even if they don't always know how to ask for contact appropriately. The teacher models acceptance of the child by responding to the child's initiative—even when s/he sees an event differently than the child.

When children report, the teacher does well to take a moment and consider which of several possible motives may be operating. A first motive is that they have experienced a problem and have come to the teacher for assistance. A second motive is that they have witnessed a problem and believe the teacher should know about it. A third motive is that they report in order to find out what the teacher will do. A fourth motive is more to make contact with the teacher than to express a concern. A fifth motive is that they wish to control the teacher's reactions. A sixth motive is that they wish to put another child in a difficult situation.

As the following figure indicates, teachers respond differently depending on the suspected motive of the child.

Table 8.4
Suggested Responses to Child-Report

Suspected Motive of Child	Suggested Response of Teacher
Child has legitimate difficulty in relations with another child.	Teacher encourages children to solve on own or mediates to extent necessary.
Child honestly reports problem situation involving other children.	Teacher thanks child for being a "caring citizen." Monitors situation. If necessary, intervenes taking a guidance approach.
Child reports to get teacher's attention or see what teacher will do (level one mistaken behavior).	Teacher reassures child that things are under control. Monitors situation in low profile manner "just in case." Notices whether reporting child seeks attention in other ways. Works on building relationship with child.
Child reports minimal problems on a regular basis (level two mistaken behavior).	Teacher thanks child for concern, but explains other children can take care of themsleves. Tells child what the serious problems are that child can report. Builds relationship.
Child reports either to manipulate teacher or get another child in "trouble" (level three mistaken behavior).	As in all cases, teacher avoids "charging into the situation." Keeps open mind about children involved. Monitors "reporter" for other level three mistaken behavior. If necessary, procedures for working with this level are followed. (See Chapter Nine)

Figure 8–6 In the mutually satisfactory resolution of problems, all learn.

Why should teachers bother with the complex, troublesome interactions that are a part of child-report? By using guidance when they respond, adults teach children to resolve their own conflicts; to respect others' efforts at problem solving; and to come to the aid of peers who are genuinely in need. We would want these capabilities in citizens of any age as we approach the twenty-first century. From this perspective, tattling becomes a teaching opportunity.

INTERVENTION WHEN FOLLOW-UP IS NEEDED

When adults disagree, the immediate resolution of differences is not assured. Yet, with children who lack the resources and experience of adults, instant resolution frequently is expected. In academic settings that emphasize decorum and academic achievement, many view teachers who mediate difficulties as using time unproductively

Time is required if differences are to be settled in ways from which all can benefit. In the mutually satisfactory resolution of problems, all learn (Wichert, 1992). In the peaceful resolution of difficulties, teachers enhance self-esteem and faith in the school—the will for educational success (Greenberg, 1988).

Ginott (1972) recognized that in some situations there should be "no hurried help." He wrote that when the teacher quickly "solves" problems for children, they feel inadequate. Ginott states:

The teacher listens to the problem, rephrases it, clarifies it, gives the child credit for formulating it, and then asks, "What options are open to you?" "What are your choices in this situation?" Often the child himself comes up with a solution. Thus, he learns that he can rely on his own judgment. When a teacher hastily offers solutions, children miss the opportunity to acquire competence in problem-solving and confidence in themselves (p. 92).

Sometimes, situations can be addressed quickly with nonverbal or verbal responses that sustain self-esteem and increase understanding. In these cases, follow-up is not necessary. In other cases, speedy resolution is not realistic. When the teacher must give time to a situation, s/he does so either at the moment of the occurrence or later in the day. (Response at a later time is due to conflicting demands on the teacher at the moment, or to the need for a **cooling down time** if emotions are high.)

This section addresses teacher-responses for when follow-up is necessary, either at the time of the intervention or later. Two follow-up strategies are explored: **mediation techniques**, and **guidance talks**.

Mediation Techniques

Teachers use mediation techniques when children cannot settle disputes on their own, or when teachers and children have disagreements. In using mediation the teacher models responses that resolve difficulties and teaches communication skills. Mediation can occur both with individual children, as a child guidance technique, or with groups—taking the form of a class meeting. An analysis of the mediation process yields at least ten steps. These are listed, but in practice, as Ginott's statement suggests, mediation has three basic components: (*a*) identifying the problem, (*b*) generating possible solutions, and (*c*) agreeing on a solution to be tried.

Table 8.5
Steps in Formal Classroom Mediation

A. Identifying the problem
    1. Decide that time should be taken for the mediation to occur.
    2. Establish that the purpose of the mediation is to resolve a problem, not to blame or label individuals.
    3. Allow each child involved to express views and feelings about the problem using reflective listening to clarify points.
    4. Summarize differing viewpoints, checking for accuracy of interpretation with participants.
B. Generating possible solutions
    5. Request cooperation in seeking a solution.
    6. Encourage the suggestion of solutions.
    7. Appreciate that each suggestion was made, even if others have difficulty with it.

C. Agreeing on a solution to be tried
    8. Work for consensus on a course of action.
    9. Avoid accusations about vested interest. Instead, point out that "others see the situation differently" and encourage further discussion.
    10. Point out that perfect solutions are not always possible, but this one is worth trying. Suggest a time when any one wanting to can talk more.

Reflective Listening. A key tool in mediation is **reflective listening**. Reflective listening means that the teacher articulates or rephrases the child's feelings and perceptions. Reflective listening conveys to the child a feeling of acceptance and teaches the use of words to describe feelings and perceptions. By feeling affirmed by the teacher, the child feels less need to defend a particular position and is more open to dialogue. Reflective listening is helpful in gaining agreement about the problem to be solved. Occasionally the practice is enough to settle a problem in itself:

Anecdote: Les was building a barn with blocks when Craig accidentally knocked it over. Les had fists clenched and teeth set when the teacher arrived. The teacher said, "Craig didn't mean to, Les, but it's too bad about your building and it's OK to feel sad about it."

Les hung his head and looked like he might cry. Then, he looked up and said, "It's not a building; it's a barn. But I'm gonna build it different this time." Les got back to work—and Craig looked relieved.

Including Children's Ideas. A second mediation tool is **involving children in the solution process**. When children contribute to the solution, they feel capable as problem solvers. Including some suggestions of Ginott, questions like these empower children to "work things out":

- What options are open to you?
- What are your choices in this situation?
- How can we solve this problem?
- Who has an idea about what we can do?
- What can we do about it?
- How could you solve this differently?
- Maybe the two of you can solve the problem together?
- What words could you use next time?

When children are asked for their views, ideas, and assistance, they are apt to show initiative and to work for a cooperative solution. The leadership of the adult here is critical (Wichert, 1991).

Anecdote: A third grader, Elaine, had a difficult time concentrating during large group activities. She visited with neighbors and showed inattentiveness to topics being discussed. At a break time, the teacher talked with the child:

Teacher: Elaine, there is a problem during large group that we need to talk about. I have to remind you to pay attention too many times.

Elaine: Well, the other kids are always talking to me.

Teacher: Yes, I know; it is hard to listen when too many people are talking. What can we do about it?

Elaine: (long pause) Maybe I could move.

Teacher: That sounds like an idea. Why don't you choose? Where could you sit where you wouldn't be bothered by other children?

Elaine: By Renee, maybe.

Teacher: All right, let's try it. But remember our guideline, one person talks at a time, OK?

Elaine: OK, teacher.

The teacher followed through by making sure Elaine sat where they agreed and by using nonverbal techniques, including smiles, to hold her attention. Two days later s/he complimented the progress that Elaine has shown.

Requesting assistance in solving a problem works with younger children as well as older ones and can be used in group and individual situations

Figure 8–7 In a group setting, a request to solve a problem becomes part of a class meeting.

(Hendrick, 1992a). In a group setting, a request to solve a problem becomes part of a **class meeting**:

Anecdote: A kindergarten teacher brings together the class for a serious discussion.

Teacher:	There is a problem during choice time that we need to talk about. A child was hurt on the climber today. Play there is getting too rough, and I am disturbed about it.
Louise:	Yeah, and I nearly fell off, too.
Dennis:	The kids was going down the slide wrong.
Elsabet:	Too many of them and it's loud.
Teacher:	Well, Mr. Stone (the janitor) and I could put the climber away for a while, or maybe you have some ideas for what we could do.
Allen:	Don't let so many on.
Louise:	No pushin' on top, and go down on your seat.
Elsabet:	No pushing and yelling.
Teacher:	It sounds like we have some guidelines for the climber the way we do for class. I will write them down. (She prints what the children have told her and reads the guidelines aloud.) We will give the climber another try, but everyone needs to remember the guidelines.

The teacher posted the guidelines near the climber. Though the children could not decode every word, they did remember the guidelines and reminded their friends about them. Play on the climber became safer and the equipment stayed up in the room.

The ability to settle differences cooperatively is a cornerstone both of individual mental health and the functioning of a democracy. Moreover, the time commitment for mediation may not be as great as one might think. Mediation is an earnest experience for children, and the motivation to solve the problem quickly tends to be high. **Even if the mediation process does take time initially, it pays off in productive problem-solving—often by children on their own—in the long run** (Wichert, 1991).

Mediation can be formalized in such procedures as talk and listen chairs and class meetings. Individual components of mediation, such as reflective listening and including children's ideas, also can be used informally. However used by the individual teacher, mediation is an important strategy in a guidance approach to discipline.

Guidance Talks

Teachers use mediation procedures to solve current classroom problems. They utilize **guidance talks** to empower children to handle difficulties more effectively in the future. Typically, while mediation occurs either with individual children or groups, guidance talks are private discussions with individuals. Guidance talks are not needed after every teacher intervention. They are needed when conflicts have been serious and a child could benefit from reconciliation. The teacher uses guidance talks after a problem has been resolved, but is still fresh in the child's mind.

The reader is familiar with two communication techniques helpful in guidance talks, **encouragement** and the **compliment sandwich**. A third technique is **reflective listening**. The teacher uses these tools informally and supportively in the guidance conversation.

Guidance talks differ from another kind of talk discussed in the previous chapter, **contact talks**. Contact talks are for the purpose of getting to know a child better. In contact talks the teacher follows the line of conversation of the child, respecting the child's interests and background, and listening.

In guidance talks, the teacher has topics that s/he wishes to cover: (*a*) an update as to how the child is feeling; (*b*) ideas about what the child might do differently next time; (*c*) suggestions about how the child might be reconciled with the group and/or the teacher. A teacher and child should have both kinds of talk, of course. Contact talks allow a teacher to continue to build a relationship after a guidance talk has occurred.

A second key distinction for the teacher is the difference between a guidance talk and "the lecture." The disciplinary lecture tends to convey a "shape up or else" message and is only marginally a discussion. The guidance talk accepts the child's perceptions and feelings, educates about the consequences of behaviors, and guides toward more productive possibilities. Its tone is supportive and conversational.

Anecdote: Curtis, a kindergartener, was given a cooling down time when he hit another child. After cooling down, he and the teacher had the following conversation:

Teacher: How are you feeling now, Curtis?

Curtis: Still mad.

Teacher: Sometimes it takes a while to feel better. Curtis, why do you suppose you hit Glen?

Curtis: 'Cause he wouldn't play.

Teacher: If you hit kids, will they want to play with you?

Curtis: Yeah, maybe.

Teacher: (Smiles.) I've been around a long time, Curtis, and I've noticed that kids mainly want to play if you're friendly. How could you be friendly to Glen?

Curtis: Not hit?

Teacher: That's an idea. You are really thinking. What else?

Curtis: Get something so he could play.

Teacher: Those are friendly ideas, Curtis. When you play with Glen, what do you and he like to do?

Curtis: Play with trucks and stuff, and he likes puzzles.

Teacher: Those are some ideas for friends to do together. Maybe, if you told Glen you were sorry, he would want to do those things now. Or, you could play with someone else if you'd like.

Curtis: OK.

Curtis gets off the chair, but does not join Glen. Instead, he does puzzles with two other children. Later, the teacher notices Curtis and Glen playing together.

Reconciliation. **Reconciliation** is an important part of the guidance talk, but the teacher does not force apologies. Children no less than adults know when they are ready to apologize and when they are not. (To children's credit, they tend to forgive more easily than most adults.) Instead, the teacher invites an apology as one possible way to get relationships back on level ground. S/he then monitors the situation, but allows children to make amends on their own. It is easier for children to apologize when they know that their feelings and points of view have been respected—this is what the guidance talk is about.

In the most serious situations, teachers physically restrain or remove children, to prevent harm (see chapter nine). In these cases, the primary focus of the child's anger may be the teacher. Whatever the focus of blame for a conflict, the teacher is the one who initiates reconciliation. The principle of unconditional positive regard means that the teacher works for reconciliation as a part of daily practice. In the guidance approach, the teacher recognizes that the act of reconciling comes not from weakness, but from strength. Guidance discipline differs from punitive discipline in this regard.

The guidance talk may not turn around mistaken behavior instantaneously. The lessons of getting along with others and expressing strong emotions acceptably take time to learn. Nonetheless, supportive conversations help children in many ways, not the least of which is the modelling of adult compassion.

WHY TAKE THE TIME?

Researchers such as Mitchell have noted a steady decline in the self-esteem of children as they progress through the grades. To quote Curwin and Mendler:

> Mitchell found that 80 percent of children enter first grade with high self-esteem. By the time they reach fifth grade, only 20 percent have high self esteem. By the time they finish high school, the number having positive self esteem has dropped to a staggering 5 percent (p. 26, 1988).

Mitchell's finding suggests that school experiences such as failure, embarrassment, and other facets of conditional acceptance have a deleterious effect.

In a *Newsweek* feature on early childhood education, Katz referred to the need for a "1st R" in educational practice: **Relationships** (Kantrowitz & Wingert, 1989). In the schooling of the 1990s, the personal/social skills of democracy need to be considered components of the curriculum no less than the education basics. (Ironically, Dewey's eloquent pleas to this end will have become 100 years old during the decade.) Katz argues persuasively that assisting children to develop personal/social skills is as valid a component of the curriculum as the academic subjects.

Guidance discipline is a part of an interactive teaching approach that includes the "1st R." Through the use of guidance to solve problems, adults are teaching children essential life skills. Children are learning:

- acceptable ways of expressing strong emotions;
- positive alternative behaviors to acting out;
- conflict resolution skills;
- consideration for the viewpoints and feelings of others;
- positive self-regard;
- appreciation for the teacher as a helping person;
- respect for the role of the teacher;
- acceptance of the role of student.

Put in terms of broad developmental outcomes, the child gains in:

- emotional development through the ability to express feelings acceptably and resolve problems constructively;
- language development through the vocabulary, phrasing, and functional communication necessary for the resolution of difficulties;
- cognitive development by the critical thinking inherent in problem-solving;
- physical development through freedom from the effects of stress, tension, and hostile feelings when problems remain unresolved or become aggravated;
- social development by learning skills important for productive functioning as a member of the group and a democratic society.

The time commitment adults give to finding solutions for mistaken behavior is an investment in the personal and educational success of the children in their care.

ASSISTANCE FROM PARENTS

As a professional, the teacher collaborates with parents and colleagues in the education of the child. Many factors make collaboration with parents a challenge for teachers (Galinsky, 1988). Parents have common perspectives and values that differ from those of teachers. Parents:

Figure 8–8 Guidance discipline is a part of an interactive teaching approach that includes the "1st R", relationships.

- have a strong emotional investment in their children;
- at times question their own effectiveness as parents (Morgan, 1989);
- have views about acceptable behavior and discipline methods influenced by their backgrounds more than formal education (Galinsky, 1988);
- may view the teacher as a "superior" who will be unreceptive to efforts at communication (Greenberg, 1989).

Unless they come to understand these differences, teachers may take personally contacts with parents that seem uncooperative, defensive, or unfriendly.

To accommodate the difference in roles and viewpoints, Galinsky suggests that, "Rather than the dispenser of correct information, the professional builds an alliance in which the parent's own expertise is strengthened" (1988, p. 11). Galinsky (1988) and Morgan (1989) provide useful suggestions for taking this collaborative approach. The following discussion builds upon points made by the authors.

1. Create a Team Concept

This step, mentioned in other chapters of the book, provides a foundation for cooperation should problems arise. The step cannot begin too early in the program year. As Morgan (1989) suggests, work with parents' emotional ties to their children, not against them.

2. Be Aware of Your Feelings Toward the Family

Just as there are children that teachers may feel uncomfortable around, so there are families. One reason for negative feelings toward a family is the view that a family has not met implicit expectations about parenting (Galinsky, 1988). In this event, it is important for the teacher to understand circumstances within the family that may make the expectations unrealistic. Cultural, economic, or social factors all contribute to life styles and values potentially different than the teacher's own. The teacher who identifies and accepts the fact of diversity is in a better position to understand and work with the family, and the child.

3. Understand Parent Development

About this topic, Galinsky states:

It is much easier to understand parents if you know the normal course of parental growth and development. For example, before decrying the superbaby phenomenon, it helps to know that all new parents want perfection for their children—that is normal. It is their definition of perfection you want to alter, not their desire for the best (1988, p. 10).

Figure 8–9 "It is much easier to understand parents if you understand the normal course of parental growth and development."

4. Choose Words That Avoid Value Judgments

Describing without labeling is a basic of the guidance approach that pertains to parents no less than children. Galinsky and Morgan use examples that may sound familiar. Here is a variation of an example used by Morgan (1989, p. 56):

Instead of: Karla was a real terror this afternoon. It was "isolation corner" for her today. After that she shaped up, and she is being a good girl now.

Say: After nap today, Karla had a problem with two children. She needed a cool down time, but then we read books and she is having an easier time now.

Note the non-judgmental tone and the recognition of progress included in the second statement, which is approaching a compliment sandwich. As contrast, in statement one the use of "value laden" language is clear (Morgan, 1989). The compliment sandwich, "I" message, and reflective listening all provide alternatives to value judgments, and are useful in communications with parents as well as children.

5. Refer for Support Services

Galinsky identifies a crucial role of the teacher as referring families to other services (Galinsky, 1988). She states, "It is just as important to know when to say no and to refer as it is to know when to say yes" (p. 10). The teacher is not a therapist or a social worker, but can refer a family to a needed service and be supportive through the referral process.

Head Start has led the way in assisting families to access health and social agencies as well as educational services. Increasingly, schools and other programs are coming to realize that not just the child, but the family is the unit of service in early childhood programs (Galinsky, 1988; Boyer, 1992). The ability to work with families to remove the stigma of special education or social service assistance is a goal of the teacher. Establishing trust with the family at the beginning of the year increases the chances of a successful referral.

Matters of teacher-parent relations such as referrals will not always go as the teacher hopes. As Galinsky comments, "Having others to turn to when there are tensions is crucial in working effectively with parents" (p. 10). The source of support might be a fellow teacher, aide, director, social worker, special educator, or principal (1988). A friend or family member outside of the school is equally important. The person serving as the "support base" should recognize the need for a teacher to privately "vent" with no repercussions. Ideally, the source of support also can assist the teacher to plan a constructive course of action.

6. Mediate with Parents

Mediation often becomes necessary when mistaken behavior grows serious. Galinsky suggests a six-step approach to **teacher-parent problem-solving**. The goal is to convert "unhealthy tension" to "healthy tension" in relations (1988). The six steps are similar to the process suggested earlier in the chapter for helping children solve problems in the classroom. The steps include:

1. Describe the situation as a problem out front. Avoid accusations or the implications that the source of the problem resides in the personality of the parent or the child.
2. Generate multiple solutions. Parents and professionals should both do this, and no one's suggestions should be ignored, put down, or denounced.
3. Discuss the pros and cons of each suggestion.
4. Come to a consensus about which solutions to try.
5. Discuss how you will implement these solutions.
6. Agree to meet again to evaluate how these solutions are working so that you can change your approach, if necessary (Galinsky, 1988, p. 11).

The teacher cannot separate the child's life at school from the child's life at home. The child's life at home is the family. Through acceptance of the family, the teacher optimizes chances of gaining the parent's trust and assistance in helping the child.

SUMMARY

Chapter eight introduces the basic theme of unit three: Rather than punish children for having problems, guidance discipline teaches children to solve them.

How do teachers apply the concept of mistaken behavior?

Ability to understand the level of a child's mistaken behavior helps the teacher with intervention decisions. Children show level one, experimentation level mistaken behavior, as a result of involvement in situations or curiosity. The teacher responds in a matter-of-fact manner to educate toward alternatives without reinforcing the behavior. Children show level two mistaken behavior, socially influenced, when they have been reinforced toward mistaken behavior by significant others. The teacher uses guidance talks or class meetings to re-establish an applicable guideline and to teach alternative behaviors. Level three, strong needs mistaken behavior, occurs when there is trouble in the child's life that is beyond the child's capacity to cope with and understand. The teacher uses the comprehensive approach to addressing level three mistaken behavior introduced earlier and discussed in chapter nine.

What goes into the decision to intervene?

The teacher is a friend to children, but an adult friend, who accepts the responsibility for leadership. The adult works to understand situations by practicing "withitness." In addition to judgments about the level of mistaken behavior, on a regular basis the teacher decides: whether problem situations involve one or two children or a number of children; whether to intervene; and the degree of firmness of the intervention. The strategy of inviting, requesting, or commanding choices illustrates the use of different degrees of firmness and at the same time grants children a measure of independence.

What are four quick intervention strategies?

Quick intervention strategies that stem problems but still protect self esteem are important in guidance discipline. Humor is one such strategy by which the teacher can defuse tense situations. A second strategy is nonverbal communication, including facial expressions and establishing proximity. Brevity is a third strategy, an effective alternative to moralizing and "lectures." A fourth strategy is direct intervention through the "describe, express, direct" and the "describe and direct" sequences.

How does the teacher respond to mistaken behaviors reported by children?

Child-report (an alternate term to tattling) is difficult to deal with because the motives of children are not always what they seem. Two reasons why teachers should neither ban nor disparage child-report are: There are times when a teacher wants a child to report—when safety is threatened. Also, child-report is a request for contact with the teacher. Children need positive contact even if they don't always know how to ask for contact appropriately. Suggestions were provided to help teachers determine motives for child-report and take an appropriate course of action.

What are strategies to use when interventions require follow-up?

Time is required if differences are to be settled in ways from which all can benefit. Teachers use mediation techniques when children cannot settle disputes on their own. Mediation has three basic components: (*a*) identifying the problem: (*b*) generating possible solutions; (*c*) agreeing on a solution to be tried. Teachers use guidance talks to teach children to handle difficulties more effectively in the future.

Why take the time to find solutions?

Assisting children to develop social skills through conflict resolution is a valid part of the curriculum of the 1990s. Individuals and the society both benefit when children have experience at solving problems of mistaken behavior.

(Courtesy of Lin Wahlberg, Early Childhood Family Education, Bemidji, Minnesota.)

How does the teacher gain assistance from parents?

Collaboration with parents is difficult for teachers due to differences in perspective and values. To accommodate these differences, Galinsky (1988) suggests that the role of the teacher is to foster an alliance in which the parent's own expertise is strengthened. To do so, the teacher builds positive relationships, monitors feelings toward the family, understands parent development, chooses words that avoid value judgments, and uses referrals for support services. The teacher uses a six-step problem-solving approach in collaboration with parents to solve problems that may arise. Through the assistance of the family, the teacher reaches the child.

FOLLOW-UP ACTIVITIES

Follow-up activities allow the student to interrelate material from the text with "real life" situations. The "observations" imply access to practicum experiences, the "interviews" access to teachers. When communicating about the activities, students need to respect the privacy of all participants in the observation or interview, as an important professional courtesy.

1. **How do teachers apply the concept of mistaken behavior?**
   a. Observe a teacher who intervenes in an instance of level one, two, or three mistaken behavior. Respecting the privacy of the teacher, how did the intervention comply with or deviate from the recommended guidance approach for that level?
   b. Interview the teacher about the kinds of mistaken behavior that s/he finds most troubling. Ask the teacher to discuss why. At what level or levels was the mistaken behavior that the teacher described?
2. **What goes into the decision to intervene?**
   a. Observe a situation when a teacher had to decide whether to intervene. Respecting the privacy of the teacher, how did the decision correspond to the discussion about intervention in the chapter? Refer to the issues of withitness, the intensity of the mistaken behavior—marginal to serious—and the degree of firmness of the intervention.
   b. Interview a teacher about how s/he decides whether intervention in a situation is needed. When there is an intervention, what difference does it make whether one or two children or a larger group is involved? How does the teacher decide how firm to be during the intervention?
3. **What are four quick intervention strategies?**
   a. Observe one of the four strategies in use. How did the teacher respond in the situation? How did the child or children respond? What did you learn from the observation about the intervention strategy?

b. Interview a teacher about whichever of the four strategies s/he has used. How conscious is the teacher of using the strategy? How often does s/he use it? How comfortable is the teacher with the strategy? Why?

4. How does the teacher respond to mistaken behaviors reported by children?

a. Observe an instance of child-report. Referring to the chapter as a guide, what seemed to be the motivations of the child in making the report? How did the teacher handle the situation? What seemed to be the effect on the child who reported?

b. Interview a teacher about tattling. How does the teacher handle child-report? How do the teacher's views compare or contrast with the material on child-report in the text?

5. What are strategies to use when interventions require follow-up?

a. Observe an instance of serious mistaken behavior. Did the teacher use mediation? Did the teacher use a guidance talk? What did you learn about working with serious mistaken behavior from your observation?

b. Interview a teacher about his or her approach when intervening during serious mistaken behavior. What does s/he try to accomplish at the point of the conflict? After the parties involved have cooled down? What do you believe the teacher uses of the mediation and guidance talk strategies based on your interview?

6. Why take the time to find solutions?

a. Observe an instance when you believe a teacher took a problem-solving approach to mistaken behavior. What was the outcome for the children involved? What was the outcome for the teacher? What did you learn from the observation about using problem-solving strategies with mistaken behavior?

b. Interview a teacher who takes a problem-solving approach to mistaken behavior. What are the priorities of the teacher when she intervenes? What does the teacher want children to learn when s/he intervenes?

7. How does the teacher gain assistance from parents?

a. Observe, and if possible participate, in an instance of parent-teacher communication outside of the classroom—a conference, parent meeting, home-visit, etc. What seemed to be the teacher's priorities in the communication effort? What seemed to be the result in terms of parent-teacher relations?

b. Interview a teacher about a family that s/he was uncomfortable with or had trouble understanding. How did the teacher communicate with the family to build relations? How satisfied was the teacher with the success of the effort?

SUGGESTED RESOURCES

Galinsky, E. (1988). "Parents and Teacher-Caregivers: Sources of Tension, Sources of Support," *Young Children, 43*(3), pp. 4-12.

Greenberg, P. (1988). "Ideas That Work With Young Children. Avoiding 'Me Against You' Discipline," *Young Children, 44*(1), pp. 24-29.

Kantrowitz, B. and Wingert, P. (April 17, 1989). "How Kids Learn," *Newsweek*, (50-56). New York: Newsweek, Inc.

Minnesota Association for the Education of Young Children. (1001). *Develop mentally Appropriate Guidance of Young Children*. St. Paul, MN: MAEYC. (In Appendix.)

Morgan, E.L. (1989). "Talking with Parents When Concerns Come Up," *Young Children, 44*(2),. pp. 52-56.

Wichort, S. (1991). "Solving Problems Together," *Scholastic Prekindergarten Today*, March, pp. 46-52.

REFERENCES

Boyer, E.L. (1992). *Ready to Learn: A Mandate for the Nation*. Princeton, NJ: The Carnegie Foundation for the Advancement of Teaching.

Bredekamp, S. (ed.) (1987). *Developmentally Appropriate Practice in Early Childhood Programs Serving Children From Birth Through Age 8*. Washington, DC: National Association for the Education of Young Children.

Canter, L. and Canter, M. (1976). *Assertive Discipline: a Take-Charge Approach for Today's Educator*. Sand Beach, CA: Canter and Associates, Inc.

Charles, C.M. (1989). *Building Classroom Discipline*. White Plains, NY: Longman, Inc.

Clewett, A.S. (1988). "Guidance and Discipline: Teaching Young Children Appropriate Behavior," *Young Children, 43*(4), pp. 26-36.

Curwin, R.L. and Mendler, A.N. (1988). *Discipline with Dignity*. Alexandria, VA: Association for Supervision and Curriculum Development.

Galinsky, E. (1988). "Parents and Teacher-Caregivers: Sources of Tension, Sources of Support," *Young Children, 43*(3), pp. 4-12.

Gartrell, D.J. (1987). "Punishment or Guidance," *Young Children, 42*(3), pp. 55-61.

Ginott, H. (1972). *Teacher and Child*. New York: MacMillan Publishing Company.

Glasser, W. (1969). *Schools Without Failure*. New York: Harper and Row.

Greenberg, P. (1988). "Ideas That Work With Young Children. Avoiding 'Me Against You' Discipline," *Young Children, 44*(1), pp. 24-29.

Greenberg, P. (1989). "Ideas That Work With Young Children. Parents as Partners in Young Children's Development and Education: A New American Fad? Why Does It Matter?" *Young Children, 44*(4), pp. 61-75.

Hendrick, J. (1992a). "Where Does It All Begin? Teaching the Principles of Democracy in the Early Years," *Young Children, 47*(3), pp. 51-53.

Hendrick, J. (1992b). *The Whole Child.* Columbus, OH: Merrill Publishing Company.

Jones, F. (1987). *Positive Classroom Discipline.* New York: McGraw Hill.

Kantrowitz, B. and Wingert, P. (April 17, 1989). "How Kids Learn," *Newsweek,* (50-56). New York: Newsweek, Inc.

Kounin, J. (1977). *Discipline and Group Management in Classrooms.* New York: Holt, Rinehart and Winston.

Morgan, E.L. (1989). "Talking With Parents When Concerns Come Up," *Young Children, 44*(2), pp. 52-56.

Wichert, S. (1991). "Solving Problems Together," *Scholastic Prekindergarten Today*, March, pp. 46-52.

9

Guidance in the Tough Times

GUIDING QUESTIONS

As you read chapter nine, you will discover answers to the following questions:

- **What conditions make intervention necessary?**
- **What are three methods of crisis management?**
- **What techniques assist the teacher to manage personal feelings of anger?**
- **What are strategies for working with level three strong needs mistaken behavior?**
- **What are considerations when teachers and parents disagree?**

From early experiences in baby-sitting or high school child development classes, some young adults gravitate toward early childhood education. After teaching older children, other adults shift to early age groups, feeling they can relate more comfortably with young children. The opportunity to be fully nurturing within the teaching role, and the rewards for being so, motivate many women and a small but growing number of men toward early childhood education.

Teachers want to be friendly and supportive toward young children. Aware of the trust that is placed in them, early childhood teachers take seriously the decision "to discipline." They worry about hurting feelings and losing children's friendship. They are concerned about what they or children might do when emotions run high. They wonder how intervention will affect other children and the atmosphere of the class. They fear the self-doubt and shame that can occur if they overreact. They may feel anxiety as well about what a child may say to a parent, and what the parent may do in response.

Figure 9–1 The opportunity to be nurturing within the teaching role motivates many toward early childhood education.

Still, sometimes intervention is necessary, and timely intervention is the measure and foundation of the authenticity of the teacher (Gartrell, 1987). There is security in enforced limits for the child, other children, and the teacher (Hendrick, 1992). To paraphrase Dreikurs (1972), reluctance to intervene in the face of harm or serious disruption marks an unproductive level of teacher permissiveness, as distinct from "democratic" [guidance] discipline.

A premise of unit three is that even in crisis situations, intervention techniques remain problem-solving in nature, intended to guide and not to punish. The previous chapter examined strategies for solving "routine" problems in the classroom. The strategies discussed were for those situations that could be resolved without undue difficulty, either immediately or with follow-up. Chapter nine, the second chapter of the unit, examines serious mistaken behavior, when strong emotions make words ineffective.

CONDITIONS THAT MAKE INTERVENTION NECESSARY

Varying tolerance levels toward mild mistaken behaviors mean that teachers differ in responses to these situations. To maintain consistency in response to mild mistaken behaviors, teachers do well to link interventions to established guidelines, work to understand the child and the situation, and self-monitor moods and response tendencies. In contrast to mild mistaken behaviors, a large majority of early childhood teachers choose to intervene when:

1. children cannot resolve a situation themselves and the situation is deteriorating;
2. one or more children cause serious disruption to the education process;
3. the danger of harm exists.

Often two or all three of these conditions are present at the same time, and virtually all teachers would then intervene.

Whenever possible, if the teacher can control the situation with quick intervention strategies discussed in the previous chapter—body language, humor, brief comments, inviting or requesting choices, describing situations and directing behaviors—such strategies are desirable. They minimize classroom disruption, cause minimum shock to children, and restore equilibrium effectively. When children have lost control, however, the nature of the intervention becomes more involved. The teacher then uses a **combination of intervention strategies** for the purpose of conflict resolution.

Figure 9–2 When children have lost control, the teacher uses a combination of intervention strategies.

Anecdote: 1. (Deterioriating situation): Nigel was in the space under a four-sided climber playing by himself. Dinee opened the door and started to come in. Nigel pushed against the door and said, "You can't come in here." Dinee pushed her way in, and the two were yelling at each other when the teacher arrived.

With firmness she said to both: "You are having a problem, so choose: Let's talk and settle this, or play somewhere else." Nigel made a fist at Dinee, who shoved his hand away. The loud voices continued. The teacher, halfway in the door, put a hand on each child's shoulder and stated: "You have decided. Go to different parts of the room and find something else to do." Dinee did, but Nigel lay down and began to cry. Outside of the climber the teacher held him for a bit and got him started on a favorite puzzle. Later, the teacher talked with the children about how they could handle the problem differently "next time."

Anecdote: 2. (Serious disruption): Though the teacher had given a "five minute warning," Randy was not ready to stop using the blocks as clean-up began. The teacher asked him to help put the blocks away, but Randy instead grabbed several loose blocks and brought them to where he was building. The teacher went over to Randy and told him he could leave his structure for later, but he would have to put the new blocks away. Randy became upset and began to kick the blocks. Lightly holding Randy's arms, the teacher knelt down to eye level; she stated firmly, "Randy, I know you are angry, but blocks are not for kicking. Let's go sit so that you can cool down." She took his hand and the two sat down. At the end of cleanup, the teacher made sure that Randy successfully joined the next activity.

Anecdote: 3. (Danger of harm): Darwin and Rita were painting on opposite sides of an easel. Darwin peeked around the side and painted some red on Rita's blue sky. Rita painted blue on Darwin's bare arm. Darwin dropped his brush and pushed Rita down. Rita yelled and while sitting began to kick Darwin's ankles. Looking furious, Darwin was in the act of pouncing when the teacher arrived and restrained him. Darwin struggled to get loose until he realized that he couldn't. After a few minutes in the teacher's "bear hug," with the teacher speaking soothingly to him, Darwin quieted down. When she felt she could leave him, the teacher tended to Rita, who was still sitting on the floor. She followed-up later by talking with each.

In these three situations the teacher chose to resolve conflicts by non-punitive intervention. In each case, the teacher reestablished limits, order, and after reconciliation, a measure of calm. Because during a conflict all involved are at risk for psychological and physical harm, crisis intervention is neither easy nor pleasant. When any or all of the three conditions is present—a situation deteriorates, serious disruption occurs, the danger of harm exists—intervention becomes necessary. **Nonpunitive intervention** is the measure of the value the teacher places in guidance discipline.

CRISIS MANAGEMENT TECHNIQUES

Crises occur when emotions are running high and the communication process is breaking down. In **crisis intervention** the teacher makes a final effort to restore communication so that mediation can occur. If this is impossible, the teacher works to restore order, so that guidance techniques can be used when emotions have cooled down.

The three previously illustrated situations constitute typical early childhood classroom crises. Among the intervention techniques the teachers used were *commanding cooperation*, *separation*, and *physical restraint*. These procedures are fundamental **crisis management techniques** and each is discussed further.

Commanding Cooperation

In a guidance approach the teacher matches the intensity of the intervention to the seriousness of the mistaken behavior. Chapter eight introduced **making choices** as a useful intervention procedure. At a prevention level, the teacher frequently works to **invite cooperation**: "I need some superstrong helpers to help move the chairs." At a problem-solving level, the teacher **requests cooperation**: "As soon as the books are on the shelves and the legos are in the box, it will be time to go outside." At the crisis level, the teacher sometimes **commands cooperation**: "Brett, you choose: Use words to express your feelings, or go to another part of the room and cool down."

When commanding cooperation, the teacher is not making an ultimatum—"Either you shape up, or I will make you" Ultimatums set up adversarial relationships between teachers and children that undermine mutual trust (Greenberg, 1988). Instead, the adult requests children to choose a personal course of action and teaches them that they have some control in the situation. The child may not like the options, but the fact that s/he can choose bestows dignity, in contrast to the "do it or else" alternative imposed by a threat.

Referring to the example of commanded cooperation above, Brett may choose to use words—the "in" choice. In this case the communication process is restored and mediation becomes possible. If Brett elects to separate from the

Figure 9–3 A common command for cooperation is that children discuss a conflict or play elsewhere. The teacher stands by to mediate in order to resolve the difficulty.

situation—the "out" choice—his decision is respected and the teacher later uses guidance methods to teach him more effective behavior alternatives.

The command for cooperation is a **method of first resort** among crisis techniques because it holds out the possibility of mediation to resolve the difficulty. This method remains nonpunitive, however, only if the "out" choice is a logical consequence of the behavior and if guidance is later offered. What seems a logical consequence to a teacher in the midst of a crisis may really be punishment, so the teacher should pose the "out" alternative with care.

For example, in a second grade situation a logical consequence of hitting on the playground might be to walk with a friendly playground supervisor during recess for a day, not to have in-school detention during recess for a week. In a preprimary setting, an "out choice" for continued reckless play on a climber might be to go to a different activity; it would not be to stay off the climber for a week. Guidance talks that follow-up by explaining the consequence and teaching more acceptable behaviors are a key part of the procedure.

Separation

Separation from the group is the crisis intervention technique of second resort. Whenever possible, the author favors the least disruptive form of separation:

diversion to alternate activity in another part of the room—**redirection**. The teacher uses redirection when s/he decides not to mediate a problem. Even when separation is "only" redirection, the teacher may still opt to follow-up with a guidance talk to ensure that young children understand the events and maintain composure. Redirection is often used with preschoolers, but has its place with older learners as well.

In-room **isolation**—commonly known as use of a "time out chair"—has received criticism for overuse in early childhood classrooms (Clewett, 1988; Gartrell, 1991). Indeed, the role of isolation in guidance discipline should be weighed carefully.

Isolation occurs when a child is removed from a situation and placed alone in a separate part of the room, usually with no alternate activity. (Isolation in either a closed-off portion of the room or outside of the room—unless in the company of an adult—are inappropriate intervention practices.)

Two distinct uses of "in-room isolation" are:

- punishment for perceived misbehavior;
- a "cool-down" time for when a child has lost control, before a guidance talk can occur.

In the past insufficient distinction has been made between these two practices, with **time-out** being the general term used. The distinction needs to be made clear.

The Time-Out. In sports, a time-out is a break from the game for the purpose of substitution and strategy. For young children the time-out should be a break from a tense situation for the purpose of regaining composure. Piaget (1937) has made the argument that young children—due to developmental egocentrism—have difficulty conceptualizing the intricacies of social situations. The ability of young children to "think about what happened" is limited, especially when put on a chair by themselves.

During the time-out young children do not logically "analyze the consequences of their actions," even if directed to do so. Instead, they are likely to internalize the shame of being separated, while sometimes simultaneously relishing the negative attention received from the teacher. This developmental reality means that periods of isolation, without adult guidance, do little to teach children "how to get along better." Even when considered a "logical consequence" by the teacher, the effect on the child is punishment.

As Clewett maintains (1988), isolation reinforces a teacher's sense of power by forcing conformity to his or her expectations. Isolation also pressures the child toward diminished self-esteem and negative feelings toward the teacher and the education environment (Clewett, 1988). **When isolation is used in retribution for unacceptable social activity rather than as a cool-down time, the separation becomes punishment and is distinct from guidance discipline**.

Unless a child has lost control, mediation or one of the quick but nonpunitive interventions methods should be used. Separation before this point is often done for the teacher's convenience—to avoid the "bother" of mediation, or to rely on the "standard discipline practice" for when a child "misbehaves." In many classrooms the use of time-outs—meaning in-room isolation—is taken for granted. Teachers attest that it is successful in "getting a child to behave" at the time, but fail to notice that they may use it several times a week with the child for this purpose.

The mark of an effective intervention technique is that it reduces the mistaken behavior. Ongoing use of the time-out for one or a group of children indicates that the technique is not working. In moving toward a guidance approach, teachers need to realize that methods taken for granted may be more punitive than commonly thought (Clewett, 1988).

The Cool-Down Time. Separation to help a child regain equilibrium is a logical consequence of loss of control. Usually, the adult sits with the child during the cool-down time, talks with the child about what happened and what the child might do differently next time, and helps the child rejoin the group. The difference between separation as punishment and separation as cooling-down time is one of teacher disposition. The self-check for this difference is a straightforward question: **Am I isolating this child because s/he deserves to be punished or because s/he needs to regain composure?**

Classrooms using a guidance approach resort to the *time-out chair* seldom if at all (Clewett, 1988), and to *cool-down times* only in the most serious situations. Guidance-oriented teachers start with developmentally appropriate, individually-responsive programs that reduce the need for mistaken behavior. They prefer the intervention techniques discussed to this point, including mediation, requesting choices, and redirecting to alternate activity.

To distinguish further **cool-down time** from **time-out**, here are some additional considerations:

1. The use of a time-out chair or worse, a "naughty chair," institutionalizes separation as a form of punishment in the classroom. The chair becomes a place of negative value and children made to sit on the chair are at-risk of being stigmatized.
2. Instead of a designated chair, a child needing to be separated should go to an unused part of the room. Use of whatever quiet space is available helps keep the cooling down time in perspective; it should be a special occurrence for which no institutionally designated chair or area is necessary.
3. Children need a cool-down time when they have lost emotional or behavioral control. Generally, an adult stays with a child while the child regains composure. If the child is unaccompanied, the time of separation should be brief; a simple guideline is no more than one minute per year of age—i.e. three minutes for a three-year-old. If more time is needed, the adult should be there.
4. Routinely, at the conclusion of the separation, the teacher engages the child in a **guidance talk** about what the child might say or do differ-

ently next time. Not a lecture, the teacher encourages the child to communicate about the situation. Part of the point of the conversation is that certain actions hurt and hurting cannot happen "in this classroom." "I cannot let you hurt anyone, and I will not let anyone hurt you."

5. The guidance talk is one part of the **reconciliation process** at the conclusion of the cool-down time. A second part is assisting the child to rejoin the group. Often, the teacher facilitates the transition by steering the child to a quiet activity alone or with one or two other children.

6. Reconciliation does not mean forcing a child to say s/he "is sorry." Premature apologies contradict honest feelings and do an injustice to this important convention. If children are helped to understand their feelings and know that they are supported by the teacher, they will reconcile on their own—usually more quickly and fully than adults.

7. Two common practices for concluding in-room isolation have been the use of a timer and the child's own judgment about when to rejoin the group (Gartrell, 1987). In agreement with Clewett (1988), the author believes that cool-down separation is a serious enough experience in a child's life that teacher assistance is important for reconciliation.

8. When it is part of the reconciliation process and not forced, **restitution** is a valuable part of reconciliation. With the teacher's assistance, a child might help clean up a mess that was made, rebuild a house that was knocked down, or get a wet towel for a bump on the head.

Anecdote: Four children were sitting down to "supper" in a housekeeping center. The pretend food was a large quantity of styrofoam "peanuts" used in packing. Mark, a developmentally delayed five-year-old, arrived to join the group. There was no room at the table, and before Ina, the teacher, could arrive to mediate the problem, the children told Mark he couldn't play. Irate, Mark swept the bowl of beads on the floor and began to scream. He was in the act of dumping the four plates upside down when Ina arrived. She stooped, put her arm around Mark, and guided him to an unoccupied bean-bag chair. Sitting by him, Ina stroked Mark's head until he quieted down.

The teacher reminded Mark to come to her when he had a problem and told him the children felt sad about what had happened. She asked Mark what he could do to make things better. Mark said, "Pick up."

Mark and the teacher went over and helped the three children who were already picking up the styrofoam. When they were done, Ina asked the children if Mark could join them for supper. "O.K.," said Shelley, "Mark can be the little kid."

Physical Restraint

Physical restraint is the crisis management technique of **last resort**; it is the passive bear hug. It is *not* any of the notorious methods of subtle or not so subtle corporal punishment used on children over the years. Physical restraint is not paddling, spanking, slapping, ear pulling, hair yanking, back-of-the-neck squeezing, knuckle whacking, retribution child-biting, mouth tapping, or binding to a chair (Stone, 1978). Neither is it pushing or pulling a child nor (in contrast to one author's view) hanging a child upside down (Cherry, 1983).

Physical restraint means holding a child, including arms, legs, and perhaps even head, so that the child can not harm you, other children, or himself (Gartrell, 1987). Physical restraint is used when a child has lost control, physically and emotionally. A child needing restraint may be attacking another child, yourself, or another adult. The child may also be having a tantrum and showing such behaviors as hitting body parts against a floor or wall.

Once the teacher decides that physical restraint is necessary, the commitment is total. Quickly removing the child's shoes is a helpful survival strategy. Sitting on a chair and clamping arms around arms and legs around legs is what physical restraint is about. Children generally will react strongly and negatively to being restrained. The teacher stays with it and often speaks soothingly to the child (Clewett, 1988). With many children calm words or even quiet singing or rocking helps; other children calm down more easily with silence.

With the realization that the teacher is reinforcing needed behavioral and emotional limits, the child calms down. Gradually, the child finds the closeness comforting and strange as it might seem, the passive restraint sometimes ends as a hug. (It is an open question at this point as to who needs the hug more.) If the child becomes able to talk about the event at the time, the teacher provides guidance. Otherwise, guidance talk is provided at a later time. After physical restraint, children (and adults) are drained. Helping the child into a quiet activity, like reading a book, promotes the reconciliation.

Anecdote: For the third time Dean had his lego structure knocked down. This time the child was Andy, and Dean began shouting. Dean threw legos at Andy and then hit and kicked at him. Diane, the teacher, approached rapidly, said firmly "You're upset, Dean, but no hurting." When he began hitting out at her, Diane took hold of his arms and legs, and sat down on the floor.

Dean shouted for Diane to let him go, but she held on and began to say quietly, "Dean, I can't let you hurt anyone, and I won't let anyone hurt you. I am holding you so that you and Andy won't be hurt."

After struggling, Dean realized the teacher would not let go and gradually calmed down. Diane told him it was no fun to have

> things destroyed by others and that he had a right to be upset. She encouraged him to next time use words and to come to her right away. After a few minutes, she suggested that Dean do some puzzles, which he did. Dean later asked to sit by her during snack—much to the teacher's relief.

From the guidance perspective, children show serious mistaken behavior when there is trouble in their lives that they cannot cope with on their own. Indeed, any child is entitled to a "level three" day when nothing goes well and emotions run high. The crisis management techniques discussed here support children so that self-esteem is not further deflated by punitive teacher reaction. When serious mistaken behavior continues, however, crisis management techniques in themselves are not enough. A comprehensive strategy for addressing repeated level three mistaken behavior is discussed later in this chapter.

WHEN TEACHERS FEEL ANGER

Because teachers are human, they feel anger. The source of the anger may be the children themselves—a child who manipulates or harms others—or a group that too many times fails to live up to expectations. The source may be beyond immediate teacher-child transactions, such as a parent who does not follow-through, a fellow staff member who does not understand, or a friend or family member who lets us down. In 1972, Ginott pointed out that teacher preparation programs rarely educate about anger and how to handle it—a shortcoming still widely true today.

The teacher of young children may feel particularly guilty about anger—because consistent nurturing is such an expected part of this role. Yet, prekindergarten teachers no less than secondary teachers face anger in themselves. The issue is not feeling guilty about the reality of this emotion; it is how we manage the anger we feel.

Teachers generally can improve their management of anger through three steps:

1. *monitoring feelings and making adjustments;*
2. *using safeguards when expressing anger;*
3. *practicing reconciliation.*

1. Monitor Feelings; Make Adjustments

An effective anger management strategy begins before a crisis occurs. Teachers need to **self-monitor** moods and predispositions. Like children, all teachers are entitled to "level three days." For physical and emotional reasons, there are days when all teachers are functioning at the survival level. Perhaps

Figure 9–4 A long-used coping strategy for down days is free time for children, when possible outside.

in the next century more contracts will include paid personal/family leave policies ("mental health days") to allow for this aspect of the human condition. In the meantime, teachers—both men and women—do well to prepare contingency plans for when they are emotionally or physically "down." These coping strategies come from early childhood classes and workshops of teachers from the upper Midwest:

a) Rather than show videos on a routine basis, a kindergarten teacher only uses them for two purposes: when they tie directly into the curriculum or when she needs relief. She talks regularly with the children about their favorite videos and for the second purpose always has a few favorites on hand.

b) A third grade teacher keeps a schedule of high-interest, largely self-directed activities that he uses when he is overtired or has sinus headaches.

c) Three first grade teachers have an agreement among themselves and with their rotating teacher aide, that for "special occurrences," the aide spends more time in a particular classroom. A level three day is an accepted "special occurrence."

d) In several preschool programs, teachers and aides work as "teaching teams," rather than in sharply defined professional and paraprofessional roles. As needed, one or the other adult can assume more leadership on a particular day.

e) In both preschool and elementary school classrooms, on level three days one member of a teaching team asks another to work with a child who shows frequent mistaken behavior.

(By way of illustration, a kindergarten teacher states: "I have a good relationship with the special education teacher who works with three children in my room. Most days, I work fine with a particular "active-alert" child. Once in a while, I rely on Jan to help with this child. We have become a real team.")

f) On days when a teacher might become easily upset, a first grade teacher intentionally soft-pedals expectations for two children in her class, whom she otherwise "might come down hard on."

g) A principal from the province of Ontario has a policy in his school that if any teacher ever needs a break, he will stop what he is doing and take over the teacher's class. He says it took a while for teachers to ask, but now he gets a request every week or two. He states the teachers like this policy—and teachers from other schools have asked to transfer to his.

h) Teachers in a particular school have a buddy system. The system was set up carefully to match teachers who get along. If a teacher feels that a day will be challenging, the two might talk about it before the children arrive or go for a walk off school grounds during a break.

i) The most frequent comment of workshop participants is that they let children, even preschoolers, know how they are feeling. In classrooms where concern for the well-being of all is modelled by the teacher, children will respond in kind. Even three-year-olds have been known to tip-toe and whisper, " 'cause teacher's not feeling good."

Chronic problems with emotions that keep teachers from being at their best need attention. Just as it is important to understand the reasons for the behavior of children, it is also important for adults. Teaching is a difficult occupation. The teacher who seeks a friendly ear, counseling, or therapy in order to improve his or her work in the classroom is acting as a true professional.

2. Using Safeguards

By monitoring feelings and adjusting the program on level three days, the teacher reduces the risk of losing emotional control. But on *any* day, a teacher may become justifiably—or at least understandably—angry, even when teaching young children. Ginott provides guidance on the expression of anger (1972). His contention is that while anger cannot always be controlled, it can be managed. He states:

The realities of teaching—the overloaded classes, the endless demands, the sudden crises—make anger inevitable. Teachers need not apologize for their angry feelings. An effective teacher is neither a masochist nor a martyr. He does not play the role of a saint or act the part of an angel. . .When angry, an enlightened teacher remains real. He describes what he sees, what he feels, what he expects. He attacks the problem, not the person. He knows that when angry, he is dealing with more elements than he can control. He protects himself and safeguards his students by using "I" messages (pp. 72-73).

In this section, Ginott referred to the communication basic, "describe, express, direct," discussed in chapter eight. This safeguard steers the teacher toward the problem, rather than the child's personality. If two children are fighting, the safeguard might well result in the comment: "You are hitting and not using words. I do not like what I see. You will separate and sit down. Then we will talk." The teacher backs up the words by establishing physical proximity and indicating where the children are to sit. As soon as feelings have "cooled" s/he and the children have a guidance talk.

"I" messages express strong feelings nonpunitively and focus children on the teacher's concerns. Ginott discusses the use of "I" messages this way:

> "I am annoyed," "I am appalled," "I am furious" are safer statements than "You are a pest," "Look what you have done," "You are so stupid," "Who do you think you are?". . .When Mrs. Brooks, the kindergarten teacher, saw five-year-old Alan throw a stone at his friend, she said loudly, "I saw it. I am indignant and dismayed. Stones are not for throwing at people. People are not for hurting" (p. 73).

Talking to the situation and not to the personality of the child is perhaps the most important safeguard of all. This "cardinal principle" pertains in many situations, but especially in the expression of anger. Ginott's contention is that when teachers express displeasure but still observe the safeguards that protect self-esteem, children listen. By using words effectively, teachers not only manage their anger, but model a nonpunitive form of conflict-resolution much needed in the society.

3. Practice Reconciliation

Teachers, like children, make mistakes. For this reason as the leaders of the classroom, when teachers overreact, they need to work for reconciliation (Gartrell, 1992). Under normal circumstances children are resilient and bounce back (Hendrick, 1992). They also forgive easily, more easily than adults. Because teachers are important in their lives, children want to be on friendly terms with them.

Soon after a conflict, children need to be reassured by the teacher that they are accepted for who they are and as members of the group. The importance of reestablishing relations is recalled by readers who can remember a conflict with a teacher when they were students. If on the following day, the teacher acted as if nothing had happened, the reader probably recalls a feeling of relief. If from that day on things never seemed the same, the year probably seemed a long one indeed.

Figure 9–5 After a cool-down time, reconciliation often occurs with the follow-up guidance talk.

Reconciliation is a matter of timing and inviting. No one is ready immediately after a confrontation to apologize and make amends. This is as true for children as it is for adults. Children may not be ready to reconcile with a teacher until they have had time to work through their feelings (Gartrell, 1987). After a cool-down time, reconciliation occurs with the follow-up guidance talk. Children are ready to talk when they are not actively resisting the conversation. Sometimes, though, they will show reluctance, unsure of their standing with the teacher.

By *inviting* reconciliation, children are more apt to oblige. The guidance techniques discussed in chapter seven, including reflective listening and the compliment sandwich, are important. With young children, apologies, and acceptance of apologies, are often expressed nonverbally. A hug from a child says a lot, "Please forgive me" and "I forgive you" all at once.

Anecdote: R.J. was holding a door open for his first grade class while they walked to another room for a special activity. He began swinging the door toward children as they passed, making believe he was closing it. As Kaye walked by, R.J. lost his grip and the door banged into her, knocking her down. After tending to Kaye, the teacher looked for R.J., but he had disappeared. She asked an aide to take the class into the room for the activity and, getting more upset by the minute, went to look for R.J. She found him in the furthest corner of their classroom, looking anxious.

Teacher: You banged the door on Kaye and I am really upset about it.

R.J.: (Crying) I didn't mean to.

Teacher: (Surprised at his reaction) What can we do about it?

R.J.: Say I'm sorry?

Teacher: All right. Anything else?

R.J. shakes his head no. The teacher decides not to pressure him. She suggests they join the group. When they sit down with the class, R.J. leans against the teacher. She puts her arm around him.

Perhaps the most difficult aspect of reconciliation is after the teacher has overreacted and crossed the boundary between firmness and harshness, between guidance and punishment. The frailty of our humanness means that this sometimes happens. Because the skills of expressing strong emotions acceptably and getting along with others are difficult even for educated adults, teachers occasionally do express anger in ways that hurt.

Perhaps a first step in learning to recover from a bad episode is to recognize our feelings and forgive *ourselves*. Only then can we figure out how to make the best of the situation and to forgive the other. Thoughts in the middle of the night may be part of this healing process and talks with others important to us certainly are. Children are forgiving and *need* us to be firm. If the undercurrent of our firmness is appreciation of the worth of each individual child, reconciliation offers the possibility of fuller understanding and more productive relations (Gartrell, 1987). As Ginott suggests in *Teacher and Child*, true reconciliation means change (1972). For professional teachers who care about young children, change means learning and growing.

STRATEGIES FOR WORKING WITH STRONG NEEDS MISTAKEN BEHAVIOR

Serious (level three) mistaken behavior is due to strong needs that a child feels and cannot meet. The strong needs arise from physical or emotional factors that the child can neither cope with nor understand. The teacher must respond firmly to serious mistaken behavior, for the well-being of all concerned. Because young children who have problems easily internalize guilt, however, strategies for assisting them cannot be reactive alone: discipline is not enough.

Experts from many related fields have recognized that a comprehensive approach is needed with children having strong unmet needs. In the last twenty years writers from the differing contexts of preschool, elementary, middle school, *secondary* and special education have advocated a comprehensive or *collaborative* approach (Boyer, 1991; 1992).

At the preschool level, Head Start has given impetus to looking at children's behavior from an **ecological perspective** (Lombardi, 1990) that includes the social, cultural, economic, health, and behavioral circumstances affecting the family. The nursery school movement also has tended to view behavior from the broader child and family context (Moore, & Kilmer, 1973). Such writers as Schickedanz et al. (1982), Essa (1983), Reynolds (1990), and Honig (in McCracken, ed., 1986) have recognized the importance of comprehensive strategies for addressing the behavior of young children having problems.

At the elementary/secondary levels, the Teacher Assistance Team procedure articulated by Chalfant et. al. (1979) has become a widely accepted model "for within building problem solving." Strengths of the model are its encouragement of teacher collaboration and non-judgmental approach to the problems of children and teachers alike.

The Contribution of Special Education

Because of the nature of learning and behavior problems, special educators have developed systematic assessment, planning, and intervention strategies to assist children with disabilities. In use nationwide since the 1970s, the Individual Education Plan (I.E.P.) is collaborative—in that it involves the input of a range of staff, as well as parents—and comprehensive, tailored to the complex of needs identified through the I.E.P. assessment. Used at an informal level, the I.E.P. provides a model for addressing strong needs mistaken behavior. Where classroom and special education teachers can freely collaborate, the basis is set for an effective problem-solving strategy for children who are having difficulties.

Over the years, a problem in many schools has been denial of the precipitating circumstances that surround children who show level three mistaken behavior. Educators instead have tended to punish these children, thinking that what they need is to learn obedience. In truth, punishment reinforces the negative feelings the children have about themselves and the world around them. Either immediately or later in life, the emotional difficulties and the acting out behaviors often become worse.

In more fortunate circumstances, special education teachers are brought in, an I.E.P. process is undertaken, and the downward spiral is slowed, if not halted. Practitioners of guidance discipline agree with many special education teachers who hold **that children showing serious mistaken behavior need comprehensive assistance, and not the stigma of an outdated, one-dimensional discipline approach**.

Labeling or Diagnosis?. Despite its promise, special education has suffered from an "image problem" that has worked against its effectiveness in the lives of children. A widespread criticism of special education intervention is that children "must be labeled to be served." The intentions behind this sentiment are humane. Reacting to the idea that "labeling is disabling," the belief is that a child labeled with a behavioral disability probably will suffer more from a negative self-fulfilling prophecy than gain from the special education assistance.

The fallacy of this view lies in adults' inability to distinguish between the processes of **labeling** and **diagnosis**. A label is a judgmental shortcut that others use to put a child in a behavioral category: "hyper," "rowdy," "withdrawn," etc. Labels do injustice because they blind adults to other behaviors and qualities of the child. By fixating on the labeled behaviors, the child becomes stigmatized and is undermined in the effort to grow and change.

Diagnosis is the process used in helping professionals to determine systematically the nature of a child's difficulty—**in order to empower the child to overcome it**. Adults have the power to interpret diagnoses in different ways. A special education diagnosis only becomes detrimental when adults use the diagnosis as a label.

As an illustration, the difference is between a child who is labeled "hyper" by his teachers and a child who receives a diagnosis of having attention deficit-

Figure 9–6 An increasing practice is special education staff working alongside regular teachers in the classroom. Where staffing is adequate, inclusion allows service for many children with disabilities in the classroom.

hyperactive disorder through a special education assessment. In the first case, teachers commonly use general isolation, enforced seatwork, and frequent rewards and punishments. The behavior does not change and remains disturbing to children and teachers alike. In the second case, the child receives counseling and perhaps diet restrictions or controlled medications. The classroom staff, special education teachers and parent(s) actively monitor the situation; and, in most cases the child's behavior changes. With the change, the label no longer fits and the child becomes more free to change and grow.

At its best, special education intervention involves close collaboration between classroom staff, specialists, parents, and the child. In such situations, adults work together to liberate children from the problems that result in level three mistaken behavior, and the effects of consequent labels. The proactive approach to young children with problems used in the guidance approach builds from the special education experience.

The Individual Guidance Plan

For many teachers, children who show level 3 mistaken behavior pose the most difficult of classroom challenges. A comprehensive strategy for addressing strong needs mistaken behavior is available for use by all teachers of young children. Specialized licenses and multiple degrees are not necessary. The plan was introduced in chapter two and discussed further in chapter seven. Of necessity, the **Individual Guidance Plan** (or I.G.P.) starts with intervention to prevent harm and disruption. In addition the plan calls for learning more about the child, collaborating with all adults concerned, improving the level of teacher-child relations, and providing opportunities for the child to experience success. (A sample I.G.P. work form is included in Appendix E.)

With due recognition to accepted special education practice, the I.G.P. follows the following six step process:

1. *Observe Pattern of Mistaken Behavior*
   The teacher notices patterns of behavior that indicate trouble in a child's life. Any child is entitled to an occasional level three day. Patterns of atypical, extreme or inappropriate behavior for more than a day or two, however, indicate serious unmet physical or emotional needs. The teacher observes when and how the mistaken behavior occurs.

2. *Use Consistent Guidance Intervention Techniques*
   The teacher responds consistently and firmly to the mistaken behavior, using guidance techniques. In a teaching team classroom, one teacher may be the "designated intervener" to ensure predictable limits for the child.

3. *Obtain Additional Information*
   The teacher seeks to understand the child's behavior and the child more fully. Incidents of mistaken behavior are charted against days

of the week, times of the day, and the daily schedule. Actions for gaining more information also include talks with the child, talks with staff, and a conference with the family.

4. *Hold I.G.P. Meeting*

If steps one-three do not result in resolution of the problem, a meeting is held with the parent, teaching staff, and other relevant adults. The team uses the problem solving process outlined in chapter eight (p.263). In developing the I.G.P., the team includes the child in the meeting or shares the I.G.P. with the child.

5. *Implement Guidance Plan*

The team works together to put the I.G.P. into operation. One necessary component of most plans is improvement in relationships between children and the adults in the classroom. A second is adaptation of the educational program to ensure increased opportunities for the child to experience success. Referral for assessment by special education or other helping professionals may be part of the I.G.P. (If special education services are warranted, an I.E.P. process may supersede the I.G.P.) Counseling or other services also may be part of the plan.

6. *Monitor Guidance Plan*

Staff continue observations, review the plan, communicate with parents, and make modifications as needed. If necessary, the staff holds second I.G.P. meeting.

Three case studies follow, each using the I.G.P. process differently. The first uses the I.G.P. on an informal basis. In working with "Sherry" the staff did not follow the formal six-step procedure, but did use a comprehensive guidance approach that reflected the steps. In the second case study, the teachers used the I.G.P. more formally, and the steps were followed. The third case study follows the steps, but needed to use a phone call in place of the formal meeting. These cases illustrate the flexibility of the I.G.P. procedure.

Case Study One—Guidance Plan Used Informally With Sherry, Aged Four

Sherry had few friends at the Head Start center. She occasionally joined children in the housekeeping area, but stayed only for short periods before she would leave to play by herself. Sometimes arguments precipitated her leaving; other times Sherry simply drifted off. The two teachers often had to coax her to stay on task during directed activities. Sherry got restless easily during large groups.

Sherry did like reading stories in small groups with a teacher. She also enjoyed small animal and people figures and engaged in extensive play with the figures. During September, Sherry's first month at the center, the teachers had to talk with her privately several times about putting the figures in her jacket pockets. The teachers discussed the problem in a staff meeting. They agreed that the mistaken behavior was a symptom of a larger problem, and rather than confront Sherry, they decided to try to learn more about her situation.

The teachers established that Sherry was the seventh of nine children from a low income family. One remembered from teaching an older brother that the father was a truck driver and often away from home. The mother sometimes had seemed overwhelmed in the family situation and perhaps was not literate. To a large degree, the children had to fend for themselves.

The two teachers met with the mother, as they tried to meet periodically with each child's parents. The staff did not directly discuss their main concern, the fact that Sherry was taking things home from the center. They believed that the parents would react punitively to this information. Instead, they used a compliment sandwich, mentioning that Sherry really seems to like reading, playing "house," and using miniature figures.

They shared that they would like to see Sherry gain confidence in relating with other children, as she tends to stay by herself. The teacher and mother discussed how the family could help Sherry gain in confidence. The staff suggested that an older member of the family might begin reading to Sherry each day. The parent identified an older sister that Sherry was close to and said the sister could start that practice. The staff set up a system with the mother by which Sherry would take home a "special book" each day and return it the next.

The teachers commented that they also would begin to spend more individual time with Sherry, reading stories and having contact talks. They agreed the teacher would call the parent in two weeks to discuss Sherry's progress.

In a separate staff meeting, the teachers decided that one teacher would check Sherry's jacket at the end of each day. She would use guidance talks to reinforce that the figures are needed at the center, and compliment sandwiches to note Sherry's progress. One of the teachers hypothesized that Sherry might be taking things as a way of looking after herself, by "giving herself presents," as others didn't seem to give Sherry all the attention she needed.

Each day the staff informally noted how Sherry was doing and after a week agreed that she was building an attachment especially with one teacher. By two weeks, her "taking things" decreased, and Sherry seemed happier at the center. She shared with the teacher that her sister was reading her the books she took home, "and the other kids read 'em too." The teacher called the parent, and expressed pleasure over the progress Sherry was making. The mother mentioned that she and her husband were trying to spend more time each day with the children; she commented that other children in addition to Sherry were enjoying the daily story time.

Case Study Two—Individual Guidance Plan with Gary, Aged Five

The playground supervisor reported to Ms. Martin, Gary's kindergarten teacher, that Gary "had a real chip on his shoulder." If Gary thought someone was teasing him, he would charge and push the child down. In the classroom, Ms. Martin noticed that Gary became restless easily and would actually need to pace for a while before he could settle down. Ms. Martin also noticed that Gary shied away from any kind of physical contact. Gradually, Gary's reactions to perceived challenges became more aggressive. On one occasion when Ms. Martin quietly asked him to resume his seat, Gary swept boxes off a shelf and sat under a table.

Ms. Martin began having daily contact talks with Gary. She used cooling-down times, but he reacted strongly to clear instances of isolation. On two occasions she had to restrain him in the isolation location. She felt that he was distancing himself from her despite her efforts to be nonpunitive.

Ms. Martin took two actions. First, she asked a special education teacher to observe Gary. During the observation, Gary had no difficulties. The special education teacher said she would come back another time.

Second, Ms. Martin called Gary's mom. Ms. Martin had met Gary's mom at the class orientation and the two had talked. Gary's mom had said she was a single parent who was working at a liquor store and going to a technical college part-time. In the phone call, Ms. Martin explained that she respected Gary's independent spirit, but that he was having difficulty managing his emotions. She asked if there were anything Gary's mom could share that would help her in working with him. Gary's mom hesitated, then said that Gary had been abused by her past boyfriend when he was four. Ms. Martin asked if she and the special education teacher could meet with the mom. Though reluctant, the mother agreed.

The mom did not show up for the first meeting. Ms. Martin called again, and the mom said she had to complete a late assignment for a class. The meeting was rescheduled after Ms. Martin emphasized that the meeting would only be about helping Gary. The meeting was held. Because of the abuse factor, Ms. Martin had reported the phone conversation to the principal. The school social worker determined from Social Services that the abuse had been verified—it had been against both mother and child. At the meeting, the mother insisted she did not want Gary to receive special education "testing," because she was afraid he would be labeled as disturbed. She said any informal support would be all right.

It was agreed that a teacher aide would spend time with Gary each day. The mother was encouraged to seek counseling for her son through Social Services. The teacher would set up some "pace space" for Gary and a private cubicle he could go to when he needed to be alone. The teacher suggested that when the aide was not present and Gary needed to, he could visit the school nurse, who was just two doors down from the class. The teacher and aide would work on helping Gary express strong feelings more acceptably.

The plan was put into place. Ms. Martin held a class meeting. She explained that sometimes children have special needs to help them get along in school. She matter-of-factly mentioned that she and the aide would be working closely with Gary and sometimes they would do things differently with him. The teacher said that if the other children felt that they ever had "special needs" that they should come and tell her; she would try to help them too. The children accepted the arrangement. Some of the children had been afraid of Gary, and the special assistance made sense to them.

Gary got so he liked both the teacher aide and the nurse. He developed enough trust in the teacher that he would come to her often when he was upset and verbally vent, which everyone thought was an improvement. He continued to pace and react violently at times when he felt threatened.

After two weeks, Gary stopped coming to school. The teacher tried to reach the mom by phone, first at home, then at work and the college. She learned through the school social worker that Gary and his mom had left the community. Gary stayed on Ms. Martin's mind. One day after school a teacher called from another town. The teacher had Gary in her class, and the mom had told her she could call Ms. Martin for background. The two teachers kept in touch every week or so for the rest of the school year.

Case Study Three—Individual Guidance Plan with Wade, Aged Seven

After a few weeks of second grade, Wade began to have difficulties. He was in three fights in a week, and showed inattentiveness toward most subjects in the classroom. The teacher, Mr. Harper, had to remind him to stay on task, and his homework assignments—a new happening for Wade—often went undone.

Two of the three fights occurred in the classroom. The first happened just as Mr. Harper returned to the classroom from lunch. The teacher quickly intervened. He described what he saw, told the two children how he felt about it, and separated them for a cooling down time. He talked with each child, and then the two of them together. Wade felt that another boy had taken his "GT Racer," and a fight had resulted. The situation was resolved after Wade found his GT car. Mr. Harper used the same intervention methods—describe-express-direct, separation for cool-down and follow-up guidance—with the other fight that occurred.

Mr. Harper observed Wade and noticed that while Wade excelled in reading, he was having a difficult time with numbers. Mr. Harper also noted that Wade became frustrated quickly if he made a simple error. Small muscle control, particularly in penmanship, also seemed to be a problem. In talking with Wade, the teacher learned that his older sister and brother teased him about "doing baby work" and "writing like a baby." From previous meetings with the parents, the teacher thought that his father might have inappropriately high standards for Wade as well. Because the source of Wade's unmet needs seemed to include his family, the teacher decided contact with the parents was important.

Wade's parents both worked, and setting up a meeting with them at the school proved difficult. Though not his preference, Mr. Harper decided to have a two part meeting. Part one was with the student teacher and foster grandparent in Mr. Harper's class. Both shared concern about Wade's situation. They agreed that the foster grandparent and student teacher would have daily individual contact with Wade, to improve his confidence and relations with him. At the student teacher's suggestion, the teacher agreed that they should do more open-ended art activities that didn't invite comparative attention to neatness. The team also came up with a few suggestions for Wade's parents.

Part two of the meeting was a lengthy phone conversation with Wade's mom during her break at work. The teacher used a compliment sandwich, saying that Wade really liked numbers and worked hard at tasks, but that lately he was showing quite a bit of frustration. Mr. Harper added that Wade seemed sensitive about his penmanship, and he was worried that some of Wade's assignments were not getting done for this reason.

Teacher and mom agreed that the family should be more encouraging toward Wade's written assignments. It was suggested that new pencils with better erasers might help Wade to make corrections. Mr. Harper also mentioned some of the teaching team's ideas and got the mother's feedback about them. At the conclusion of the phone call, the mother agreed that Mr. Harper would call with a progress report during the second week and that she and her husband would come in for a follow-up meeting in three weeks.

Wade came to school with the new pencils. He and Mr. Harper had a guidance talk about how the teacher, the family, and Wade were all going to work together to make school go better for him. He mentioned that Bill, the foster grandparent, and Kendra, the student teacher, would each be visiting with Wade to see how things were going. Kendra especially gave Wade lots of encouragement about his writing skills. The teacher asked for new pictures to hang on the "kids' art" bulletin board each week. Bill got Wade to volunteer his fall collage and his "whatever you like to do outside in the fall" theme picture.

Mr. Harper provided private encouragement to Wade about his reading and writing assignments. Instead of stickers on his papers, the teacher gave more specific feedback in the form of written compliment sandwiches. On occasion, Wade still expressed his frustration graphically, but he used words and there were no more fights. Mr. Harper called the mom and shared his progress. The mother stated that she was working on the rest of the family to be more encouraging of Wade's efforts.

In the follow-up meeting with the mother and father, Mr. Harper remarked about the progress that Wade had made. He explained to the parents that Wade had high standards and had convinced himself that he could not meet them. The teacher commented that Wade did not respond well to criticism and that instead he needed encouragement and recognition in order to succeed. For the father, who was concerned about "spoiling the boy," the teacher showed Wade's portfolio with sample assignments from early in the year and the preceding day. Dad could see a difference, and grudgingly agreed that the "positive approach" should be continued. Mr. Harper left the meeting feeling that progress had been made (and with an agreement that a special education teacher could be brought in to assess Wade's learning characteristics.)

I.G.P. Afterthoughts

In these case studies, immediate intervention was given to address the mistaken behavior shown by each child. Beyond immediate intervention, however, the teachers recognized the mistaken behavior as symptomatic of larger problems in the children's lives. The use of an **Individual Guidance Plan**, either informally or formally, allowed the teachers to learn more about the child. Such information is crucial if the teacher is to build a relationship and alter the environment in ways that allow the child to overcome mistaken behavior and to grow.

Teaching that uses the guidance approach can be difficult; it calls for teachers to go beyond their immediate feelings and reaction tendencies and to view children—and family situations—nonjudgmentally. Sometimes, as happened in Case Study Two, the I.G.P. will not work out as a teacher would wish. We may not be able to change life circumstances for a child, but we can make the child's life a little easier. The professional teacher does not win every battle, but learns as s/he tries.

Figure 9–7 Teachers who use the guidance approach work to accept children and view them nonjudgmentally.

WHEN TEACHERS AND PARENTS DISAGREE

At one time or another, teachers and parents will have differences in viewpoints about program priorities, program content, teaching style, behaviors of the parents' own children, or the actions of other children. Boutte et al. (1992), Galinsky (1988), Lightfoot (1978), and Powell (1989) make similar points about such differences: They need not become **negative dissonances**, but can serve as **creative conflicts** (Lightfoot, 1978).

Lightfoot distinguishes between these terms by maintaining that negative dissonance is the result of differences that alienate the parent from the teacher. In such cases, the teacher typically asserts the power of the educational institution over the parent, often on the basis of the parent's social or cultural background. Views, values and communication styles of the parent are considered of lesser importance than those of the teacher, as an "official representative" of the school or center (Powell, 1989).

Creative conflicts arise from the diversity of life in a complex, pluralistic society in which the right of the individual to his or her own views is accepted (Lightfoot, 1978). The teacher who respects parents, whatever their background, realizes that differences in values or viewpoint need not terminate positive teacher-parent relations. The common ground of the child whose life they share makes differences an opportunity for creative communication, and not inevitably a point of division (Galinsky, 1988).

Figure 9–8 At one time or another teachers and parents will have differences in viewpoints. (Courtesy of Richard Faulkner, Family Service Center, Koochiching-Itasca Head Start, Grand Rapids, Minnesota.)

Yet, the reality remains that some parents are difficult to communicate with and most teachers are underprepared for this part of the job (Boutte, et al., 1992). The tendency to selectively support the involvement of parents, dependent on the teacher's feelings toward them, is an example of the "negative dissonance" experts in this area believe important to avoid (Powell, 1989).

In the article, "Effective Techniques for Involving 'Difficult' Parents," Boutte et al. (1992) identify and provide suggestions for working with parents showing any of six different patterns of behavior. Though the teacher's approach differs whether a parent is antagonistic or unresponsive, a few basic guidelines assist in a variety of situations when teachers and parents disagree.

Encourage Mutual Respect

Warren (1977) makes the case that parents who seem unworthy were once children whose unmet needs have prevented them from a healthy adulthood. The teacher who does not let personal judgments get in the way of involving parents in their children's education understands the importance of Warren's words.

Parents from backgrounds different than the teacher's have legitimate points of pride and values that their children share. Remaining open to learning about customs and lifestyles new to the teacher conveys respect for the family and the child.

At the same time, the teacher can take pride in being a professional and need not be defensive about educational practice that s/he knows to be appropriate. Regardless of differences in age or experience, self-respect is a right of the early childhood teacher. As a professional, the teacher uses appropriate practice in relations with parents, no less than with children. Appropriate practice means an invitation to parents to become involved and to collaborate in the education process of the child (Boutte, et al., 1992; Galinsky, 1986).

2. Model Listening

When parents feel strongly about a view to the point of anger or confrontation, the teacher needs to listen, allow them to cool off, and not dispute or "block out" what they say (Boutte, et al., 1992). The teacher is flexible about accepting specifics in the argument, but stops personal abuse, redirecting communication to the point of the meeting. Reflective listening shows the parent that the teacher is trying to understand. Use of parents' ideas when deciding on follow-up shows that listening was at work. As part of the listening process, it may be important to reiterate that everyone wants what is best for the child. Invitation for another contact in the future communicates that the teacher is serious about having parents involved. Parents who know they are being listened to become more likely to listen in return.

3. Talk to Situations

In conferences the teacher should have specific information at hand about the child and the situation being discussed: observations, samples of the child's work, written accounts of situations. The teacher describes events and does not judgmentally evaluate the child, the child's behaviors, or the child's family background. Citing a workshop she attended, Galinsky notes,

Figure 9–9 Honestly meant, open-ended questions make conversations with parents more friendly.

Certain statements tend to create distrust and worry rather than an alliance. For example: If a teacher says, "Is something going on at home?" the parent may feel accused. Instead, try, "Did Arthur have a hard time getting up today? He seems tired". (1988, p. 11).

Basic guidance communication techniques like compliment sandwiches highlight progress and pose problems from a constructive context. Honestly meant, open-ended questions make conversations more friendly. A goal is to generate possible solutions to problems together, discussing the pros and cons of each. (The problem solving process outlined in the previous chapter provides a guide.)

4. Invite Continued Involvement

For parents who are assertive, the teacher can work with these energies. Positive strategies include: providing current literature to discuss later, encouraging attendance at parent meetings, and seeking active involvement in the classroom. Such measures give the parent a respectful opportunity to learn more about, and contribute to, the program. As Boutte, et al. state:

> Parents usually will feel less alienated and will be more willing to participate if they are involved more in the decision making regarding their children. All parents should be allowed to contribute to the program in some significant way (1992, p. 20).

In inviting continued involvement in the child's education, the teacher makes hypotheses about the level and type of involvement the parent may accept. S/he adjusts expectations as necessary to keep the communication going. The teacher who works around a point of difference and wins an ally has truly mastered the principle of "creative conflict."

5. Communicate with Other Staff

If a teacher suspects a problem may arise—and certainly if a problem occurs— s/he should discuss the situation with other staff. The communication may range from asking for information from a colleague who knows a parent to requesting that an administrator be present at a meeting. Fellow staff can be a great source of support in a difficult situation. Venting to trusted others is important, but communication about families needs self-monitoring to avoid the "teachers lounge phenomenon" (gossip). When the purpose is to improve relations with a parent, the communication marks the professionalism of the teacher. In the complex world of the 1990s, teachers need collaboration in order to extend their ability to assist children, and their parents, to learn and to grow.

SUMMARY

What conditions make intervention necessary?

Three conditions make intervention necessary:

- Children cannot resolve a situation themselves and the situation is deteriorating;
- One or more children cause serious disruption to the education process;
- The danger of harm exists.

In these situations the teacher uses nonpunitive crisis management techniques in order to reestablish limits, accomplish reconciliation, and restore calm.

What are three methods of crisis management?

Commanding choices is the method of first resort because it holds out the possibility of mediation to resolve the difficulty. Not an ultimatum, the teacher uses the method to encourage the child to choose an acceptable behavior alternative.

Separation is the crisis intervention method of second resort. The teacher first opts to redirect the child's behavior to a more constructive alternative. If the child has lost control, the teacher uses a **cool-down time**, as distinct from a time out. The teacher follows up with a guidance talk in order to help the child understand the situation and become reunited with the group.

Physical restraint is the method of last resort. It is the passive bear hug that communicates to the child that the teacher will reestablish limits. Physical restraint is exhausting but important to use with a child who has lost complete control. After the child has quieted down, the adult helps the child through reconciliation.

What techniques assist the teacher to manage personal feelings of anger?

An effective anger management strategy begins before a crisis occurs, as the teacher **self-monitors feelings and makes adjustments** in the program. Teachers do well to prepare contingency plans for when they are emotionally or physically "down" and are at-risk for loss of control.

The teacher uses **safeguards** in the expression of anger. The teacher uses "I" messages that express feelings without humiliating others. S/he uses the describe-express-direct technique to address the problem without disparaging personality.

The teacher **practices reconciliation**. Teachers, like children, make mistakes. For this reason, after a confrontation, the teacher works to invite reconciliation. A first step is forgiving oneself for whatever happened. Then, the teacher works to reestablish positive relations with the child or group. Reconciliation initiated by the teacher testifies to the right of the professional to change and to grow, no less than the child.

What are strategies for working with level three strong needs mistaken behavior?

When working with children who show serious mistaken behavior, the teacher takes a comprehensive approach that is loosely modelled after the special education *Individual Education Plan*. Either formally or informally, teachers use the **Individual Guidance Plan**, which has six steps:

- Observe the pattern of mistaken behavior;
- Use consistent guidance intervention techniques;
- Obtain additional information about the child;
- Hold an I.G.P. meeting;
- Implement the guidance plan;
- Monitor the guidance plan.

What are considerations for when teachers and parents disagree!

At one time or another, teachers and parents will have differences. The teacher works to avoid having those differences become divisive. **Negative dissonances** occur when the teacher asserts the authority of the institution over the parent. Such division occurs most often when parents are of differing social or cultural circumstances than the teacher.

Instead, the teacher needs to keep positive relations with the parent, as the goal of each is the same, the best interests of the child. The teacher keeps in mind these considerations in order to turn different viewpoints into **creative conflicts**. The teacher:

- encourages mutual respect;
- models effective listening;
- talks to the specific situation;
- invites continued involvement;
- communicates with other staff.

FOLLOW-UP ACTIVITIES

Follow-up activities allow the student to interrelate material from the text with "real life" situations. The "observations" imply access to practicum experiences, the "interviews" access to teachers and parents. When communicating about the activities, students need to respect the privacy of all participants in the observation or interview, as an important professional courtesy.

1. **What conditions make intervention necessary?**
   a. Observe an instance when a teacher chose to intervene in a situation. Talk with the teacher about the decision. (Make sure that the teacher understands your reasons for the discussion is to understand more about conditions that make intervention necessary.)
   b. Interview a teacher about the reasons a teacher has for when to intervene. Compare the reasons with the conditions in the chapter.

2. **What are three methods of crisis management?**
   a. Recall from your own experience as a student an incident when a teacher intervened in a crisis. Were the methods the teacher used closer to a guidance or a punishment orientation? Why? (In communication about the events, respect the privacy of the parties involved.)
   b. Interview two different teachers about how they use separation in their classrooms. Ask their thoughts about this crisis intervention method and other methods they use when children's emotions are running high. (Let the teachers know that the purpose of the discussion is to learn about the use of crisis management methods.)
3. **What techniques assist the teacher to manage feelings of anger?**
   Talk with two teachers about one of the following:
   a. Adjustments they make on days when they are encountering physical or emotional difficulties.
   b. How they manage angry feelings toward a child or a situation.
   c. How they communicate with a child after they have intervened in a crisis situation.
4. **What are strategies for working with level three strong needs mistaken behavior?**
   a. Discuss with a teacher how s/he worked with fellow staff, or other professionals, to help a child overcome level three mistaken behavior. Which steps of the I.G.P. were formally or informally followed in the approach used.

b. Discuss with a teacher how s/he worked with a parent to help a child overcome level three mistaken behavior. Which steps of the I.G.P. were formally or informally followed in the approach used.

5. **What are considerations for when teachers and parents disagree?**

a. Interview a parent you are comfortable with and will give you open feedback. Reminding of the importance of protecting identities, talk about a time the parent disagreed with a teacher. Discuss whether the parent felt the disagreement got resolved successfully. Why or why not? What does the parent think a teacher should do to resolve a difference in view with a parent?

b. Interview a teacher about a time s/he and a parent disagreed. Reminding of the importance of protecting identities, discuss how the teacher tried to resolve the disagreement. Did the teacher feel the effort was successful? Why or why not? What does the teacher think is important to do in order to successfully resolve a difference in view with a parent?

SUGGESTED RESOURCES

Boutte, G.S., Keepler, D.L., Tyler, V.S. and Terry, B.Z., (1992). "Dealing with Difficult Parents," *Young Children, 47* (3), pp. 19-24.

Chalfant, J., Pysh, M. and Moultrie, R. (1979). "Teacher Assistance Teams: A Model for Within Building Problem Solving," *Learning Disabilities Quarterly, 2* (3), pp. 85-96.

Clewett, A.S. (1988). "Guidance and Discipline: Teaching Young Children Appropriate Behavior," *Young Children, 43* (4), pp. 26-36.

Ginott, H. (1972). *Teacher and Child.* New York: Avon Books

Gestwicki, C. (1992). "Section IV. Making a Partnership Work," in *Home, School, Community Relations.* Albany, NY: Delmar Publishers, Inc.

Stone, J.G. (1987). *Teacher-Parent Relationships.* Washington, DC: National Association for the Education of Young Children.

Warren, R.M. (1977). *Caring.* Washington, DC: National Association for the Education of Young Children.

REFERENCES

Boutte, G.S., Keepler, D.L., Tyler, V.S. and Terry, B.Z. (1992). "Dealing with Difficult Parents," *Young Children 47* (3), pp. 19-24.

Boyer, E. (1991). "Education: A New Look for the 1990s, Westminster Town Forum, (November 14, 1991). St. Paul, MN: Public Radio.

Boyer, E. (1992). *Ready to Learn.* Princeton, NJ: Carnegie Foundation for the Advancement of Teaching.

Chalfant, J., Pysh, M. and Moultrie, R. (1979). "Teacher Assistance Teams: A Model for Within Building Problem Solving," *Learning Disabilities Quarterly, 2* (3), pp. 85-96.

Cherry, C. (1983). *Please Don't Sit on the Kids.* Belmont, CA: David S. Lake Publishers.

Clewett, A.S. (1988). "Guidance and Discipline: Teaching Young Children Appropriate Behavior," *Young Children, 43* (4), pp. 25-36.

Dreikurs, T. (1972). *Discipline Without Tears.* New York: Hawthorn Books, Inc. Publishers.

Essa, E. (1983). *A Practical Guide to Solving Preschool Behavior Problems.* Albany, NY: Delmar Publishers Inc.

Galinsky, E. (1988). "Parents and Teacher-Caregivers: Sources of Tension, Sources of Support," *Young Children, 43* (3), pp. 4-12.

Gartrell, D. (1987). "Punishment or Guidance?" *Young Children, 42* (3), pp. 55-61.

Gartrell, D. (1991). "Developmentally Appropriate Guidance of Young Children." St. Paul: Minnesota Association for the Education of Young Chilren (In Appendix).

Gartrell, D. (1992). "Discipline," in Williams, L.R. and Fromber, D.P. (eds). *Encyclopedia of Early Childhood Education.* Hamden, CT: Garland Publishing.

Ginott, H. (1972). *Teacher and Child.* New York: Avon Books.

Greenberg, P.O. (1988). "Ideas that Work With Young Children. Avoiding 'Me Against You' Discipline," *Young Children, 44* (1), pp. 24-29.

Hendrick, J. (1992). *The Whole Child.* Columbus, OH: Merrill Publishing Company.

Honig, A.S. (1986). "Research in Review. Stress and Coping in Children," in McCracken, J.B. (ed). *Reducing Stress in Young Children's Lives.* Washington, DC: National Association for the Education of Young Children.

Lightfoot, S.L. (1978). *Worlds Apart: Relationships Between Families and Schools.* New York: Basic.

Lombardi, J. (1990). "Head Start: The Nation's Pride, A Nation's Challenge," *Young Children, 45* (6), pp. 22-29.

Moore, S. and Kilmer, S. (1973). *Contemporary Preschool Education.* New York: John Wiley and Sons, Inc.

Piaget, J. (1937; reprinted 1960). *The Moral Judgment of the Child.* Glencoe, IL: The Free Press.

Powell, D.R., (1989). *Families and Early Childhood Programs.* Washington, DC: National Association for the Education of Young Children.

Reynolds, E. (1990). *Guiding Young Children: A Child Centered Approach.* Mountain View, CA: Mayfield Publishing.

Schickedanz, J.A., Schickedanz, D.I. and Forsyth, P.D. (1982). *Toward Understanding Children.* Boston: Little, Brown.

Stone, J.G. (1978). *A Guide to Discipline*. Washington, DC: National Association for the Education of Young Children.

Warren, R.M. (1977). *Caring*. Washington, DC: National Association for the Education of Young Children.

10
Liberation Teaching

GUIDING QUESTIONS

As you read chapter ten, you will discover answers to the following questions:

- **What is liberation teaching?**
- **What is the connection between liberation teaching and anti-bias curriculum?**
- **Why is liberation teaching important for a guidance approach to discipline?**
- **How does liberation teaching apply to relations with parents?**

In the "olden days" of teacher preparation, an instructor sometimes told education majors: "You can divide any class into three groups. The top third will learn even if they are not taught. The middle third will learn if they are well taught. The bottom third will not learn however they are taught." Today, this callous view of education is rejected by early childhood teachers.

Liberation teaching means that the teacher does not give up on any child. In Ginott's terms, the teacher who practices liberation teaching sees children beyond the frailties they may show (Ginott, 1972). The methodology of liberating teachers is developmentally appropriate, culturally responsive, and guidance-oriented. The teacher realizes that the child is an extension of the family system and works with the family to benefit the child.

As the capstone of unit three, chapter ten brings together the different strands of the guidance approach, that it:

- views human nature positively and builds self-esteem;
- prevents problems by accommodating the developmental and cultural characteristics of young children;

295

Figure 10–1 The methodology of liberating teachers is developmentally appropriate, culturally responsive, and guidance-oriented.

- teaches children empathy and problem-solving skills;
- practices nonpunitive intervention to resolve difficulties;
- builds a team relationship with the parent and other adults.

The concept that integrates these strands of guidance discipline is liberation teaching.

LIBERATION TEACHING, WHAT IT IS

As introduced in chapter four, liberation teaching has its roots in the social psychology of the 1960s and 1970s. The term derives from such disparate sources as liberal Catholic theology and the writings of Mazlich and Faber (1974). Maslow provides a useful dynamic for the concept (1962) in his statement that all individuals have two sets of needs, one for safety and one for growth. To the extent that children feel that safety needs—security, belonging, self-esteem—are unmet, they are likely to exhibit mistaken behavior and personal development becomes difficult. Unmet needs can be caused or aggravated in the classroom. In Maslow's terms liberation teaching is assisting the child to meet safety needs and empowering the child toward growth.

The work of other psychologists also applies to the liberation concept. In Piaget's writings liberation teaching is teaching for autonomy (Piaget, 1932; Kamii, 1984). In Elkind's refinement of Erickson's work, liberation teaching enables the child to move away from shame, doubt, and inferiority toward initiative, intimacy, and industry (1989). For Harlow, cited in chapter two, liberation teaching is assisting the child to rise from the social relations of survival and adjustment toward encountering.

Parents and teachers might recognize liberation teaching as "plain old good teaching." The term "liberation" is useful because it identifies attributes of good teaching that are a part of the guidance approach. As well, it provides a goal for the use of guidance in the classroom.

Stigma or Liberation

To understand liberation, one must recognize **stigma**. In the classroom situation, stigma occurs when a teacher fixates on a vulnerability of a child and separates the child from the group. The separation at times may be physical, but at bottom is psychological, first in the mind of the teacher, then in the mind of the child and other children (Goffman, 1963). Thereafter for the child, full participation in the group becomes difficult. The effect is debasement of the self-concept of the victim and pressure on the group to condone and even support the act of stigmatization (Goffman, 1963).

Children most at-risk for stigma are those who show chronic mistaken behavior. These are the children who need a positive relationship the most, but often are the most difficult for the teacher to like and accept. There is an irony here. Young children at level three mistaken behavior are already the victim of circumstances. (Children show serious mistaken behavior as a result of difficulty in their lives that is beyond their capacity to cope with and understand.) Through the mistaken behavior they show, they are vulnerable for further victimization by the teacher's act of stigma.

Mistaken behavior is a primary cause of stigma, but young children come into the classroom vulnerable in other ways.

1. Even when mistaken behavior is not the sole cause, *personality factors* can result in stigma. Children with unique temperaments, learning styles, verbalization abilities, experience backgrounds, or developmental characteristics can be a burden, and so objectionable, to some teachers. Likewise, children with a high need for attention or for independence may prove difficult for some teachers to accept.

2. Teachers also may react in a rejecting fashion to children with *physical vulnerabilities*. A major group is children with disabilities:
   - established, such as a hearing loss or cerebral palsy;
   - recently identified, such as fetal alcohol syndrome or infantile crack addiction;
   - less easily diagnosed, such as allergies (or even potential disabilities, like a child with a positive HIV diagnosis).

Figure 10–2 Gender differences that are expressed in nonstereotyped ways sometimes put children at-risk for stigma.

As well, some teachers may be discriminatory toward children who are of unusual facial appearance, short or tall of stature, underweight or overweight, or unclean. Gender differences, especially when manifested in exaggerated or non-stereotyped behaviors, sometimes "rub teachers the wrong way." Any of these physical vulnerabilities that a teacher finds inconvenient or displeasing can result in a child's being negatively separated from the group.

3. A third category of risk is the *social factor*. Increasingly even in rural communities, children come from nontraditional family situations. Teachers uncomfortable with family backgrounds "out of the mainstream" may distance themselves from these children and their family members. Examples of social circumstances that put children at-risk for stigma include:
   - income differences, when a family noticeably is low-income or sometimes high-income;
   - religious differences, when a family holds beliefs and regards holidays differently than the teacher;
   - family differences, when a family structure is troubling to the teacher, such as with families that are out of the traditional marriage pattern;

- characteristics of family dynamics, when a teacher perceives parenting behaviors to be suspect.

4. The fourth category is the *cultural factor*. Books and articles have been written about the importance of avoiding "culturally assaultive" classroom practices. (See Suggested Readings.) It is now commonly understood that children and their families are at-risk for stigma when cultural differences are emotionally charged for the teacher (Greenberg, 1989). Recent works in the anti-bias literature (Derman-Sparks, 1989; York, 1991) suggest that teacher-denial in relation to cultural differences also constitutes stigmatizing behavior.

Stigmatized children are influenced toward perceiving the disparaged quality as central to their personalities. In such cases self-esteem suffers and faith in one's potential diminishes. Whatever the child's behavior patterns, personality, physical condition, social background, or cultural heritage, stigmatizing teacher-responses aggravate a child's need for safety and undermine the possibility of growth, and increase the likelihood of mistaken behavior.

Behaviors that Stigmatize. Similar to Purkey's concept of **disinviting** reactions (1978), stigmatizing behaviors by a teacher can be intentional or unintentional. Stigmatizing behaviors are those which:

- fixate on a vulnerability as a limiting factor in the child's development;
- establish psychological distance between the teacher and the child;
- tolerate or tacitly encourage stigmatizing responses by children or other adults;
- fail to alter the physical or social environment to include the child;
- stress competition, so establishing patterns of winning and losing (winners and losers) in the group;
- show preference for some in the class over others on the basis of social, academic, or behavioral criteria;
- ignore or disparge the background and lifestyle of a family and the child;
- use forms of discipline that punish and fail to teach conflict resolution skills.

Teachers are apt to show stigmatizing behaviors if they feel marginal acceptance in the teaching situation. When support is inadequate, teachers are likely to find reasons why children do not "perform." If the reason is "the child's fault" or "the family's," then the teacher is "not to blame". Administration sensitivity to the difficulty of the job is an essential first step in assisting the teacher to overcome tendencies toward stigma. Support systems for teachers are important.

Liberating Responses. With the practice of liberation teaching, the teacher helps each child to feel accepted as a welcome member of the group. Supported in the setting, children come to accept perceived vulnerabilities as a part of but not dominating their identities. With acceptance assured, children become more understanding of the human qualities of others (Greenberg, 1992; Hendrick, 1992). Liberating responses also can be unintentional or intentional. Liberating responses:

- show clear acceptance of the child as a worthwhile individual and member of the group;
- empower the child's abilities;
- educate others away from rejecting responses and toward empathetic responses;
- alter the physical and social environment so that all are included;
- facilitate cooperative and individual activities in which each child can experience success;
- appreciate elements of the child's family background;
- sensitively incorporate elements of the child's family background into the program;
- use forms of discipline that guide rather than punish and that teach **conflict resolution skills.**

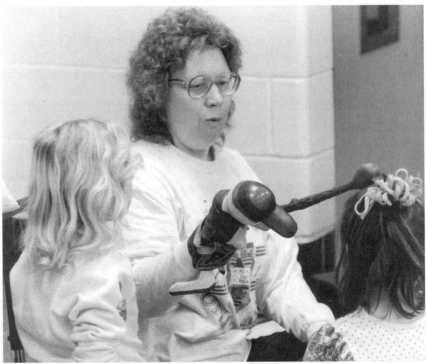

Figure 10–3 One way to encourage the acceptance of differing human qualities is through the use of puppets. (Courtesy of Richard Faulkner, Family Service Center, Koochiching-Itasca Head Start, Grand Rapids, Minnesota.)

The teacher effectively uses liberation teaching when differing human qualities do not polarize the class, but instead become opportunities for learning personal affirmation and mutual enrichment. The classrooms of liberating teachers tend to be caring communities.

LIBERATION TEACHING AND ANTI-BIAS CURRICULUM

Liberation teaching has much in common with the concept of **anti-bias curriculum**. As defined by Louise Derman-Sparks (1989), **anti-bias** is:

> . . . An active/activist approach to challenging prejudice, stereotyping, bias, and the "isms." In a society in which institutional structures create and maintain sexism, racism, and handicappism, it is not sufficient to be nonbiased (and also highly unlikely), nor is it sufficient to be an observer. It is necessary for each individual to actively intervene, to challenge and counter the personal and institutional behaviors that perpetuate oppression (Derman-Sparks, p. 3, 1989).

The term, **curriculum**, means that the anti-bias disposition is institutionalized in the educational program of the school or center. Derman-Sparks comments that anti-bias curriculum incorporates the positive intent of **multicultural education**, but avoids the surface treatment of other cultures—such as using the "Mexican Hat Dance" in order to "study" Mexico—which she regards as **tourist curriculum** (Derman-Sparks, p. 7, 1989). The author adds:

> At the same time anti-bias curriculum provides a more inclusive education: (a) it addresses more than cultural diversity by including gender and differences in physical abilities; (b) it is based on children's tasks as they construct identity and attitudes; and (c) it directly addresses the impact of stereotyping, bias and discriminatory behavior in young children's development and interactions (Derman-Sparks, pp. 7-8).

A contemporary feature of anti-bias curriculum is its active involvement of parents in planning and implementing the program and its problem-solving approach to differences between parent and teacher (Derman-Sparks, 1989; York, 1991; McCracken, 1992; Wardle, 1992).

Liberation Teaching, An Additional Step

Liberation teaching is in harmony with the ideas of anti-bias curriculum. The basis of the anti-bias approach is the creation of an affirming environment in the classroom, in which children learn to appreciate others and themselves. This too is the goal of liberation teaching. Liberation teaching goes beyond the definition—though not the spirit—of anti-bias curriculum in one respect. Along with factors of race, gender, and disability, liberation teaching focuses on an additional element that leads to stigmatization in the classroom—behavioral and personality characteristics of the individual child.

According to a study by Bullock (1992), aggressive behavior is the most prevalent reason for stigmatization in the classroom. Children who are withdrawn and lack social skills also tend to experience the "passive oppression" of being ignored (Bullock, 1992). Though Bullock found differences for children "rejected" versus "neglected," his review of the research indicates that "many adolescents who drop out of school experience poor peer adjustments in their earlier years of school" (1992, p. 93). Oppression as a result of cultural, physical, **or behavioral** factors is not acceptable in the guidance-oriented classroom. Liberation teaching seeks to reduce the effects of stigma, both to children oppressed by the mistaken behavior of others and to children showing the mistaken behavior themselves.

The Contribution of Anti-Bias Curriculum

Anti-bias curriculum empowers liberation teaching. In the anti-bias view, the teacher is an activist who intervenes to halt discriminatory acts. In her discussion of the power of silence, Stacy York criticizes teaching practices that prevent open discussion of tacitly oppressive (mistaken) behavior:

> Teachers and schools create "no-talk" rules for classrooms. Controversial situations occur, and questionable things are said or done. A Euro-American child calls a Native American child a "dumb Indian." Three boys in the block corner won't let a Laotian boy join them. They chant, "Go away, poopy boy. You talk funny." Everyone in the classroom hears it and sees it. Children may even look at each other as the situation occurs, but nothing is said then or thereafter.

Figure 10–4 Oppression as a result of cultural, physical, or behavioral factors is not acceptable in the guidance-oriented classroom.

Many times, people feel paralyzed and make no response. [Teachers] have told us that they fail to act because they are uncertain of the right thing to say; or they fear making a mountain out of a molehill; or because they feel they should not be influencing children with their ideas. But the silence only serves to reinforce the hurt, pain, fear, hatred, and distorted thinking (York, pp. 197-198, 1991).

York's examples illustrate the overlap of mistaken and stigmatizing behavior. In such situations, teachers need to intervene. Using nonpunitive, problem-solving techniques, they explain the unacceptable behaviors and teach prosocial alternatives. They may follow-up as well with a class meeting, a planned activity, or a discussion with a parent in order to reinforce the message that different human qualities are not to be feared or scorned, but learned from and understood. The activist message in the writings about anti-bias curriculum offers much to guidance discipline by empowering teachers to be liberating.

Anecdote: In a kindergarten classroom some boys were playing "fireman," using the climber for their station and the dramatic play areas for the "house on fire." Charlene asked to play, but was told, "You can't 'cause you're a girl. Only boys can be firemen." Charlene tried to get on the climber anyway, but was pushed at by the boys who began yelling.

The teacher intervened: "Hey, guys, do you remember our book about firefighters? Men and women can both be firefighters. If you are going to put out fires, you need to have Charlene's help."

The other boys didn't object when Steve said, "OK, Charlene, you can steer on the back." The teacher watched as the four got on their long wooden "fire truck" and "sped off" to the fire. Charlene turned a make-believe steering wheel in the back, helped to fight the fire, and even found a baby that needed to be saved. After the fire was out, the boys included Charlene on the climber fire station, " 'Cause Charlene saved the baby."

That Friday, a female fire-fighter who was a friend of the teacher visited the class. She arrived in street clothes and with the class's participation discussed, put on, and demonstrated her gear. There were no comments the next week when Charlene and Della played firefighter with two boys.

THE IMPORTANCE OF LIBERATION TEACHING FOR GUIDANCE DISCIPLINE

Traditionally, discipline systems have played a support function for the content of the educational program. The purpose of the discipline system was to allow

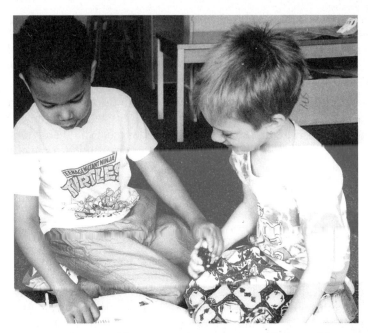

Figure 10–5 Liberation teaching engenders an appreciation of human qualities in the self and the other.

the teacher to present a smooth and positive education program. Guidance discipline rises a notch above the usual support function. The reason is that the guidance approach teaches vital social skills: expressing strong feelings in acceptable ways, cooperating with others, resolving problems through the use of words. As the world becomes more complex and interconnected, communication skills are paramount. The skills learned in classrooms practicing guidance discipline are the skills of social studies and the language arts, practice for life in a democracy.

Liberation teaching raises the importance of guidance discipline further. Liberation teaching links the prevention of oppression occurring around mistaken behavior with the cultural and physical factors that also cause children to be stigmatized. If guidance discipline encourages democratic life in the classroom, liberation teaching provides a foundation for that democracy in human relations—the appreciation of human qualities in the self and the other.

By empowering the child to overcome a vulnerability for stigma—and helping others to see the child as more than a social problem—the teacher models a precept of democracy: acceptance of the humanity of the other, with differing human qualities not a source of anxiety, but of learning. Human relations abilities are becoming ever more important in our culturally diverse society. There can be no higher purpose for modern education than to nurture this basic outcome.

Anecdote: In a suburban first grade, Tom, a member of an all European-American class, approached his teacher, an African American. Without looking directly at her, but with some emotion, Tom declared: "Teacher, somebody's different in here."

The teacher responded, "Do you mean me, Tom? My skin is a darker color than yours and that's one of the special things that makes me who I am." Tom frowned and shook his head, but the teacher thought that her skin color was probably what Tom had on his mind.

The next day Tom's Mother, an occasional classroom volunteer, called the teacher and said, "Annie, I just have to tell you what happened last night. Tom and I were in the supermarket when an African American woman went by with a shopping cart. Tom turned to me and said, "Look, Mom, there goes a teacher."

Liberating teachers accept the child behind the behavior. In refusing to demean, they model human relations and communication skills that encourage the child to learn and to grow. Guidance, developmentally appropriate practice, and anti-bias curriculum infuse liberation teaching. Liberation teaching contributes an appreciation for the humanity of the child to the guidance approach to discipline.

LIBERATION TEACHING AND PARENT PARTICIPATION

The practice of liberation teaching means that the teacher accepts the fundamental connection between the life of the child and the family. The teacher works with and seeks to understand the family in order to benefit the child. The sections of previous chapters addressing parent involvement are based on this premise of liberation teaching. Liberation teaching with parents means that the teacher encourages the maximum participation in the education of the child possible for each family. Over time, as trust builds between teacher and parent, the amount of parent involvement grows. Recapping information from previous chapters, a strategy for increasing involvement is suggested, using as reference points three levels.

Level One—Sharing of Information

At the beginning of the school year, the teacher introduces parents as well as children to the program. The teacher becomes acquainted with each family and seeks out ways to involve the family in the child's education. Families differ in the level of participation they are ready to accept. Most families are at least

Figure 10–6 Liberation teaching with parents means that the teacher encourages their maximum participation in the education of the child. (Courtesy of Richard Faulkner, Family Service Center, Koochiching-Itasca Head Start, Grand Rapids, Minnesota.)

willing to share information. The teacher makes the most of this willingness, recognizing the two sources of information the parent will have: the teacher and the child.

On the teacher's part, s/he uses the many methods of communication discussed in previous chapters—phone calls, happy-grams, orientation meetings, home visits, and parent conferences. The teacher works for three outcomes at this level of involvement:

- understanding by the parent that the teacher accepts and appreciates the child;
- comfort felt by the parent in communicating with the teacher about family background, including information about the child;
- willingness on the part of the parent for increased involvement.

The child is the second source of information for the parent. If the child wants to come to school when sick, the foundation is set for further parent involvement. If the child does not want to come to school when well, participation beyond the passive receipt of information may be the best the teacher can expect. Through the foundation provided by a successful program for the child and active inviting by the teacher, parent participation is encouraged at additional levels.

Level Two—Active Educational Involvement

The nature of active educational involvement will differ with each parent and with the program. Working parents may not be able to come into the classroom, except possibly on a special occasion. They may be able to contribute materials, read or do other enriching activities with children, or arrange for a nonworking family member to attend the class. The use of a home-school journal—a running dialogue in writing between the teacher and parent—is a clear indication of active educational involvement with some parents who cannot participate with the group.

With parents who can come into the classroom, McCracken (1992) suggests a **tossed salad approach** in which parents from differing backgrounds add to the program in informal but important ways. Rather than focus on parent presentations around holidays or specific customs, parents interact informally with children and other adults—with friendships and discovered mutual

Figure 10–7 One approach is to ask each family to have members come in and share something of their background.

interests providing incidental educational opportunities. As McCracken points out, when there is diversity in the families served, the tossed salad approach allows for multicultural education in a natural and supportive way. For such a program to work, parents must feel welcome and comfortable in the classroom—the job of the teacher, as leader of the teaching team (McCracken, 1992).

Another approach, a bit more formal, is to ask each family to have a member come in for a day and share something of its background (Gestwicki, 1992). Every family would be asked, not just those with an "exotic" heritage, and the member could share anything that was important to the family, not just a cultural icon. The teacher might ask families who were comfortable with the idea to share at the beginning of the year. Use of the tossed salad approach would help other parents become used to being in the classroom before being asked to present. As mentioned, working parents might be able to have a nonworking member participate.

With planning and coordination, the teacher can provide follow-up activities for children around the themes of individual parent visits. For instance, integrated curriculum activities could be set up around pets if one or more parents brought pets to share. One benefit of a family-share program is that it introduces cultural differences in functional ways for the children—even two Swedish American families would have different items and activities to share. A second benefit is that it allows each child to bridge the gap between home and school in personally satisfying ways. Some parents, who came only to share, might be encouraged to come back to the class at other times.

Level Three—Policy Participation

A third level of participation is in policy activities: program committees, advisory councils, policy boards. Some parents start at level one, but prefer policy participation to educational participation. Each parent is different and progress to either level two or level three should be supported. The importance of policy participation is that it means the parent is taking a leadership role in the education of *all* children in the school or center. If the parent has begun at level one and progressed to level three, the children, the program, and the parent all stand to benefit.

The model that Head Start has provided for encouraging low income, often low-esteem parents, to become active participants in their children's education is one of liberation teaching on a broad scale (Collins, 1993). A single parent who over time comes to a meeting, volunteers in a class, gets elected to a policy council, and enrolls in a postsecondary school is what liberation teaching with parents is about. The parent who says, "I sent my child and hoped that she would benefit, but I have benefitted as much or more," indicates liberation teaching at its fullest.

SUMMARY

What is liberation teaching?

Liberation teaching is helping each child to learn and to grow, despite vulnerabilities that could lead to stigma. Psychologists such as Maslow, Piaget, and Erikson provide concepts regarding healthy development that are the outcomes of liberation teaching. The term **liberation teaching** is useful because it provides a goal for the use of guidance in the classroom.

To understand liberation teaching, one must recognize **stigma**. Stigma occurs when a teacher fixates on the vulnerability of a child and causes the child to become psychologically separated from the group. The effect of stigma is debasement of the self-concept of the victim and pressure on the group to condone and even support the act of stigmatization.

Because their behaviors make them easy to dislike, children most at-risk for stigma are those who show chronic mistaken behavior. Children also are vulnerable for stigma in other ways: (*a*) Personality characteristics that "rub the wrong way" can cause teachers to show rejecting behaviors. (*b*) Physical factors that put children at-risk include gender differences, physical disabilities or atypical physical characteristics. (*c*) Stigma due to social factors can result when nontraditional family situations cause discomfort in teachers. (*d*) Cultural factors constitute a fourth factor, family backgrounds that cause teacher distancing and discrimination toward a child or family.

With the practice of liberation teaching, children come to accept their own personal qualities and to understand the human qualities of others.

What is the connection between liberation teaching and anti-bias curriculum?

Anti-bias curriculum teaches alternatives to oppressive behaviors that perpetuate sexism, racism, and handicappism. Anti-bias curriculum incorporates the positive intentions of multicultural education but addresses more than cultural diversity by including gender and differences in physical abilities. Active involvement of parents in planning and implementing the program is a part of anti-bias curriculum.

Liberation teaching is in harmony with anti-bias curriculum, but goes a step beyond by addressing additional factors that lead to stigmatization: behavioral and personality characteristics. Liberation teaching holds that oppression as a result of cultural, physical, or *behavioral factors* is not acceptable in the guidance-oriented classroom. The teacher protects from stigma both the child who is oppressed by mistaken behavior and the child who displays it.

Anti-bias curriculum empowers liberation teaching by casting the teacher in an active role in the face of mistaken behaviors. The teacher intervenes nonpunitively, explaining unacceptable behaviors and teaching alternatives. S/he may follow-up as well with a class meeting, a planned activity, or a discussion with a parent in order to reinforce the message that differing human qualities are not to be feared or scorned, but learned from and understood.

Why is liberation teaching important for a guidance approach to discipline?

Guidance discipline raises the matter of discipline a notch above its usual support function by teaching vital social skills important for life in modern society. Liberation teaching raises the importance of guidance discipline further. Liberation teaching puts a premium on the acceptance of the humanity of the other, with differing human qualities a source of learning and understanding, rather than anxiety. Liberation teaching infuses guidance discipline with a foundation in human relations.

How does liberation teaching apply to relations with parents?

The practice of liberation teaching means that the teacher accepts the fundamental connection between the life of the child and the family. The teacher encourages the maximum participation acceptable to each family, and over time, as trust builds, invites increased participation. The teacher encourages the parent to move from the sharing of information to active educational involvement to participation in program policy decisions. The Head Start practice of empowering parents toward productive action provides a broad-based model for the practice of liberation teaching.

FOLLOW-UP ACTIVITIES

Follow-up activities allow the student to interrelate material from the text with "real life" situations. The "observations" imply access to practicum experiences, the "interviews" access to teachers. When communicating about the activities, students need to respect the privacy of all participants in the observation or interview, as an important professional courtesy.

1. **What is liberation teaching?**
   Discuss with two teachers a "success story" each has had in helping a child to overcome vulnerabilities and succeed in the program. Reflect about what was common in the two teachers' approaches.
2. **What is the connection between liberation teaching and anti-bias curriculum?**
   Talk with two teachers about an incident when each intervened to stop an act of oppression or discrimination. Analyze whether each intervention was guidance discipline, liberation teaching, anti-bias activism, or a combination of the three.
3. **Why is liberation teaching important for a guidance approach to discipline?**
   Observe an instance of intervention when a teacher intervened using principles of the guidance approach. Reflect about the likely meaning of the experience for each child involved and for the teacher. Was liberation teaching at work? Why or why not?
4. **How does liberation teaching apply to relations with parents?**
   Discuss with a teacher a situation in which s/he helped a parent overcome initial reluctance to participate in the program and the parent grew from the experience. Ask the teacher to reflect about the likely effect of the experience for the parent, the child, and the teacher.

SUGGESTED RESOURCES

Boutte, G.S. and McCormick, C.B. (1992). "Authentic Multicultural Activities: Avoiding Pseudomulticulturalism," *Childhood Education, 68*(3), pp. 140-144.

Bullock, J.R. (1992). "Reviews of Research: Children Without Friends," *Childhood Education, 69*(2), pp. 92-96.

Clark, L., DeWolf, S. and Clark, C. (1992). "Teaching Teachers to Avoid Having Culturally Assaultive Classrooms," *Young Children, 47* (5), pp. 4-9.

Collins, R.C. (1993). "Head Start: Steps Toward a Two-Generation Program Strategy," *Young Children, 48*(2), pp. 25-33; 72-73.

Derman-Sparks, L. (1989). *Anti-Bias Curriculum: Tools for Empowering Young Children*. Washington, DC: National Association for the Education of Young Children.

Hendrick, J. (1992). "Where Does It All Begin? Teaching the Principles of Democracy in the Early Years," *Young Children, 47* (3), pp. 51-53.

Koeppel, J. with Mulrooney, M. (1992). "The Sister Schools Program: A Way for Children to Learn About Cultural Diversity—When There Isn't Any in Their School," *Young Children, 48* (1), pp. 44-47.

York, S. (1991). *Roots and Wings: Affirming Culture in Early Childhood Programs.* St. Paul, MN: Redleaf Press.

REFERENCES

Bullock, J.R. (1992). "Reviews of Research: Children Without Friends," *Childhood Education, 69*(2), pp. 92-96.

Collins, R.C. (1992). "Head Start: Steps Toward a Two-Generation Program Strategy," *Young Children, 48*(2), pp. 24-33; 72-73.

Derman-Sparks, L. (1989). *Anti-Bias Curriculum: Tools for Empowering Young Children.* Washington, DC: National Association for the Education of Young Children.

Elkind, D. (1989). *Miseducation: Preschoolers at Risk.* New York: Alfred A. Knopf.

Faber, A. and Mazlish, E. (1974). *Liberated Parents Liberated Children.* New York: Avon Books.

Gestwicki, C. (1992). *Home, School and Community Relations: A Guide to Working With Parents.* Albany, NY: Delmar Publishers Inc.

Ginott, H. (1972). *Teacher and Child.* New York: Avon Books.

Goffman, E. (1963). *Stigma: Notes on the Management of Spoiled Identity.* Englewood Cliffs, NJ: Prentice-Hall, Inc.

Greenberg, P. (1989). "Ideas That Work With Young Children. Parents as Partners in Young Children's Development and Education: A New American Fad? Why Does It Matter?" *Young Children, 44* (4), pp. 61-75.

Greenberg, P. (1992). "Ideas That Work With Young Children. How to Institute Some Simple Democratic Practices Pertaining to Respect, Rights, Responsibilities, and Roots in Any Classroom (Without Losing Your Leadership Position)," *Young Children, 47* (5), pp. 10-21.

Hendrick, J. (1992). "Where Does It All Begin? Teaching the Principles of Democracy in the Early Years," *Young Children, 47* (3), pp. 51-53.

Kamii, C., (1984). "Autonomy: The Aim of Education Envisioned by Piaget," *Phi Delta Kappan, 65* (6), pp. 410-415.

Maslow, A.H. (1962). *Toward a Psychology of Being.* Princeton, NJ: D. Van Nostrand Company, Inc.

McCracken, J.B. (1992). "Tossed Salad is Terrific: Values of Multicultural Programs for Children and Families," *Alike and Different: Exploring Our Humanity With Young Children.* Washington, DC: National Association for the Education of Young Children.

Piaget, J. (1937, reprinted 1960). *The Moral Judgement of the Child*. Glencoe, IL: The Free Press.

Purkey, W.W. (1978). *Inviting School Success: A Self-Concept Approach to Teaching and Learning*. Belmont, CA: Wadsworth Publishing Company, Inc.

Wardle, F. (1992). "Building Positive Images: Interracial Children and Their Families," *Alike and Different: Exploring Our Humanity With Young Children*. Washington, DC: National Association for the Education of Young Children.

York, S. (1991). *Roots and Wings: Affirming Culture in Early Childhood Programs*. St. Paul, MN: Redleaf Press.

Appendix **A**
Sample Greeting Letters and Surveys to Children and their Families

SAMPLE INTRODUCTORY LETTERS TO CHILDREN AND THEIR FAMILIES

The following letters were composed by small groups of students in early childhood education classes at Bemidji State University. Many of the groups included experienced teachers. In a few cases the author combined wording from more than one letter. Readers may prefer some letters over others; the samples are intended to provide "starter ideas" for doing introductory correspondence with families. Some of the letters were done on computers and included computer drawings, such as animals, to give them a friendly appearance. Stickers could also be used for this purpose.

To personalize the letters, the name "Shawn" is used for the child. The name given to the teacher is "Ann Gilbert." The university students recommend that the teacher locate and use the actual name of the parent or care giver, rather than generic terms like, "Dear Parent(s)," or "To the Parent(s) of _____." In the samples the name of a single parent, "Ms. Reno," appears. The school name, "Central," is used, though the program might be a prekindergarten center as well.

The sample letters are in four types:

1. Greeting letters to children
2. Greeting letters to families
3. Survey letters to help the teacher learn about the child and family
4. Survey letters to obtain information about how parents might be involved.

314

1. Greeting Letters to Children

These letters are sent together with letters to parents. Usually the correspondence would be mailed a week or two before the start of the program year. A day care program may modify the greeting to send as soon as a child begins attending.

Dear Shawn,

Welcome to our kindergarten class. I am excited about this year and have a lot of fun learning activities planned. I look forward to having you in our classroom and am sure we will have a successful year together.

Your teacher,

Ann Gilbert

(Elephant computer drawing)

Dear Shawn,

Hello, my name is Ann Gilbert. I will be your teacher this fall. I am very pleased to have you in our classroom. We will be doing many fun things this year. On the first day of school we are going to start talking about elephants. When you come to school the first day, I will have a picture of an elephant on my door so you know where to go. Be sure to let your family know they can visit our classroom anytime. See you soon!

Your teacher and friend,

Ann Gilbert

(Elephant computer drawing repeated with the words, "See you at School"!)

Dear Shawn,

I was very happy to hear that you will be coming to my class this year. I know starting school can be a little scary, but you will be meeting new friends and doing many fun things.

Your mother told me she would like to come to our class with you. That is just great. If you like, you are also welcome to bring your favorite toy to play with during play time.

I am really looking forward to seeing you and your mother next week. This year is going to be great fun. I hope you are as excited to come to school as I am. A big welcome, Shawn.

Your teacher,

Ann Gilbert

2. Greeting Letters to Families

Greeting letters to families accompany the letters to children. They should let parents know they are welcome participants in their child's education. Often, the letters invite parents to "get acquainted" meetings, "open house" class days, or introductory conferences—at home or school. Not all parents have an easy time with reading, and teachers need to be alert to this possibility. A transition meeting that includes last year's and this year's teachers or care givers can often provide helpful information about the child and family.

Dear Ms. Reno,

Welcome to the world of Central School! I am looking forward to having your child in our classroom this year. I am also very happy to welcome you into our classroom.

Room visitation will be all of next week, and I would like to invite you to join us and learn about our "developmentally appropriate" classroom. Parents are always welcome in my class, and if next week is inconvenient, or there is anything you would like to talk with me about, my number at school is _____. At home, you can call me anytime before ten at _____.

Again, I am looking forward to working with you and your child throughout the school year.

Sincerely,

Ann Gilbert

Dear Ms. Reno,

Hi, I will be Shawn's teacher this year. I am pleased that Shawn is going to be in my class.

I would like to set up a time when we could meet sometime soon.

Whatever time is available for you, I'll be happy to set up a meeting. I could come to your home if that would be convenient. I would like to get to know the families before the school year starts. I will be getting in touch with you in the next few days to set up a meeting.

I look forward to getting acquainted with both you and Shawn.

Sincerely,

Ann Gilbert

Dear Ms. Reno,

Hello! It is the start of a new year and I'm excited about having Shawn in our classroom. This fall I have many activities planned, and I would like to invite you to come in and join us. Next week I am going to have two "Get Acquainted" meetings for parents to learn about our program. They will be in our classroom on Wednesday and Thursday evenings at 7PM and won't go over an hour. <u>Feel free to attend either evening</u>.

At the meetings, we will discuss the activities and projects your child will be doing and also talk about things that you can do to help at home and perhaps at school. I believe that active parents are very important in children's education and want parents to feel welcome in our class.

If you can not make it to either meeting or if there is anything else you would like to talk about, my number at school is _____. At home, you can call me anytime before ten at _____.

Feel free to stop by whenever you have time to visit the classroom.

Thanks,

Ann Gilbert

3. Survey Letters to Help the Teacher Learn about the Child and Family

Survey letters of this type help the teacher to better understand and work with the child and the family. Teachers who use surveys need to be careful not to give the impression of "prying." Instead, they need to convey that the information requested is optional and will help the teacher get acquainted with the child. Teachers might wait until after they have met families before asking parents to complete surveys. Some teachers prefer not to mail these surveys out at all, but have them completed at orientation meetings or use them to structure the initial parent-teacher conference.

A request for health information is included in some of the letters. This information usually is collected more officially by the school, or program, but sometimes immediate information about health situations can be important.

Dear Shawn and Family,

My name is Ann Gilbert. I am looking forward to this year and what it will bring. I would like to tell you a little about myself. I graduated from Bemidji State University with an Elementary and Early Childhood degree. I have a family of my own, and I am looking forward to sharing things about them with you.

In order for me to get to know you better, will you and someone in your family complete this "open letter"? It will be used to say "hello" to me and your classmates.

If there is anything else you or your family would like to tell me, please feel free to write on the back. You can return it in the addressed envelope.

_____

Your Teacher

Dear Teacher and Friends,
The long official name I was given when I was born is
_____. But my favorite name I like to be called is
_____. I am ___ years old. My birthday is _____.

When I grow up I want to be _____ _____.
My favorite TV show, video, or book is _____.
Some things I like to do are _____.
My favorite food is _____. Something that makes
me happy is _____.
Something that makes me sad is _____.

I am excited to see you on the first day of school.

Your Friend,

_____

(Please invite child to write name.
Any way s/he wants to is fine.)

(COMPUTER PICTURE LOGO)
School to Home Family News
Issue Number One, September, 19__

To the family of _____

    This first issue of our class newsletter is a survey to help me get to know your child and the rest of your family better. It would be helpful if you fill out the information below and bring it to our first conference (already scheduled on_____). The survey is optional, but it will help me to work with your child and also with a lesson we will be doing on "Ourselves and Our Families." We will be talking about the survey at our conference.

The name your child would like to be called at school
_____

Your child's age_____ Your child's birthdate _____
The people in your family are:
Name_____Relation to child _____
Name_____Relation to child _____
Name_____Relation to child _____
Name_____Relation to child _____
(If others, write on back.)
Home phone_____Emergency phone_____
Name and phone of emergency contact person _____
_____
Any allergies or health concerns you want me to know about _____
_____
_____

Your child's:
Favorite toy_____
Favorite TV show, Video or Book _____
Special Pet(s) _____
Favorite story_____
Favorite things to do/play _____
Names and ages of special friends_____
_____
Holidays your family does/does not celebrate_____
_____
_____
_____

Please share any cultural or religious traditions that are important
to your family _____
_____
_____
_____

Please feel free to share anything else about your family that will
help me to work with your child _____

_____

_____

_____

4. Surveys about Parent Involvement

Surveys about parent involvement should also be done after the teacher has met the parent. Two ways to distribute the surveys are either at or by mail after the get acquainted meeting. The flyer, "Suggestions for Parent Involvement" (Appendix B) might be used with this survey.

Dear Ms. Reno,

Parent involvement is a very important part of our program. There are many ways that parents can be involved, and they are all important. I invite you to participate in any way that you can.

I would be willing to:
Read a story to a small group or the class___
Make materials at home___
Save materials at home___
Share my career___
Help with special occasions, parties, field trips___
Share a talent or hobby___
Share something of our family's cultural background___
Help with small groups in centers/stations___
Please comment on the choices you selected_____

_____

___Right now, I can only help at home
___I can volunteer in the classroom. The time(s) best for me
are_____

**Please feel free to visit the class any time you can. You do not
need to sign up in advance. I will help you find activities that you
are comfortable with.**

Thank you,

Ann Gilbert

Dear Ms. Reno,

I enjoyed meeting you and Shawn at the Open House last Tuesday. I am happy to have Shawn in my class and am looking forward to an exciting year for all of us.

Children and parents alike really seem to benefit from working together in their children's education. There are many ways that parents and caregivers can be involved, and they are all important. I invite you to participate in any way you can.

Here are a few things that parents have done in the past. Please check any ways in which you would like to help:
___Share or read a story
___Help with small group activities
___Help with special events (field trips, etc.)
___Donate materials, such as buttons or milk cartons
___Talk about my job
___Bring snacks
___Other, I can help by_____.

I can:
___come in on a regular basis.
___come in once in awhile.
___not come in due to my schedule, but can help in other ways.
___not sure at this time.

Parents are always welcome to come into the classroom to visit or help out. Two great times to come in would be at either 10AM or 2PM when we have learning centers.

Please call me if you have any questions:
Home phone_____ School phone_____.

Just return this letter in the enclosed envelope. I am looking forward to a fulfilling school year for all of us.

Sincerely,

Ann Gilbert

Appendix B
Sample Brochure:
The Education Program
In Our Class

Sample Flyer: Suggestions
for Parent Involvement

The following brochure was developed with input from undergraduate and graduate students in early childhood education at Bemidji State University. The brochure, with the accompanying flyer, might be discussed at a Get Acquainted Evening—an orientation meeting for parents.

PARENT'S GUIDE: THE EDUCATION PROGRAM IN OUR CLASS

Parents sometimes have questions about our education program. In our class, we use something called **developmentally appropriate practice**. This means that the teaching we do and the materials we use are tailored to the "age, stage, and needs" of each child in the class. Young children learn best when they have active, hands-on experiences that they can personally understand. In our class, we use practices that encourage problem-solving, cooperation with others, and individual expression. Children who become active, confident learners when they are young do better in school when they are older. Our program is designed to help your child learn that s/he can succeed at school.

This brochure tells about our education program. We go over the brochure during the Get Acquainted Evening with parents at the beginning of the year. If you have questions or concerns, feel free to call me at home or school.

322

Parents are important in their children's education. You are welcome to visit our classroom and become a part of our education program. You, your child, and I are all on the same team. We share common goals. I look forward to working with you this year.

Why Play Is A Daily Part Of Our Program

As a parent you may ask how children learn while they are playing. Through play children learn things that cannot be easily taught. In play children are forced to use their minds. They make decisions and solve problems. They figure out how to make things work and how to put things together. They have experiences from painting to hammering nails to reading books that help them learn how to think. Play helps children to understand symbols—like designs and pictures—that are needed for reading, writing, and arithmetic. Science skills learned through play include observing, guessing what will happen next, gathering information, and testing their guesses. Children use words in their play to share thoughts and feelings, and so their language skills develop.

Through play children master control of their bodies. By playing with dolls or blocks or Legos, children are developing eye-hand coordination. By running and climbing and moving to music, they are developing large muscles and becoming physically fit.

They also learn to get along with others. Children have different ideas when they play. They learn how to listen to others' views, how to lead, and how to follow. They also learn to cope when things don't go the way they planned—for themselves or others. They learn how to solve conflicts with words rather than fists—a very important life skill. They learn to get along with others who have backgrounds different than themselves. Through play, children learn to control and express their emotions.

It is important for children to feel free to learn without fear of making errors. Play allows them to do this. (We have a saying in our class, "Mistakes are OK to make. We just try to learn from them.") Play is more than fun and games. It involves many types of learning and should be a part of every child's life—at school as well as at home.

Why Our Art Is Creative

Teachers in sixth grade would never give a class an essay to copy. They want children to do their own work. It is the same with art in the early years. A teacher who provides a model for children to duplicate encourages copying, and discourages children from thinking for themselves.

Nowadays teachers know more about the importance of art than they did when we were in school. Teachers know that even before children can read and write, they tell stories through their art. Art is the young child's essay, the young child's journal. If we ask a child to tell us about a creative picture, even if it doesn't look like "something" to us, the child often has a story about it. The making and telling of stories through art is important for the development of later skills in reading, writing, and self-expression. But this can only happen if the art is creative, if each child's picture is unique—truly the child's "own work."

Teachers who let children explore freely with materials are using art in a developmentally appropriate way. So are teachers who use spoken words rather than models to motivate children to draw their own pictures. Teachers frequently use themes to encourage creative art. Some popular themes are "what I like to do outdoors in the spring" and "who the people are in my family."

One of the things we now know about art is that children go through stages in their art development. Art that is creative, so that each child's work is accepted, lets each child work at his or her stage of development. Children develop important thinking skills, as well as eye-hand coordination, by doing creative pictures.

Though popular, coloring books and dittoes are *not* developmentally appropriate activities. They do not let young children work at their stage of development. Coloring in lines and using realistic colors are easier for children in a later art stage that happens at about age seven. Children who are in earlier stages, such as the scribbling stage or the early picture stage, do not have the skills necessary for coloring in—or cutting out—lines accurately. Such experiences often lead to frustration and feelings that "I'm no good at art." We do not ask a kindergarten child to print like a third grader. For the same reason, we should not ask young children to work at a stage of art development that they have not yet reached. It is better for their development to give them blank paper and encourage creative pictures.

Please appreciate the original art work your child brings home from our class. Save samples and you will see your child's skills progress. Ask your children to tell you about their pictures. Enjoy their responses even if they tell you, "This is not a story to tell; it's a picture to look at." Your enjoyment of their creative art will help them gain ability to express their thoughts and feelings—important skills for school success. Their work will still be charming, and it will be **their own**.

Why We Use The Whole Language Approach

Whole language is an approach to teaching writing and reading. It is based on the idea that children learn language best by using all of its parts together. With whole language, children use all of their communication skills, speaking, listening, singing, art, and beginning writing and reading. In a whole language classroom there is less emphasis on drill of separate skills than in the past.

Here are some important whole language ideas so that you can see what it is all about.

1. Whole language surrounds children with the printed word through story books, labels of objects, lists of words and letters, and opportunities to write. Children learn to read by making sense of the pictures and printed words around them, including their own.
2. Children learn to write by using creative spelling and printing on a daily basis in their journals. With experience they eventually learn how to spell and write correctly.
3. Writing by children helps them: learn thinking skills, develop their expressive abilities, develop a sense of "authorship," and practice writing mechanics. Important writing mechanics include sound-letter relationships, sentence structure, and the meanings of words.
4. Reading to and with children acquaints them with printed words, teaches children to love books and reading, and encourages positive attachments between adults and children.
5. Whole language stresses "parents as partners." By encouraging writing and reading in home and school, parents contribute to their children's "literacy development." The whole language team includes the parent, teacher, and child working together.
6. Whole language builds confidence, skill, and self-esteem. It is the "natural approach" to learning to read and write.

Why We Use Real Objects In Our Mathematics Program

Children are very quick at learning to count from 1 to 20 or even 1 to 100. Until they are older in second or third grade, though, they have a difficult time understanding what numbers stand for. They can hold up four or five fingers when you ask them how old they are, but don't really understand what "five years" means. (Ask them how old they think you or other people they know are—and enjoy their responses.) They can count twelve flowers on a worksheet perhaps, but not fully understand what the words "12 flowers" mean.

To help them build a concept of number, children need to sort, compare, match and count **real objects**. The objects provide a "concrete clue" as to what 12 objects really are and later what "12 take away six" is. Manipulating objects encourages problem-solving and enhances logical thinking. The children will enjoy math and want to experiment more in mathematics.

In our class we begin by using materials that are familiar to the children. (Examples: buttons, keys, rocks, shoes, etc.) One way to get the children excited and involved is to have them bring items from home. These materials will be used for motivation as well as tools for exploring and learning. (I will be talking more about how you can help your child develop a "collection.") When the children are comfortable with the materials in the lessons, they will have an easier time learning basic mathematics concepts. Skills that will aid them in mathematics later include forming sets, matching items, and understanding numeral to number correspondence (2 = **; 3 = ***).

We are very excited about our mathematics program. Through manipulating objects, children will have an easier time understanding and enjoying
mathematics. (We want to prevent the development of "math anxiety.") We
would like to see all components of the education program be positive experiences for the children.

Why We Use a Guidance Approach to Discipline

Some forms of discipline may stop classroom problems temporarily, but they
tend to have negative side effects. These forms of discipline often lower
children's self-esteem, cause children to feel negatively toward school and
learning, and lead to behavior or personal problems in the long run. Our class
uses a guidance approach to discipline. This is what a teacher does who uses
"guidance discipline." She:

1. Provides a developmentally appropriate program that encourages
   children to be active, involved learners.
2. Teaches children to appreciate themselves and others as worthwhile
   individuals.
3. Builds a group spirit in which all children know they are important
   members of the class.
4. Provides children with a few clear guidelines for behavior and a
   reliable classroom environment so that they can learn from their
   mistakes.
5. Guides children to use words to settle problems, as much as possible
   on their own.
6. Addresses problems directly, but respects the individual child by not
   embarrassing or humiliating.
7. Builds partnerships with parents, so that the teacher and parent can
   work together to help the child learn and develop.

If you would like more information about guidance discipline, please feel free
to get in touch. [The teacher may wish to provide other materials such as the
position statement, **Developmentally Appropriate Guidance of Young
Children**, by the Minnesota Association for the Education of Young Children—Appendix C.]

Why Parents Are Important In Our Program

As you may have figured out from the rest of this brochure, **parents are very
important in our education program**. You are the first and foremost
educator of your child. Teachers only help. We both want the same thing for
your child, that s/he has a successful, productive year in our class—one that
will help your child become an effective learner and a happy classmate. To
reach this goal, parents and teachers need to work together as a team.

There are three things you can do as this school year begins: First, read over the flyer on how to get involved. Second, complete and return the Family Survey [Appendix A]. Third, to the extent you can, please do get involved. Together, we can make this a great year.

The following is a sample flyer, Suggestions for Parent Involvement. It might be distributed with the Family Survey [Appendix A] at the Get Acquainted Evening.

SUGGESTIONS FOR PARENT INVOLVEMENT

There are many ways that parents can be involved in our program this year. Each parent's involvement will be a bit different. This pamphlet is to let you know what some of the ways are. Remember, you are the first and foremost educator of your child. To whatever extent you can be involved, your child (and our whole class) will benefit.

At Home

1. Appreciate the work your child brings home. Talk with your child about what s/he is doing in school.
2. Read over the newsletters and notices that come home. Note special school events and suggested at-home activities.
3. Read with your child each day. Limit TV viewing and help your child find other activities. Model reading (and writing) in the home.
4. Talk with your child for a few minutes each day about anything s/he would like to talk about. Use your listening skills.
5. Do joint activities with your child on a regular basis.
6. Save things that we could use in class. We have a need for everything from jars of buttons to items of clothing for "dress-up." Let me know about anything you think we might be able to use. I may ask in the newsletter or by phone for special items from time to time.

With The Teacher

7. Feel free to call me. At school my phone is _____. Best times to reach me are _____. At home my phone is _____. Best times to reach me are _____.
8. I try to make a home visit to each family during the year. I will be contacting you to discuss whether this would be possible.
9. We have four regularly scheduled parent-teacher conferences during the year. These are very important in order for us to work

as a team. If you can't make a conference, let's talk about another time or place that would be more convenient.

10. On occasion an additional parent-teacher conference may be necessary. I will contact you directly to arrange the conference and will let you know then what the conference would be about.

11. From time to time we have parent meetings, such as the Get Acquainted Evening. These are optional, but we would love to have you attend.

In The Classroom

12. Because I have an "open classroom" policy, you are welcome to visit any time. We have a special "parents' area" set up in the room. You are welcome to just observe or to join in. I would be happy to talk with you about things you could do when you visit.

13. Help with special events. We sometimes have class parties, events, and field trips. Parents who can help at these special times are much appreciated.

14. Each week we invite a family to come in and share with the class something that is special to one or more family members. We invite all families to do our "Family Share" sometime during the year. Members can share something of their heritage, a hobby or special interest. I will be talking with you about this.

15. Another way to volunteer is as a Very Important Parent. VIPs come in on a weekly basis for a short period of time and help with such activities as learning centers or small group reading. We try to accommodate the schedules of anyone who would like to come in on a regular basis, but some times work better than others. Let me know if you would like to become a VIP. We'd love to have you do this.

16. Our program has committees, councils, and an Association. I will be talking about these at the Get Acquainted Evening. Your participation at this "policy level" will help make our total program run better.

As you can see, there are many ways you can be involved. Please fill out the Parent Survey to sign-up. Your involvement on our team will be much appreciated!

Appendix C
Developmentally Appropriate Guidance of Young Children

(Position Statement of the Minnesota Association for the Education of Young Children

*Reprinted with permission of the
Minnesota Association for the Education
of Young Children)*

DEVELOPMENTALLY APPROPRIATE GUIDANCE OF YOUNG CHILDREN

A Position Statement of the Minnesota Association for the Education of Young Children

This position statement by the Minnesota Association for the Education of Young Children (MNAEYC) addresses developmentally appropriate guidance techniques for children aged birth to eight.

The importance of guidance techniques which are based on sound child development principles has been well established. Research on self-concept development and the self-fulfilling prophecy demonstrates the necessity of using guidance approaches that respect the course of child development and do not label children as behavioral failures.

This document is intended for use by administrators, teachers, providers and other caregivers of young children. The term "teacher" is used in a generic sense to refer to all adults who care for young children.

SUMMARY OF PRINCIPLES FOR DEVELOPMENTALLY APPROPRIATE GUIDANCE

Principle One

Children are in the process of learning acceptable behavior.

Principle Two

An effective guidance approach is preventive because it respects feelings even while it addresses behavior.

Principle Three

Adults need to understand the reasons for children's behavior.

Principle Four

A supportive relationship between an adult and a child is the most critical component of effective guidance.

Principle Five

Adults use forms of guidance and group management that help children learn self-control and responsiveness to the needs of others.

Principle Six

Adults model appropriate expression of their feelings.

Principle Seven

Adults continue to learn even as they teach.

PRINCIPLE ONE

Children Are In the Process of Learning Acceptable Behavior

It takes individuals many years to learn appropriate ways to express strong emotions and interact appropriately with others. Young children are just beginning to learn these difficult personal and social skills. MNAEYC holds that teachers of young children should take a guidance approach that is educational in tone and responsive to the child's individual level of development rather than using punitive discipline.

Application. Think of behavior traditionally considered "bad" or "rowdy" as mistaken. The behavior may be unacceptable, but it is the result of the child's developmental immaturity, of not yet understanding how to act "appropriately." In reinforcing reasonable limits, adults need to teach children "what to do instead," and not just "what not to do."

Examples. Recognize that everyone makes mistakes: "We all spill sometimes, even teachers. The sponge is in the bucket. Let me know if you need help."

Reinforce limits and teach alternatives: "People are not for hitting. When you hit people it hurts them. Use your words when you are angry. Then people will know what you're upset about."

PRINCIPLE TWO

An Effective Guidance Approach is Preventive Because it Respects Feelings Even While it Addresses Behavior

Most adults can remember instances of discipline in their childhood that caused pain and affected self-concept. The teacher may have thought that s/he was dealing only with "a problem of the moment," but the effects of the punishment stayed with the individual for years. An approach to discipline that is guidance rather than punishment-oriented respects the feelings and self-concept of the child, even while it addressed mistaken behaviors.

Application. 2a. The adult structures the environment and sets expectations that enable children to succeed. Taking turns, sharing, losing at games, waiting for long periods and sustained attention to teacher-led activities are difficult skills for young children. Teachers need to use developmentally appropriate practices to reduce mistaken behavior caused by a mis-match of the child and the educational program.

Example. Teachers de-emphasize winning and losing in games and stress successful participation by all.

Teachers use open-ended art, rather than dittoes and product-centered crafts.

Teachers emphasize individual choice in learning centers and structure organized activities with children's attention spans in mind.

Application. 2b. In group situations, the adult avoids discipline methods that publicly embarrass an individual such as writing a child's name on the blackboard or scolding a child in front of others. Instead, the adult uses problem solving strategies that show respect for the child's feelings while reinforcing limits.

Example. Teacher to group: "As soon as we are all ready, the story can begin."

Teacher to aide (quietly): "Maybe you can sit by Sally and help her focus on the story."

Teacher to child. Teacher silently moves close to child who needs a reminder and then continues activity.

Application. 2c. In individual situations, the adult accepts the child's feelings, addresses the child's behavior, and avoids references to the child's personality . The adult avoids labeling a child as a "trouble-maker" or "problem child."

Example. "Mary, it's all right to be upset. Use your words to tell Jake how you feel."

"Larry, I know you're angry, but I can't let you throw blocks."

Application. 2d. The adult recognizes that measures such as physically restraining a child or removing a child from the group are taken only when preventive and problem solving methods have not worked or when a child has lost control. Because these measures of last resort can be punishing for all concerned, the adult needs to help the child: reconcile with the adult, feel welcome in rejoining the group and learn more effective ways of expressing strong emotions. To reduce the punitive effects of "timeouts," they should be kept brief and be considered "cooling down times" that are followed up by discussion. The adult may want to stay with a child during a timeout.

Example. "You need to use words instead of biting. You and I need to spend some time alone until you've calmed down. Then I'll help you figure out how to use the blocks with Carl."

"Nancy, we're glad you're ready to come to the art table now. We need some help with these paper chains."

Physical punishment is never appropriate. Repeated use of timeouts, physical restraint or other crisis interventions with an individual indicate trouble in the child's life and a need to better understand the child. Repeated use of crisis interventions with a group indicates an over-reliance on them and a need to develop new guidance techniques.

PRINCIPLE THREE

Adults Need to Understand the Reasons for Children's Behavior

There are always reasons for children's behavior. Working to understand these reasons can assist the adult in helping the child. Although we can never know another person fully, we can increase our understanding and that effort in itself can lead to better relations and more mature behavior.

Application. 3a. Children do things to see what will happen. Children learn from such actions, and from others' reactions. Sometimes "experimentation mistaken behavior," if harmless, should be ignored. If the adult decides to intervene, s/he should do so in a way that teaches the child about consequences and alternatives, but also appreciates the child's natural curiosity: the child's need to learn.

Example. A child marks on a table. "Mary, you can color on the paper. Let's get some soapy water and wash the table nice and clean. Then we'll get some paper to use with those markers."

Application. 3b. Children do things because they have been influenced by others to do them, either at home or in the classroom. With "socially influenced" mistaken behavior, the adult firmly but matter-of-factly reinforces a limit, but also teaches an acceptable alternative for next time.

Example. Child says, "that damned kid makes me so mad." Teacher (hiding smile) responds: "Peter made you feel mad and you can tell him or me, but you don't need to call names. We'll get the message."

Application. 3c. Children who show serious mistaken behavior almost always have trouble in their lives that is beyond their ability to understand and manage. Sometimes the trouble can be physical, such as a hearing loss. Other times, the trouble may be caused by a serious situation at home, center, or school. When a child shows rigid or exaggerated behavior, the adult should be alerted to the need for more information, especially if the behavior continues for more than a day or two. Observing and talking with the child can often add to an adult's understanding. Meeting with other staff can be helpful. A phone call or conference with parents may well be essential to better understanding the problem. Occasionally, consulting with an outside professional can help. When staff fully use their resources for understanding what is going on, an effective, coordinated plan for assisting the child is much easier to construct.

Example. A teacher notices that a child shows uncharacteristic irritability especially toward the beginning and end of each week. Talks with a parent determine that the parents have separated and the child is living with the mother during the week and the father on the weekends. The staff works together with the parents to make the transitions more understandable and less traumatic for the child.

PRINCIPLE FOUR

A Supportive Relationship Between an Adult and a Child Is the Most Critical Component of Effective Guidance

Trust and acceptance are the prerequisite foundation of the relationship between an adult and a child. Not only do children learn about behavior from an adult, they also learn about themselves. It is generally understood that children who are labelled "behavior problems" tend to see themselves as the adult does and to show more mistaken behavior than before they were labelled. On the other hand, children who gain the understanding that they are valued and belong tend to develop positive self-concepts and have less need to act out against the world.

Application. An irony of teaching is that the children who act the "worst" need a helping relationship the most, and are often the hardest to accept. Building relationships with such children is a challenge for the early childhood teacher and yet it is a critical task. In constructing productive relations with children who show troubling behavior, teachers need not "love" them, but do need to find ways to accept them as individuals and as members of the group.

Example. The teacher talks with the child, the child's parents, other staff, and outside professionals to gain a better understanding of the child.
   The teacher lists qualities of the child that she likes, appreciates, respects and can affirm. The teacher finds times during the day to focus positive attention on the child.
   The teacher helps the child into activities where s/he can succeed.

   REMINDER: An adult cannot build a supportive relationship primarily on acts of discipline.

PRINCIPLE FIVE

Adults Use Forms of Guidance and Group Management that Help Children Learn Self-control and Responsiveness to the Needs of Others

Children need to be able to decide between "right and wrong" not on the basis of fear of authority or peer pressure but on the basis of careful thought. The more we can help children to make thoughtful decisions in social situations when they are young, the more we are assisting them to become caring, responsible adults.

Application. Children need many appropriate opportunities to solve problems, make decisions and learn from their experiences.

Example. Teacher to two arguing children: "You two seem to be having a problem. You can either work it out yourselves with words or I can help you. Which do you want?"

Teacher to child: "Karen, you choose. Let everyone have a turn or find an empty table and work by yourself."

PRINCIPLE SIX

Adults Model Appropriate Expression of Their Feelings

As professionals, teachers make decisions about how to respond to behavior based on their judgments of the events at the time. Because we are human, sometimes we may jump in too quickly, over-react, show inconsistency, lose our tempers, or otherwise disclose our human frailties. Teachers who are professionals attempt to learn from their mistakes. They know that their job is challenging because young children are just at the beginning of learning very difficult social skills—skills that take into adulthood to fully master. They have accepted the fact that being a caring teacher is a life-long task.

Application. When upset, teachers use methods to diffuse and express their feelings that do not put down the other person. They may pay attention to a "victim" first and talk with the child who did the hurting after they've cooled down. They may use "I messages" to describe their feelings rather than accuse and disparage the "culprits." They may firmly request more information before they make a hasty judgment. They may check themselves before responding to a child who is difficult for them to understand. Finally, they monitor their moods and feelings and are aware of their impact on teaching effectiveness.

Examples. "Skip, I saw what happened. You need to wait here until I find out if Jenny is all right. We'll talk about it in a few minutes when I've calmed down."

"I am really bothered that the water got spilled out of the aquarium. We need to fill it up quickly and then we'll talk about what happened."

"When I see puzzle pieces spilled on the floor, I'm worried that we'll lose them and then we won't be able to do the puzzle anymore. Please tell me what happened."

PRINCIPLE SEVEN

Teachers Continue to Learn Even As They Teach

Application. Teachers recognize that they are learners even as they are teachers.

Examples. Teachers and caregivers should observe, and be observed by other professionals, in order to get feedback for personal review of teaching practices.

Teachers use collaborations with parents, staff, and outside professionals in order to continue learning about the children they work with.

Teachers read, attend courses, conferences, and workshops in order to update their store of ideas.

Teachers use observation and communication skills to learn from the best of all teachers, the children themselves.

REFERENCES

Bullock, J. "Understanding and Altering Aggression." *Day Care and Early Education*, (Spring, 1988), Human Sciences Press.

Clewett, A.S. "Guidance and Discipline." *Young Children* (May, 1988), NAEYC.

Elkind, D. *The Hurried Child: Growing Up Too Fast Too Soon*. Reading, MA: Addison-Wesley, 1982.

Gartrell, D. "Punishment or Guidance?" *Young Children* (March, 1987), NAEYC.

Ginot, H.G. *Teacher and Child*. New York: Macmillan, 1972.

Goffin, S.G. "How Well Do We Respect the Children in Our Care?" *Childhood Education* (Winter, 1989), ACEI.

Greenberg, P. "Avoiding 'Me Against You' Discipline" *Young Children* (November, 1988), NAEYC.

Hendrick, J. *The Whole Child*. Columbus, OH: Merrill Publishing Company, 1988.

Kostelnik, M.J., Stein, L.C., Whiren, A.P. "Children's Self-Esteem: The Verbal Environment." *Childhood Education* (Fall, 1988), ACEI.

Marion, M. *Guidance of Young Children* (2nd Ed). Columbus, OH: Merrill Publishing Company, 1987.

Stone, J.G. *What About Discipline?* Cambridge, MA: Educational Development Center, 1973.

Warren, R. *Caring: Supporting Children's Growth*. Washington, D.C.: NAEYC, 1977.

Weber-Schwartz, N. "Patience or Understanding?" *Young Children* (March, 1987), NAEYC.

APPROVED BY THE MNAEYC BOARD - JANUARY 30, 1988

DEVELOPMENTALLY APPROPRIATE GUIDANCE COMMITTEE:

Dan Gartrell, Author
Diane McLinn, Chair
Roz Anderson
Mary Holub
Vickie Iverson
Ginny Petty
Zoe Ann Wignall
Katie Williams

Revised by Dan Gartrell and Nancy Johnson—October, 1991
Designed by Michele Wolfel—(612) 483-4335
Printing by SPI Printing & Graphics

MNAEYC
1821 University Ave.
Suite 296-S
St. Paul, MN 55104
(612) 646-8689

Copies in booklet form are available by calling MNAEYC

Appendix **D**
Individual Guidance Plan Worksheet

The use of a structured system may not be necessary with all children who show level three mistaken behavior. Still, some teachers find a set plan helpful. Appendix D includes an Individual Service Plan Worksheet. The worksheet can be used without permission. The author does ask for feedback on its use by letter: Dr. Dan Gartrell, Professional Education Department, Bemidji State University, Bemidji, MN 56601.

INDIVIDUAL SERVICE PLAN WORKSHEET

Child's name_____

Initial Write-up Date_____

1. Noted Behaviors

Behavior Observed: Thoughts about Behavior:

2. Additional Information

Check procedures used. Then summarize information gained.

_____Discussion with child. Date:_____

_____Discussion with other staff. Date:_____

_____Discussion with parent. Date:_____

_____Discussion with other professionals. Date:_____

3. Cooperative Strategy Meeting   Date
Persons attending meeting:

Strategy to be tried:

4. Follow-up Meeting or Review   Date:
Effort/progress shown by child:

Progress still needed:

Any change in strategy:

5. Summary of Results/Changes as of (Date)_____

6. Summary of Results/Changes as of (Date)_____

7. Summary of Results/Changes as of (Date)_____

Index